MIGRANTS NO MORE

International African Library
General Editors: David Parkin and J. D. Y. Peel

For Agnès, Samuel, Timothy Arne and Fifi Jeanne Uwimana

MIGRANTS NO MORE

SETTLEMENT AND SURVIVAL IN MAMBWE VILLAGES, ZAMBIA

Johan Pottier

INDIANA UNIVERSITY PRESS
Bloomington and Indianapolis

in association with the
INTERNATIONAL AFRICAN INSTITUTE
London

Copyright © Johan Pottier 1988

All rights reserved

No part of this book may be reproduced or utilized in any form or by any means, electronic or mechanical, including photocopying and recording, or by any information storage and retrieval system, without permission in writing from the publisher. The Association of American University Presses' Resolution on Permissions constitutes the only exception to this prohibition.

Library of Congress Cataloging in Publication Data

Pottier, Johan.
  Migrants no more.

  (International African library)
  Bibliography: p. 198
  Includes index.
  1. Mambwe (African people) — Social conditions.
2. Mambwe (African people) — Economic conditions.
I. Title. II. Series.
DT963.42.P68   1988   306'.089963   88–9373

ISBN 0-253-33894-8

1 2 3 4 5   92 91 90 89 88

Manufactured in Great Britain

CONTENTS

List of maps and diagrams	*page* vi
Preface	vii
1 Introduction	1
2 A peripheral setting	20
3 Migration today: viewed from a rural district town	31
4 Cohesion today: Kowa revisited	58
5 Food security, food trading and local administration	86
6 Land, labour and cash	111
7 Kinship and the border economy	138
8 New developments in shifting agriculture	158
9 Settlement and survival: conclusions	174
Appendices	186
Notes	189
Glossary	197
Bibliography	198
Index	207

MAPS AND DIAGRAMS

Maps

1	Mbala district: Mambwe hinterland	*page* 27
2	Kowa (1978) - dispersal of households 1973-78	62
3	Kowa 1935-78	71
4	Chele regrouped	120
5	Land acquisition in Chele: the VPC gardens	121

Diagrams

1	Romance's effective network	50
2	Kinship and affinal links of M-01 (Romance) within the three UNIP sections surveyed	52
3	Trade partners of M-01 (Romance)	53
4	Kowa 1950s	61
5	Skeleton genealogy of Kowa village 1978	64-5
6	Linkages between Siuluta and Simpungwe in Kowa	66
7	Ward representation	105
8	Chivunzila village, summer 1978	142-3
9	Chivunzila women 'in residence' (skeleton genealogy)	152-3
10	Succession in Kowa	186
11	Succession in Kowa (my evidence)	186

PREFACE

Zambia is no longer Northern Rhodesia, as I hope this book will show. The struggle for independence has changed much more than the country's name. Nonetheless, certain economic imperatives have survived from the colonial past to the present, primarily the importance of mining copper and selling it on the world market. The vagaries of the copper market are such that they affect the lives of every Zambian, whether living on the Copperbelt or in the rural areas, and necessarily affect the policies of the Zambian government.

During fieldwork I have sought to collect data that are of interest to Zambia's policy makers, whilst also seeking a link-up with Professor Watson's widely read *Tribal Cohesion in a Money Economy: A Study of the Mambwe People of Zambia*. Research conditions in independent Africa demand from the fieldworker that he or she follows an appropriate code of conduct. The issue is not unproblematic, as Professor Simons has emphasized in his 'Prologue' to the *African Social Research* volume that marked the fortieth anniversary of the Rhodes-Livingstone Institute. Researchers on contemporary Africa, he explained, must expect to face a particular uncertainty.

Social scientists in liberated Africa are permitted, even expected, to provide radical interpretations of the colonial past. Researchers probe colonial systems, even traditional societies, for signs of class formation. Concepts formerly tabooed, such as class struggle, oppression, alienation, exploitation and revolution, are freely used as the focus and basis of analysis. It is less certain, however, whether as much licence is allowed in the study of contemporary self-governing states (H.J. Simons 1977: 272).

Fieldwork among the Mambwe of Mbala District was a testcase with regard to the 'licence' that would, or could, be allowed. I have tried to record and to interpret my observations from the perspective of the people who inhabit the district of Mbala. The book focuses on ordinary people, both in a rural and an urban setting. Working within those two worlds, I enjoyed total freedom of movement, and never was there any attempt to impose that invisible hand of 'informal but pervasive censorship' – a constraint so typical of fieldwork conditions in colonial Zambia (Simons 1977: 271-72; Epstein 1958). With this book I hope to pay tribute to the principle of freedom of discourse, a principle honoured by Zambian Humanism.

Unfortunately, tension did develop and damage was inflicted, when fieldwork ended abruptly in the aftermath of atrocious onslaughts by Rhodesian soldiers at Old Mkushi and other refugee camps. This occurred in November 1978, after I had spent 13 months in Mbala district. At that time extra security forces moved in to check on the activities of Mbala's residents. The peaceful town suffered intolerable frustrations. The white Rhodesian regime had aimed to strain peaceful relations within Zambia, and seemed to have succeeded. While I express my understanding of the immense problem which the Zambian authorities faced in late 1978, I equally express indignation at the way in which the growing tension led to unnecessary violations of the spirit of Zambian Humanism. I strongly regret that Mr Pearson Amon Simpungwe, who had been a committed and loyal assistant during the entire period of fieldwork, became subjected to brutal treatment during interrogations by the Zambian Air Force. Various authorities, including the Office of the President, were informed about the incident immediately after it had occurred. Despite the irreparable injuries he sustained, physical and mental, Mr Simpungwe remained in all his statements truthful about the objectives of my research. May his courage to uphold the truth never be forgotten.

My debt to Pearson Simpungwe is not solely for his courage during the final stages of fieldwork. All too often, I feel, the role of the assistant-interpreter is belittled, and the debt acknowledged perfunctorily. When the fieldwork started we were total strangers to each other, but we learned to share joy and sorrow, hopes and fears, 'deep talk' and boredom, and also (rather too frequently) vexation over punctured bicycle tyres and empty stomachs. This sharing I can never forget.

There was a time when anthropologists went into the field to study other people's myths. Many still do so today. Increasingly, however, fieldworkers find they are confronted with their own myths: the myth of objectivity, the myth of the perfectly integrated researcher, the myth that male ethnographers must content themselves with male-biased notes (Gregory 1984). All three myths affected my fieldwork.

Informants routinely demanded to know my point of view - on domestic labour, gender, wealth, morality. It was therefore impossible not to be conscious of my own myths and my worst assumptions. Interaction during fieldwork was a two-way affair: 'your views against my (our) own'. I was never allowed to hide from personal opinion. Except for basic etiquette that was strongly enforced (how I hated the rule that men must not stretch their legs when sitting down!), I was entitled and expected to remain myself. My 'self' changed as a result of my living among the Mambwe, but I never needed to worry about 'becoming one of them'.

Being constantly encouraged to express my views on 'the world' meant that interaction developed into occasional sessions for introspection; within myself and within some of the people with whom I lived. How I remember the many hours I spent in the company of David Sitbet Kowa, that keen historian and wise councillor in village matters. Matching his views on the 'true' history of Kowa village against my own 'true' views on lineage manipulation, we were able to spend some unique moments in what Rabinow has called the liminal, self-conscious world between cultures (Rabinow 1977: 39).

Most of the time, however, it was not possible to reach that cultural middle-ground. The exchange of views was so often restricted to 'this is what I know' and 'this is what you tell me', that I was mostly unable to assess the impact which the interaction had made on the other party. Also, my own views rarely went unchallenged, especially where they touched on matters of immediate concern. During such challenges irritating laughter was a habitual substitute for words. I did not like it. But responding to giggles, I learned, was also excellent training in the art of reflection.

Coping with laughter was *not always* painful. Marriage celebrations, for example, are a good time for letting one's hair down. In fact, it was after a wedding, after a long night of drinking, singing and dancing, that my presence in the village where I then researched (Kasunga) became more acceptable. My dancing style had given away my 'true' indentity. Now everyone knew it: I was Watson's son! My denying the relationship only confirmed it. I gave up. It seemed harmless enough. (Never before had I suspected that anthropologists too could be tempted into manipulating their own lineages.) There was one drawback. If Watson was my father, then I could be expected to know a good deal about Mambwe history and about the Mambwe way of life. And indeed I did. I had read *Tribal Cohesion*, possessed a copy of the book, and was soon known to ogle at my father's genealogies at night. I 'knew much' – the Mambwe euphemism for sorcery.

During fieldwork I thought it necessary, for ethical and other reasons, to tell informants about the existence of *Tribal Cohesion*. It was only natural to want to do so. The book, which gives names and places, was news to the Mambwe, but they did not usually regard the disclosure of identities as an infringement of privacy. After all, 'who out there in England would want to read about us?'. My 'knowing much', on the other hand, did cause suspicion and made me, at times, hesitant to mention the book. The 'knowing much' was inappropriate for a man of (relative) young age. The book had advantages too: if Watson had written a book, then I was likely also to want to write one. And thus, being put on the spot, I was able to discuss 'privacy' with some degree of frankness.

As fieldwork progressed my 'knowing' increased. I learned about cross-border trading. What, and how, would I report? Most informants thought that concealing places or the names of traders was unnecessary. Cross-border trade was not a taboo, not something to be ashamed of. 'We all know what is going on; we have been doing it for as long as I can remember', an older man once said. But I was asked not to write and not to know about cattle moving across the border. I accepted the restriction on reporting. I did, however, stick to my decision to change or omit the names of traders. Some informants thought it necessary, others did not. I remained with one dilemma. My attempts to link up my own genealogies with those collected by Watson - an activity I found both stimulating and legitimate - meant that people could still be identified, even when I omitted their names. This caused delay in processing the full data on cross-border trading (Chapter 7).

How did I solve this dilemma? Genealogical developments, as I shall show, reveal a good deal about local adjustment to economic crisis. The more I think about this, the more I feel that the structural adjustments I witnessed were a major strength of Mambwe organization, a mechanism for coping against the odds, a credit to their culture. On occasion the coping mechanism is very effective. It is therefore desirable that the ins-and-outs of cross-border trading be understood. Furthermore, from the point of view of policy and survival, cross-border trading has now been identified (in the general literature) as inevitable, so long as price differentials between adjacent countries exist. Scott recently took that position vis-à-vis grain leakages across Mali's borders (Scott 1984: 19-20). The new perspective compels me to agree with those informants who claimed that cross-border trade was nothing to be ashamed of. It is practice the outside world should not just know about (which it does), but also be brought to understand. If cross-border food leakages are harmful to achieving internal, national food security, a point I concede, then it is up to the planners and the politicians to see to it that differentials are evened out. People in peripheral areas must not themselves be blamed for food leakages. To them, such practices are both natural and legitimate. It is within such a frame of reference that I have written up the more sensitive data this book contains.

From a more strictly academic point of view, the study of small-scale trading also reveals the importance of links that in the past have been undervalued by anthropologists, such as links between women and their parents, or between women and their sisters and brothers (Ardener 1984: 123; also Van Donge 1985). To be able to contribute to this debate is exciting and provides an opportue occasion for reminding readers that Watson too emphasized the relationship between Mambwe women and their brothers. Today this link assumes great importance, because of the escalating divorce rate and the practice of home-coming for women. My data on cross-border trade also reveal that Mambwe women do have some control over this important sector of the economy. Their lives *are* burdened with heavy chores, but Mambwe women are not powerless. To withhold this type of information would be to consciously distort reality. Informants usually insisted that I should speak my mind; not to do so with regard to power relations would amount to injustice.

What prompted me to write this book, several years after completing my doctoral thesis, was the awareness that some of the data I had collected were of the 'cryptic' type which, once decoded, enable re-interpretation of previous analysis (Kaplan 1964: 134). When writing the thesis I had decided not to exhaust my data on cross-border transactions, to limit myself to a discussion of their general importance for economic survival. I stated that women played a central role in cross-border activities, but thinking the information too sensitive, refrained from discussing the mechanisms underlying the trade.

The experience gained from teaching and research on African food systems recently caused me to suspect that the data I had left unprocessed could have wider relevance. Increasingly I came to realize that certain observations suggested processes of symbiotic complementarity, of the kind that sometimes exists between specialized eco-systems. Such complementarity, which may involve several forms of exchange between specialized producers, is often portrayed as an effective strategy for survival, as in *Life Before The Drought* (Scott 1984). I grew curious and impatient to know the full story. Then, after accepting to speak at the workshop on 'African Regions, Frontiers and Boundaries' (New York, February 1985), I began to study unprocessed details of cross-border trading. At first I was merely concerned with 'getting the facts right'; later on I became aware of theoretical implications.

Being more explicit about the principles underlying cross-border trading has helped me understand why some of the views I expressed during fieldwork caused informants to be so amused. My re-living the fascinating world of cross-border trading has forced me to reconsider in particular my thoughts on the nature of agricultural labour relations. This rethinking was a welcome by-product of the decision to process 'the old data'. But I must not run ahead of the arguments presented in this book. At present, I merely want to state that the exercise of looking at existing data in a new light does not only lead to greater analytic clarity, as philosophers of science have argued (Kuhn 1970; Feyerabend 1975), but that the exercise can also be thoroughly enjoyable. It is in the hope that my rethinking may encourage others to do likewise that I have now written up the fuller story of my fieldwork among the Mambwe.

Tribal Cohesion lives on as a rich source. In the last decade or so it has been referred to by many: in order to challenge deterministic views about the migratory process (Amselle 1976: 32; Parkin 1975:10); to refine our understanding of modes of production and their articulation (Long 1975: 266); to rethink gender in the context of African agriculture (Cliffe 1978); to argue that the concept 'tribe' masks a complex array of social processes (Murray 1980: 141); and most recently, to demonstrate that the work of the Rhodes-Livingstone Institute remains 'remarkably relevant for understanding contemporary Zambian society' (Van Donge 1985: 61). The ongoing debate around *Tribal Cohesion* has proved a formidable spark towards the rethinking of my own data and towards the writing of this book, which I for one cannot think of as 'final'.

For the realization of fieldwork and for writing this book, I shall remain indebted to many people, many more than space allows me to mention by name. Sincere thanks are due to everyone who took an active interest in my research, offered hospitality or assisted in any other way. Before starting fieldwork I consulted representatives of the United National Independence Party (UNIP), at provincial and district level. Not only were these consultations rewarding, I was also impressed that so much understanding was shown for my enthusiasm and limited experience as a researcher. Party officials encouraged me to maintain regular contact throughout the period of research, and I wish to express to them my gratitude for that privilege. I am especially obliged to Mr A.D. Musawa, then District Governor for Mbala, and Mr E.D. Nkaka, District Secretary, for their practical advice and immeasurable assistance when security forces questioned the nature of my research. I extend these feelings of gratitude to Mr E. Claus, then Chancellor at the Belgian Embassy in Lusaka. All showed genuine interest, trust and understanding. Thanks must also go to the congregation of White Fathers in Mbala, and in particular to Mgr A. Furstenberg for granting the mission's library facilities. In addition, I incurred debts to a host of local departmental employees. Mr F.M. Sichilima, Assistant District Agricultural Officer, and Mr B. Phiri, District Community Development Officer, are among the many whom I wish to thank for their considerable help with tracing records and clarifying policy.

As I ventured farther afield and stayed away from the district town for longer periods, I came to rely heavily upon the support of Ottar Maelen, teacher at Mbala's Centre for Adult Education. His regular visits during my stays in Kasunga and Kaka, his readiness to help out, and the hospitality in his home, have all contributed greatly to the successful ending of the fieldwork. Dr John Pollock and Gaelen Joseph are also thanked for providing general assistance and the work space ('peace and quiet', including hi-fi and coffee) which I needed from time to time.

At every stage during the writing of this monograph - from fieldwork to thesis, from thesis to book - I have enjoyed the constant encouragement of former tutors in the University of Sussex, and of colleagues in the School of Oriental and African Studies, University of London. Special thanks go to Professors A.Cohen, A.L.Epstein and David Parkin, and to Dr R.D.Grillo who supervised my doctoral thesis. Professor W.Watson, of the University of Oklahoma, has assisted me with witty comments on various research papers and on an earlier draft of this book, as have Professors M. Wright (Columbia University, New York) and N.Long (University of Wageningen, Holland). A cordial 'Thank You' to all.

For technical assistance with the writing of this book I wish to thank Stella Cardus, who skilfully drafted maps and diagrams, and Peter Barker, who extended computer facilities. Simple thanks are not enough for friends who so generously gave of their time when I desperately needed it.

Funds for the field trip were scarce, alas. Part of the financial burden was carried by my parents (this concept has an extensive quality), part came from the ceaseless hard work of my wife, Agnès. To my 'sponsors' I owe debts that will never be completely cancelled out. I also wish to acknowledge a small but very welcome grant from the Radcliffe-Brown Fund, received when writing the first draft of my thesis.

The energetic support of Agnès has been the greatest help of all. My children Samuel and Tim Arne, the latter *in utero* during fieldwork, have been adorable young allies who made social contacts so much easier. *Twataeziya mukwai!* Very recently I enjoyed their support again when on a field trip to the Republic of Rwanda, during which time we welcomed Jeanne Fifi Uwimana into our midst. Fifi has made the relationship with Africa a permanent one.

CHAPTER ONE
INTRODUCTION

Zambia moved into the 1980s as a nation on the brink of famine. Poor harvests in 1979 and 1980 had forced the Zambian authorities to import maize – expensive maize – from the U.S., Kenya, Zimbabwe (then Rhodesia), and even South Africa. The cost of importation, paid in precious foreign exchange, was well above the usual cost of paying local farmers for their maize. The 1970s had been a decade marked by loss of revenue due to falling copper prices, massive borrowing from the international market and repeated currency devaluations.

The huge maize deficits demanded a fresh appraisal of Zambia's agrarian policy. One inquiry, by French agronomist René Dumont, called for a grass-roots solution: a path to progress which honoured local traditions, local values and local know-how. Zambian agriculture, Dumont thought, suffered from an excessive dependence on foreign models and costly external inputs (Dumont 1979; Woldring 1984). Zambia did not lack in resources. High-level bureaucratization and consumerism were at the root of its problems. Both stood in the way of a scheme for meeting the 'basic needs' of small-scale producers. Dumont recommended that the 'forgotten' subsistence farmers be reached via programmes that emphasized appropriate, labour-intensive technology.

The Zambian response was to ignore Dumont's approach and philosophy. Operation Food Production, the 10-year revival plan launched in 1980, aimed to reinstate large-scale commercial food farming. In spite of the very mediocre past record, state farms were given a new lease of life. But public opinion differed. The State Farm Project, as Woldring has noted, 'was received generally with a good deal of scepticism. The *Times of Zambia* came out against it and made a strong plea for multi-purpose cooperatives based on *the village structure*', (Woldring 1984: 109, emphasis added; *Times of Zambia*, 5 October 1980). Paradoxically perhaps, Operation Food Production did state some faith in 'peasant and family farms' that would cooperate 'through common funds, common dipping tanks, common marketing facilities and a common machine centre' (Woldring 1984: 107). For Dumont's followers this was a move in the right direction: a long-term 'basic needs' approach, in line with earlier proposals by the International Labour Office (ILO 1977) and tuned to 'the village structure'.

This hope-giving view is not without its reverse argument. As interested observers have noted, the new policy depends on the spread of development schemes run by foreign donor countries. Although their personnel, when based 'in the field', may well be committed to showing respect for tradition, local values or 'the village structure' (the latter being a poorly understood concept), it remains probable that some price is being paid at another level of organization. Bornwell Chikulo, a Zambian political scientist, believes this to be the case. He argues that the proliferation of projects since 1980 points to 'the centrality of international capital in rural development' and exposes the fact that foreign 'donors and agencies have become the major consideration in the choice of development policy' (Chikulo 1986: 6).

Zambia's search for a viable food strategy is still hampered by ideological uncertainty and confusion. There is support for increasing broad-based producer participation, as can be seen from the agenda for Operation Food Production (which includes the revival of cooperatives), yet there is also increased reliance on state farms and large capital inputs (Chikulo 1986; Woldring 1984:107). The uncertainty at the base of this paradox may relate to the persistent references to 'the village structure'. The concept of a village structure is being used, in my opinion, to raise hope, while the concept itself is difficult to grasp and far from static. When hope for a recovery in the food sector is expressed in terms of a positive response to 'the village structure' (*Times of Zambia*) or with praise for 'African values and traditions' (Dumont 1979), then one must consider that such notions may well impress primarily because they have never been put into practice (in Zambia), and because their content is 'vague' and presumed 'noble'.

There is consensus amongst academics that the part replacement of traditional farming with a western package-approach has created the condition for rural poverty and malnutrition (Chikulo 1986; Dumont 1979; Klepper 1979; Woldring 1984; and many others). Within this debate no-one would dare suggest that rural food production systems might have survived in some pristine state. With 'village structures', on the other hand, the assumption is often made that these structures are self-perpetuating and static. I would like to see the awareness of change extended to the debate about local social structures. Whatever the degree of egalitarianism these village structures may have contributed to in the past (which is debatable), they currently testify to the occurrence of significant organizational changes and even disruptions, particularly since the post-independence adoption of a capital-based policy for rural development. It is preposterous, as I hope to show in this book, to talk of 'the village structure' or of 'traditional values' without acknowledging that such social variables need to be qualified in the light of recent history. I shall describe and clarify aspects of 'village structures' as I observed them in one remote area of Zambia, during the turbulent late 1970s. The area, inhabited by the Mambwe people, lies in Mbala district, Northern Province.

The Mambwe area is important for assessing the relationship between local culture and national programmes for development, since we are now able to build a historic profile for that relationship. The area had been the focus of a 1950s investigation into how so-called 'labour reserves' changed under the impact of industrialization. In those days, migration was the officially endorsed road to 'progress'. William Watson, who researched the Mambwe economy, suggested that the relative material success of the Mambwe and their ability to cope with migration lay in their social structure. The patrilineal structure of the Mambwe village enabled households to deploy their labour on two fronts, mining and village agriculture, in such a way that households benefitted from both. Watson's account provides first-hand information on the structure of Mambwe villages.

Tradition, cultural norms and values do change over time. If these variables are to play a meaningful role in policy re-orientation, as Operation Food Production suggests, then they must first be understood as part of an evolving structure. One of the aims of this book then is to highlight the evolving structure of Mambwe villages and to clarify some of the values held by the inhabitants.

Mambwe villages straddle the border between Zambia and Tanzania. Increasingly, these villages (on both sides of the border) suffer from population pressure and environmental bankruptcy. Today many qualify as rather good examples of how 'rural neglect has to be understood within the context of labour demands for the mining sector' (Chikulo 1986:2). Of course, at this stage in my own argument, the topic of such a relationship is among the issues that require examination. In the 1950s, however, when the Mambwe homeland came to the attention of anthropologists, its relationship with the mining sector became a *cause célèbre* in countering the idea of a negative link: the Mambwe people benefitted from the engagement as miners.

The situation did not last. When access to the mines became restricted, shortly after independence, the Mambwe homeland had to turn to alternative sources for generating cash. Initially, there was hope that the Zambian leadership would redistribute the 'fruits of independence' via programmes for aiding the neglected rural sector. But independence changed little in terms of the inherited, colonial pattern of resource allocations. By the late 1970s, cut off not only from the mining sector but also from urban employment generally, Mambwe villagers had in a sense been thrown back on the land. When I lived and researched in Mambwe country, the villagers were working out their own solution to the economic downturn and rural stagnation. Theirs was a homemade attempt to bring about recovery; an attempt largely unaided and almost wholly outside the spheres of influence laid down by local government. My observations, therefore, are about the impact of non-impact, about the outcome of the administrative failure to reach the 'forgotten' subsistence farmers.

During the late 1970s, in the wake of a national economic crisis caused by falling prices for copper (Zambia's dominant export), social change in Mambwe villages was progressing at a fast pace, in relation to agriculture, village and neighbourhood solidarity, food production, trading, politics, morale, gender, religious tolerance... Many changes related directly to the economic downturn. What I am concerned with in this book is the implication of such changes for understanding 'the village structure' and everything this entails. When my manuscript was virtually completed, I came across the following village-level social sketch by Thayer Scudder, based on his return to the Gwembe Valley, Southern Zambia, in 1981. The sketch may exemplify the fast rate at which village lives are changing.

'Drunkenness was common, while relationships at household, village and neighborhood levels had deteriorated. Especially noticeable was an increase in neighborhood violence and sorcery suspicions and accusations, with disgruntled villagers venting their frustration in a number of highly destabilizing ways. Returning home drunk, they frequently insulted those whom they passed, and periodically, from the edge of their homestead, heaped insults and threats on the unnamed person or persons whom they accused of undermining the wealth of their homestead. ... [It was very common] to seek the services of witch finders or to retaliate violently.

Though village violence had always occurred sporadically in the past, its incidence and malevolence appears to have increased significantly in recent years. During 1981, there were a number of cases ... where men died after the insecticide Rogor had been added to their beer. Rogor was also being used more frequently to poison an adversary's livestock, including cattle, smallstock, dogs, ducks and chickens. No household that was trying to better itself during trying times could consider itself immune from the possibility of attack by jealous neighbors. (...)

I do not know the extent to which the community responses noted above can be generalized to the rest of the district, if at all (Scudder 1985: 54-55).'

Scudder's telling description points to dramatic changes in the Gwembe value system and leaves little room for optimism with regard to 'recovery' programmes based on 'the village structure'. My own account of Mambwe reactions to Zambia's economic downturn is a little more hopeful, but there are significant parallels.

I have opened this introductory chapter with a summary of the current debate on rural policy in Zambia. This debate underscores the central importance recently accorded to local cultures and calls for analysis of structural and conceptual changes, especially since the economic depression that hit Zambia from about the mid-1970s onwards. To understand the dynamics of 'village structures' with reference to the Mambwe economy, I must now turn to Watson's account of rural life in the 1950s.

WATSON'S THESIS: THE 1950s

When I left for Mambwe country in 1977, I sensed that I was heading for the area of exception. The labour-sending 'reserve' I was about to visit had 'survived' circulatory migration, had even prospered from it. Watson's monograph, and the commentary by Gluckman, had established such a positive view – maybe not once and for all, but certainly with persuasive arguments. In its more extreme version, their theory held that the positive Mambwe response had come about not in spite of migration, but because of it. There were signs of improvement in the material culture. Migrants invested in clothing and household goods, better houses, ploughs, agricultural implements and cattle (Watson 1958:220). Moreover, and most crucially, with regard to its internal politics, family life and its food production capacity, Mambwe culture had preserved its integrity. There were only gains. Traditional values lived on, and had in some cases even become stronger, while cash flows were welcomed and enjoyed by all. The Mambwe economy of the 1950s was a fine contrast to earlier studies of rural Zambia under the impact of industrialization (Richards 1939; Wilson 1941/2).

I shall now present a brief summary of Watson's thesis, focusing on the parameters he chose for framing the 'survival' debate: food production capacity, family life and internal politics.

1. FOOD PRODUCTION

First, I wish to recall how Watson accounted for the maintenance of the Mambwe food production capacity, which in the eyes of many critics today could only have suffered from the exodus of migrant labour. There is, readers will note, discrepancy between Watson's analytic conclusions and my own interpretation of the evidence he presented. However, and much to Watson's credit, it is equally important to stress that his concern with the capacity for achieving local food-sufficiency remains central to any debate of rural development.

Watson argued, in the final analysis, that the maintenance of village-level food productivity hinged on whether or not male labour could be redeployed during the stage of field preparation. He affirmed that such was indeed the case in Mambwe country generally, provided the exodus of migrant labour remained within limits. Initially, though, Watson had stressed the lack of gender-based specializations as the key to understanding the ability to maintain food production at the village level. The initial position read:

The absence of large numbers of men has not meant less food for those at home, owing to the lack of specialization in the work of men and women. Even when the proportion of women to men in a village is high, they are able to provide their own subsistence, although there is a limit to this disproportion. A connection undoubtedly exists between the number of women in a village and the maintenance of subsistence production; when the men are too few the women cannot carry on by themselves (1958: 225).

His calculations suggested that the critical ratio was 2:1.

'This critical point is reached when there are more than two women to each man in the village: anything higher than this disrupts both the economy and social life' (1958: 34).

The argument that Mambwe food organization had remained intact in the face of heavy outmigration provided a contrast with Audrey Richards' account of economic decline in Bemba villages, where the matrilineal mode of organization prevailed (Richards 1939, 1961). As a result of that ethnographic contrast Watson decided to push his argument further: the Mambwe capacity for food-sufficiency had remained intact because of their patrilineal organization. In the 1950s, residence in Mambwe villages was virilocal and migrant men had a strong allegiance to the parental home. Watson considered this practice superior to the uxorilocal arrangement common in matrilineal societies. Matrilineal villages, he suggested, lacked a cohesive element, since they were organized 'around a core of women' (1958: 227).

To reach this final conclusion, Watson shifted the analytic focus away from the evidence that women's labour was dominant in Mambwe agriculture. His earlier suggestion – that lack of gender-specific specialization facilitated survival – carried surprisingly little weight in the final analysis. Instead, he moved towards the idea that the permanence of the Mambwe village, with its principles of patrilineal organization and virilocal residence, accounted for the survival and heightened cohesion of the Mambwe 'reserve'. Two principles of patriliny stood out as most instrumental in this survival: father-son inheritance, and the specific mode of land-holding and usage (1958: 226-7).

The formidable contrast between, on the one hand, Watson's evidence about agricultural task performance and work-party organization, and on the other, the construed gloss offered at the end of *Tribal Cohesion* (and taken over by Gluckman in his Foreword to the book) remains something of an enigma. While his descriptions portrayed a mode based upon the mobilization of women's labour - which dominated collective and individual tasks - his final thought focused on the redeployment of male labour. Watson's model reduced the viability of the Mambwe food system to just one variable: availability of men.

The contrast between evidence and theory does not need to be elaborated here, since it is a central issue in Cliffe's well-known paper on labour migration and peasant differentiation in rural Zambia. I deplore the condescending tone in Cliffe's paper, as does Van Donge (1985:61), yet feel that the reductionism and sexist overtones in the concluding chapter of *Tribal Cohesion* must be acknowledged. Admittedly, the critical 2:1 ratio applied mainly to food production under woodland conditions (where men climb trees to lop branches), but there remains nonetheless a wide gap between Watson's rich observations and the paucity of the theoretical model.

The sexism in *Tribal Cohesion* is not restricted to that remarkably reductionist ending. It also permeates certain claims about the division of labour – for example, the claim that the women and men of grassland villages were 'interchangeable units' for the task of hoeing (1958: 33). I doubt that this statement was based on observation. Rather, as is true for other parts of rural Zambia, it is more likely that men were *technically* capable of undertaking women's work. But for men to actually have done so might well have been shameful. As Crehan observed for the Kaonde, such practice is very rare and only eccentric men go to the extent of actually taking up the hoe, say, for the purpose of weeding (Crehan 1985: 86-89). Watson takes the point: weeding is a task almost entirely left to women (1958:23). What Watson had in mind was a different kind of interchangeability. He argued that women could take on male tasks, which they most certainly did when men were not available for clearing fallow land. However, such willingness on the part of women does not make the sexes interchangeable units.

My critique relates to explanation, not to the facts Watson recorded. At the start of this book, the all-important reference point is that Mambwe villages in the 1950s were self-sufficient in food, in spite of the demands made by copper mining.

2. LOCAL POLITICS

The above critique reduces the importance of residential stability for men in matters of food production. The critique does not, however, invalidate the importance of male residential stability as a key variable in any argument about how labour outflows are controlled. It remains a major – and convincing – part of Watson's thesis that residential stability for men facilitated regulation of the flow of migrant labour. In Mambwe land in the 1950s, such regulation was achieved via the local political system.

Watson linked the position of the chief with the effective control of the flow of migrant labour. After careful scrutiny of the evidence in *Tribal Cohesion*, French anthropologist Jean-Loup Amselle summarized Watson's position:

une lecture attentive de l'ouvrage de Watson permet de constater ... [que] la mise en place de l'"administration indirecte' et le soutien accordé aux chefs par les Britanniques, avaient pour but d'accroître le pouvoir de ces derniers sur la terre et donc de leur permettre de contrôler la circulation des migrants entre les zones rurales et les régions minières (Amselle 1976: 32)

As with food-sufficiency, the political aspect too deserves further discussion in the light of more recent debate. Central in that debate is the question of how the flow of migrant labour perpetuates itself. Indeed, the flow of labour is not necessarily linked to the position of the chief. Chiefs may control the actual flow of labour, by having a say in decisions about which individuals may leave, but the *raison d'être* for a continuous supply of labour could well lie elsewhere, for example in the predicament that labour-sending households remain in a no-win situation. Gregory and Piché explain the logic behind this reasoning and argue that it applies to both migrant labour and cash cropping. Looking at past developments in Central and Southern Africa, they write:

Wages for unskilled labour and prices for cash crops being so low, little if any surplus revenue was generated for the household. Yet the production of basic food crops declined, as did other types of noncapitalist production, leading to an even greater dependence on outside sources of income in order to meet basic needs.
A vicious circle is thus initiated ..., a vicious circle which demands a specific demographic response (Gregory and Piché 1983: 177)

The centralist stand taken by Gregory and Piché is the very position Watson attempted to counter in *Tribal Cohesion*. No vicious circle seemed to be developing in Mambwe land during the 1950s. Thanks to their patrilineal ideology, the Mambwe elders and their chiefs were able to control the migratory process *from within*. Whatever the conditions of urban wage work, chiefs controlled the exodus of men, while rural land and the ethos of communal labour lived on as the migrant's ultimate sources of security.

But for how much longer would the chiefs and elders remain in control? Were there any signs of imminent change? The answer to the latter question is 'yes'. Watson did not fail to record some of the more visible signs. For example, when discussing the role of cash in bridewealth, he pointed out that Mambwe elders were unable to control this new institution (Watson 1958:40). Bridewealth had largely replaced the previous custom of brideservice, which had declined from the moment cash was introduced in the region (1958: 40). This lack of control, as other anthropologists have since shown, erodes the power base of the elders, who then become economically dependent upon subordinates (e.g. Mendonsa 1982:7). Under such conditions, the elders cannot continue to exert control over the movement of youngsters. Mambwe elders and chiefs were no exception to this rule.

3. FAMILY LIFE

Although he could not verify whether divorce was on the increase or not (1958: 226), Watson isolated the comparative stability in family life as a factor contributing to village cohesion and prosperity. Marital stability itself was ensured, amongst other things, by high marriage payments and virilocal residence. It is worth recalling, however, that this stability in marriage was merely comparative: greater than for the matrilineal Bemba (1958: 226).

4. OTHER SIGNS OF CHANGE

Watson also reflected on the notion that returning migrants may accelerate the process of rural differentiation. In their study of African return migration,

Gregory and Piché describe the return of the migrant as 'one of the principal mechanisms of articulation between capitalist and noncapitalist spheres' (Gregory and Piché 1983:170). This is not unlike Watson's approach to that small group of farmer-traders created by the cash economy (Watson 1958: 211). Watson, however, carefully pointed out that

> the growth in wealth of this group [was] inhibited by the distance of the Mambwe area from the large industrial markets and the poverty of the soil, both of which ... hindered the development of a local market of any size. [Consequently,] the economic activities of the traders [had] not developed on a scale large enough to bring them into politics as a separate class, seeking the protection and furtherance of their specific interests (1958: 211-12).

The success of the farmer-traders remained embryonic. Watson did not expect that the emerging differentiation would proceed in a fast or drastic manner. His caution proved remarkably justified against the background of living conditions in the late 1970s.

Tribal Cohesion was a landmark in that it seemed to contain evidence to counter Wilson's misgivings about rural-urban migration and its inevitably negative impact on rural production and standards of living. Together with Van Velsen's account of Tonga society (Van Velsen 1960), the Mambwe evidence could be read to mean that rural communities did benefit from migration, provided certain conditions were fulfilled. Watson, and later Van Velsen, introduced a single variable – lineage organization – to stem the tide of the deterministic argument that all migration was necessarily damaging for all sending communities in Central and Southern Africa. Watson thought Mambwe interaction with the money economy sound because the labour-sending reserve had improved its material culture, while it had also maintained its institutional cohesion (e.g. political integrity; relative stability of marriage) and food production capacity.

The major socio-technical arrangements described in *Tribal Cohesion* support the view that Mambwe villagers pursued a 'food first' policy. Crop rotation, accurate timing, resting of the soil and work-sharing based on reciprocity were among the arrangements that ensured adequate food without damage to the resources at hand. No unnecessary surplus was produced. Whatever millet surplus existed was redistributed in ways that were socially and ecologically justified. Surplus was turned into beer for rewarding work-parties, for the purpose of community ritual (1958: 162-3) or for barter. Although Watson did not discuss the latter practice, except for a reference to specialized hunters, we now have evidence that a fish-for-grain barter system existed on the Northern plateau. The practice, which is only one of several kinds of exchange, has a long history (Wright 1977) and its importance continues today, both in the grasslands, where I observed it, and in the woodlands (Hedlund 1977).

The low level of surplus production in the 1950s parallelled the rational utilization of labour power. Not only did shifting cultivators like the Mambwe 'tend to cultivate an area large enough to ensure the food supply in a season of poor yields' (Allan 1965: 38); Mambwe communities also retained sufficient labour in any 'season' of heavy outmigration. Both these aspects underwrote the 'food first' strategy of Mambwe villagers. Watson was aware, however, that the situation in Mambwe country might be short-lived. He isolated various factors to be taken into account when assessing the long-term impact of a collective response to circulatory migration. Thus he wrote:

Whether the system of migrant labour will cause a tribal society to collapse or allow it to survive... depends on the interplay of a large number of factors: the internal system of organization and the solution of conflicts that arise within the tribe, the pressure of outside influences on these, the mode of agriculture, the degree of participation etc. (Watson 1959: 41; also Watson 1958: 226).

And he was explicit that,

The present system of wage-labour is profitable to the Mambwe only as long as they have *sufficient land* to cultivate (1958: 135; emphasis added).

Pressure on the land was a further sign of changes to come (1958: 224). Watson warned that this pressure was growing due to population increase (1958: 224) and because of the interests of commercially-oriented returning migrants. He expressed concern about possible ecological consequences, for example, should cash cropping be introduced. The soil, he remarked, was 'not rich and could not stand a continuous cereal crop' (1958: 24). The 'food first' strategy was under threat, and the threat had already become the subject of debate (1958: 224). But Watson did not think that over-utilization of land and woodland was imminent. A cash crop, he believed, would be compatible with Mambwe notions of land tenure (1958: 223).

MAMBWE ECONOMY IN THE LATE 1970s: SOME THEMES

When starting my own fieldwork, some twenty-five years after Watson's, I was aware that the political and economic scene had changed. Zambia's urban and industrial labour force had stabilized; the dismantling of the colonial Native Authority had reduced the power of chiefs; the One-Party state pursued a strategy of political penetration in all rural areas. I wondered about the impact such developments had had upon the rate of outmigration.

If chiefs had lost some of their judicial powers, would they also have lost control over the process of migration? And what might the result have been?... Anarchy? Anarchy perhaps of the kind Todaro writes about? – the anarchy of that ongoing stream of migrants departing for congested towns, irrespective of whether there are jobs for them (Todaro 1969). Not necessarily. As far as Zambia was concerned, I knew of Van Velsen's alternative: that migrants do not proceed to the towns when jobs are non-existent or hard to come by (Van Velsen 1975). Van Velsen's position seemed more in line with the evidence from West Africa (Addo 1975; Byerlee *et al.* 1976; de Graft-Johnson 1974), which suggested that rural-*rural* migration now served as an alternative to the rural-urban exodus (Adepoju 1979: 211). Which way for the Zambian Mambwe?

Reflecting on developments in West Africa, Adepoju once suggested that migrants who choose the rural-rural option 'appear to have minimized risks by their decision to live and work within the rural sector' (*ibid*: 211). At the time I started fieldwork there was no evidence in the literature that a similar development had taken place in rural Zambia. I returned from Zambia in the full knowledge that rural-urban migration from Mambwe land had come to a standstill. But had rural-rural migration become the alternative? The answer, which is far from straightforward, depends on several interrelated developments. Among those I shall describe – and my account is not exhaustive – are the expansion of the local district town (Chapter 3) and the recent increase in opportunities for small-scale trading (Chapters 3 and 7). I cannot argue that rural-rural migration has become the dominant response, since this requires evidence of a type I did not collect, but my data certainly point to a demise of the classical rural-urban pattern of migrancy.

1. MIGRATION AND RETURN MIGRATION

My evidence on this demise, presented in Chapter 3, has now gained in importance, because the literature to date continues to assume that rural-urban migration from outlying Zambian regions goes on unchecked. Hedlund and Lundahl (1983), Van Donge (1982) and Stromgaard (1985) all argue or assume that circulatory migration is still the norm in Zambia. Only Scudder presents data that counter the view: 'because costs of urban living had increased significantly, those seeking employment were less able than in the past to spend prolonged time periods job hunting'(Scudder 1985: 53). My own findings corroborate Scudder's position.

The demise of the migrant economy, with stabilization of major labour markets, was almost certainly to have made an impact on the value of village land. Since Watson had linked the land factor with the pattern of migration, it was only normal that I wanted to continue research into that relationship. Would the prospect of permanent employment on the Copperbelt (a reality soon after independence) have altered the role of land as a controlling agent? Amselle, whom I have already quoted, did not think so. In his view, land does not lose any of its importance when the urban-industrial workforce becomes stabilized: 'même lorsque l'absence se prolonge, des liens sont en général maintenus avec le pays' (Amselle 1976: 31). Applied to the situation in Mbala district, Amselle's view has turned out to be partly right and partly off the mark. I found truth in his position, since village Mambwe foster an ideology of return migration by persistently claiming that close male kin will return. Whether such claims are based on strong probabilities or weak ones, they have become an effective tool for securing access to extra land. On the other hand,

Amselle's view is also misleading because the rate of return migration for Mambwe who left in the period prior to independence is very low. And I have no evidence to argue that established urbanites make conscious efforts to maintain their links.

The low rate of return migration, to be documented with data on lineage organization for 'revisited' villages (Chapter 4), raises the question of how well the chiefs and elders controlled the flow of migrant labour. The evidence suggests that the controlling agents were not as effective as Watson had presumed. On the other hand, chiefs and elders are not necessarily the sole or ultimate agents of control. Other scholars writing on migration as a controlled system of behaviour have isolated different control elements; marriage being the more important variable after land. But just as there are contrasting views on whether urban unemployment reduces the flow of out-migration, so there exist directly opposed statements about the importance of marriage as an internal agent of control. Whereas Gregory and Piché argue that 'the maintenance of control over marriage arrangements permits household heads to encourage young migrants to return' (1983: 179), so Van Donge, on the basis of his research in Eastern Zambia, holds that same control to be a decisive means in the young men's decision to leave the rural home (Van Donge 1982: 90). The problem with the view of Gregory and Piché on the one hand, and that of Van Donge on the other, is not that they take up extreme positions, but rather that the very issue of control over the process of marriage needs to be reconsidered. Watson himself, as I have indicated, stressed the central role of cash in bridewealth, and showed that Mambwe elders were unable to control the new trend (Watson 1958:40).

I do not intend to develop this point, since it was not a focus of my field study. However, I did look into other issues that touched on marriage and paid attention to decisions regarding post-marital residence. My research on the settlement pattern of villages provides some clue as to the extent to which the notion of 'control' remains applicable. The occurrence of female-headed households, much in evidence today, and the now quite common practice of uxorilocal residence for young grooms, are some indication that decisions pertaining to marriage have recently gained in complexity. Unlike in the 1950s, when residence was patrilocal and migrants seemed to have a strong allegiance to the parental home, choice of residence today is less straightforward. Uxorilocal marriage, the practice whereby a groom joins the village of his wife's parents, has become a feasible option.

2. PATTERNS OF VILLAGE RESIDENCE

Residence remains a central theme in my discussion of the Mambwe economy, even though the debate is now divorced from questions on how the labour exodus is controlled. Instead I shall focus on how the recent change in the choice of residence has given a 'new look' to village communities. The new option in residential choice – uxorilocal residence – will be discussed in relation to current prospects for household food production and food trading.

The decision where to reside centres on a number of variables. Prominent among them are the woman's marital status (e.g. separated but still legally married; divorced with a court certificate), the bridewealth requirements and the man's ability to meet them, the availability of land in potential places of residence, and the labour needs of the respective families. Uxorilocal marriage is compatible with a return to the custom of brideservice, previously reduced in importance as a result of the introduction of cash (Watson 1958: 40). So, even though I can neither confirm nor challenge the view that there is now greater flexibility in the choice of marital partners, I am in a position to show how one related issue – the choice of residence – has definitely become less streamlined.

Residence after marriage remains mostly patrilocal, yet the alternative has established itself. Young Mambwe men now speculate more about the conditions of farming 'at home' than about those of urban work. The Mambwe area has ceased to be preoccupied with the reproduction of its urban migrant labour force. This is a response to wider developments, such as the nationalization of Tanzanian sisal estates (now closed to foreign seasonal labourers) and the saturation of labour markets on the Copperbelt. Younger Mambwe now live and work in predominantly rural surroundings. The land is still (and perhaps more than ever before) a household's ultimate security; it is also increasingly a means of maintaining that foothold in the cash economy. The changes and the uncertainties call for speculations, that in turn call for greater flexibility in matters of residence.

What makes the residential scene in Mambwe land today so different from the 1950s is the development in respect of women's residence. Unlike in the 1950s, there is now a growing tendency for women in middle age to return to villages where they have male kin. Disadvantaged by their not having any *de facto* rights in land, such women can only hope to acquire land through the intervention of a father or a brother. If land is thus acquired, it does not follow that the supportive male kin will take on any responsibility for land clearing. Some will, others will not. But the women who return to live with male kin are increasing in numbers, so much so that they now benefit from the presence and support of other women with whom they are agnatically related. I shall demonstrate the importance of such ties and benefits in relation to trading (Chapter 7). At the time of fieldwork there were few villages that did not have some distinct 'core of women'. I shall discuss this new trend and will assess its potential for organizing alternative inroads into the money economy. The presence of 'a core of women', typical of the colonial Bemba village and conceptualized by Watson (and Gluckman) as not conducive to a successful economy, can now be found in many Mambwe villages.

Besides establishing the current degree of participation in migrant work and the implications for residence, I aspired during fieldwork to find out whether sufficient land was still available, and whether the mode of agriculture had remained intact. Access to land and expenditure of labour became important themes in the course of my research.

3. THE LAND RESOURCE

I pose two basic questions with regard to resource management. First, to what extent are natural resources being stretched? Secondly, how do Mambwe villagers organize themselves in the face of dwindling resources? A further question relates to lineage organization. It will be added in the final chapter, where I shall ask whether it is still useful, in the context of resource management, to compare societies on the basis of their being matrilineal or patrilineal.

Any discussion of changes in the physical landscape must turn to consider the cost of human intervention. One aspect of implemented policy has already been noted: the demise of the system of circulatory migration. Also of importance are the nationwide ban on moving village sites, and the (now aborted) strategy of village regroupment. These three changes in policy have heightened the concentration of people in certain areas and have added to the pressure on land. The first two also triggered the cash shortages now experienced by both men and women. The cash needs of men relate to the collapse of the system of migration; those of women to the loss of fertility in kitchen gardens (*ivizule*). It was in such gardens that women previously grew the traditional maize they traded (Watson 1958: 110). The two developments have accelerated the need for cash, as well as the need for a quick, effective solution. One strategy is to grow the new marketable crops, hybrid maize and beans, in spite of the fact that local soil conditions for maize are not wholly favourable. Moreover, increases in the production of marketable crops have stepped up the pressure on two vital resources: wood and land.

Environmental degradation through excessive 'mining' of the land base did not start until after independence. Not until after the Mambwe reserve had been 'laid off', so to speak, and government had started to intervene through policy (the stumping programme; hybrid maize; village regroupment) did the pressure on land lead to accelerated soil depletion. By the second half of the seventies, acute land shortage had not yet set in, but good land had become scarce. The long-term ecological dangers that accrue to extensive ploughing and hybrid maize cropping, which is often accompanied by the haphazard use of chemical inputs, were not in evidence during the early phase of cash cropping. Potential dangers such as soil salinization or decline in organic matter concentration, both of which may be caused by the repeated use of nitrogen (Bury 1983: 284), were not locally recognized, not even by the late seventies.

Deforestation is another noteworthy feature of the changing landscape. The boundary between woodland (*miombo*) and grassland, which in the fifties followed roughly the course of the river Saisi, must now be situated several miles to the east of that river. The recession of the forest line has had implications for the food strategies of those villages that subsequently 'emerged' out of the woodland. How villagers cope with the disappearance of woodland will be examined for the village of Chikoti; a site where woodland swiddening (*citemene*) was practised until three decades ago. The line separating the two ecological zones is receding because of the high demand for wood, as a resource for cultivation and fuel. Charcoal burning is taking its toll. The demand for charcoal is high, in villages and in the towns of Mbala and Kasama. The demand provides villagers with one of their scarce-but-vital sources of income. Although the open grassland is still interspersed with clumps of trees, their prevalence has diminished and it is not uncommon to see gardens where trees have been cut at breast height, a sign that they are soon to be disposed of (also Bury 1983: 71).

Watson warned that pressure on the land was growing due to population increase (1958: 224) and because of the activities of commercially-oriented returning migrants. He also expressed concern about possible ecological consequences, when he wrote: 'the soil is not rich and could not stand a continuous cereal crop' (1958: 24). There must have been indications that monocropping was already being resorted to, since a few men used 'ploughs to cultivate land they [held] under the tribal system of tenure' (1958:224). The introduction of monocropping is often related to ploughing, but may also result, as indicated in Chapter 2, from an unprecedented need for labour power in main gardens, where millet is grown.

Today the land resource has become stretched to the limit. This is not much of a surprise. The development, however, has also led to a second form of resource stretching because of the extra demands it has placed on human labour power. I shall consider these changes in detail, in the light of Zambia's current search for a suitable rural policy.

4. THE LABOUR RESOURCE

The declining availability of land has now brought into the open a number of interrelated symptoms. By the second decade of political independence, Mambwe households had already lost control over the production of 'normal' surplus, the millet staple had been displaced, and there was a tendency towards monocropping and shorter fallow periods, while surpluses had acquired the ambiguous status of being both food and a source of cash. In addition, agriculture had become individualized, with work-sharing confined to members of the immediate extended family. Labour selling was on the increase. Opportunities for selling labour varied, but they were plentiful in villages where ploughing had become popular. Opinion on whether ploughing itself increases the demand for labour is divided (Muntemba 1977:355), yet as I could see for myself, many plough-owners had extended their acreages to the point where they were obliged to draw in paid labour (Chapter 6).

A heightened demand for labour power now accompanies the overutilization of natural resources. Exploitation of labour, along lines of class or gender or both, has become a recurrent feature of the Mambwe system of production. Although I do not think that the process of social differentiation at the top of the social ladder has moved beyond the embryonic stage described in *Tribal Cohesion*, it is nevertheless clear that the social stratum 'lower down' has widened its membership. There is now a greater tendency for the poor to sell their labour in return for cash or basic foodstuffs, particularly where 'project intervention' has occurred. Their desperate need for cash or food means that not only women but some men too now face the 'double workload'.

Given the extent to which the ecological resource is being depleted, it becomes essential to consider how people cope. The issue, which is crucial to Zambia's policy debate, is as follows: if natural resources are under threat, is it still possible that the organization of networks can overcome the constraint? In regional terms: can something still be done to change the no-win position of the ex-reserve?

In his inaugural lecture, 'Creating Space for Change: A Perspective on the Sociology of Development', Long (1984) suggests that we depart from deterministic and centralistic thinking on development. As an alternative, he proposes that we opt for 'types of analysis that take more serious account of the dynamic processes by which ordinary people - peasants, workers, entrepreneurs, bureaucrats, and others - actively engage in shaping the outcomes of processes of development' (Long 1984: 2). The approach Long advocates focuses on the interplay and mutual determination of external and internal factors and relationships (*ibid*: 2-3).

The pedigree of Long's approach goes back to the pioneering work of the Manchester School of Anthropology. As already stated, the earlier literature on Central African migration and its impact on rural society (Richards 1939; Wilson 1941/2) made for depressing reading, but the tone changed during the 1950s. The impetus for the new approach came mainly from the field experiences of Watson and Van Velsen, who adopted wide perspectives and injected a good dose of optimism into their assessments of how patrilineal labour-sending societies coped with the cash economy. Unfortunately, contemporary theories of agrarian social change carry on in the earlier depressing vein.

Dissatisfied with the depressing nature and reductionist approach in current writings on development, Long proposes a fuller and more optimistic assessment. He recognizes that the members of a society, wherever they may live, are never passive onlookers, that they co-author their own social history. This has implications for analysis:

If we are to avoid the determinism of existing general theories of social change ... we must ... look closely at the ways in which different individuals or social groups deal with changing circumstances and attempt to create space for themselves so that they might benefit from new factors entering their environment (Long 1984: 3).

The approach echoes Watson's own overall assessment of the Mambwe: 'a patrilineal, cattle-keeping people, [who] have retained their cohesion and appear to be gaining materially from migrant labour' (Watson 1959: 41).

Long illustrates the need for a more balanced approach to development by referring to his 1984 return visit to Zambia; during which time he became struck by the intensive co-operation that now exists between Watch Tower members (Jehovah's Witnesses) and non-members. The church organization of Witnesses, as Long had shown in earlier work, is strongly linked to commercial farming and protects its members from the demands of relatives (Long 1968; also Poewe 1978, 1979). Returning to the scene of his first research, at a time of protracted economic crisis and low output in the domestic food sector, Long 'discovered that Witnesses and non-Witnesses had worked out a way of accommodating to each other's ideological point of view' (*ibid*: 5). The observation reinforced his earlier criticism of dependency theory, when he argued that the analysis of exploitative relationships should be 'matched by some account of the patterns of cooperation and collaboration that also exist' (Long 1975:262). Especially relevant were types of horizontal relations (or exchanges) that occur between groups and individuals at the far end of the structures of vertical dependency.

Patterns of cooperation at the periphery do not just relate to coping with the effects of the spread of capitalism. Horizontal relations may also emerge as a strategy for coping with periodic environmental stress. This applies to Mambwe country, where prior to British rule, the Mambwe and their neighbours had worked out ways of coping with their harsh, locust-infested environment. They had achieved this through the development of cultural and economic linkages on Zambia's Northern Plateau – a region I shall refer to as South Rukwa. Essentially, the system was based on the periodic movement of people and on seasonal exchanges of surplus (Chapter 2). With colonialism and later with independence, such 'horizontal' interactions became restricted.

Mutual cooperation through networks of horizontal linkages have also been described for the Savanna-Sahel, in the days before the drought of 1968-74. Scott recalls one very common strategy:

During periods of unusually severe droughts, farmers and herders would migrate to more bountiful areas where migrants engaged in wage employment or temporary cultivation of marketable crops. This kind of response to drought, called *cin rani* in Hausaland, is quite common throughout the Savanna-Sahel zones. But historically, migration has been seasonal or temporary. ... The essential point is that these cultural adjustments even out food supply problems resulting from periodic food shortages, and droughts were far less destructive in the past than they are now (Baier 1980) (Scott 1984: 4).

Today the evening out of food supply problems can no longer be taken for granted, especially not in regions that skirt international borders. As Scott shows for Mali, pricing mechanisms may divert local surpluses away from neighbouring areas that experience deficit. Or exchanges between complementary zones may lapse, when one zone is unable to maintain its production capacity, as I have demonstrated for another part of Africa, Western Rwanda (Pottier 1986a). What happened over the last century or so in Western Rwanda is that a very elaborate organizational structure for pooling foodstuffs from outside the region (i.e., from what was once a very fertile Eastern Zaire) has become inoperative. The break-down of coping mechanisms based on symbiotic relationships is now regularly reported for Africa (Demesse 1978; Silberfein 1984), so there is no reason why a similar 'development' could not have taken place in South Rukwa.

Africa's struggle to achieve food security must be fought on two fronts. The continent's agricultural resource base needs to be revitalized and better ways must be found for co-ordinating existing food supplies. The question therefore arises whether the strength of co-operation, based on socio-cultural exchanges, can be relied upon in an environment where natural resources are rapidly being depleted.

In this book I attempt to achieve a balance between, on the one hand, an approach to development which stresses the strategies pursued by mobile, manipulative, resource-conscious, organizational networks, and on the other, an assessment of the cost of policy intervention in terms of the management of vital resources, such as land and human labour. Anthropologists and sociologists interested in development need to explore the viability of agrarian societies from both these angles. Students of resource management need to evaluate the phenomenon of resource manipulation through the deployment of multiple linkages, just as they must examine whether the natural resource base is managed in ways conducive to long-term renewal.

What is at stake, in the case of the Mambwe economy, is that existing networks for the acquisition of complementary foodstuffs 'from across the border' may collapse. The threat, in relation to food security for Mambwe villages, might come from a tighter control of cross-border commerce and/or from rapidly declining levels of local food production. Moreover, the active mobilization of 'horizontal' linkages may itself stimulate the process of resource depletion. Where this happens, local people will have to live with the awkward reality that wealth, as Berger has said, 'must first exist in order to be equitably distributed' (Berger 1974: 113). If nothing is done in South Rukwa to stimulate food production in a manner which reverses the process of environmental degradation, then, we may soon have to admit for the whole of this region that there is not much left to be exchanged. Looking back to life before the drought in the Savanna-Sahel, Scott showed how over time, the people there 'lost entitlement to food, especially through an inability to produce it and to purchase it' (Scott 1984: 16). The two sides to survival - the ability to produce; the ability to organize - must be recognized. I take them to be among my major themes.

CHAPTER TWO

A PERIPHERAL SETTING

The industrial complex is a new thing, and for all they know may disappear as quickly as it came (Watson 1958: 8)

If a suitable cash crop were introduced, and capital for tools, fertilizers, seeds, etc., made available, the possibility of a more intensive use of the available soil would be created. Such specialized development of Mambwe land is not incompatible with the tribal system of land tenure, and would probably be acceptable to the Mambwe, but so far no suitable cash crop has been discovered (*ibid*: 223).

The discovery of a cash crop, a hybrid maize deemed suitable for the entire nation, came in the early seventies. The hybrid SR-52, tested out by researchers at the Mount Makulu agricultural research station (Klepper 1980), gained rapid popularity and soon found its way up the Northern Plateau. At about that same time, the people on the plateau realized that industrial employment in its circulatory form had come to an end (see Chapter 3).

The campaign for hybrid production was backed by politicians who spoke of loans for agricultural inputs and who exhorted villagers everywhere 'to feed the nation'. The country's leader, President Kenneth Kaunda, stood firmly behind the idea that Zambia could become self-sufficient in maize. The hybrid programme was also supported, vigorously on occasion, by local administrators and field-based extension workers who promised to pass on the 'magic' of this technological wonder. Many returning migrants declared their interest in taking up small-scale commercial farming (1-10 ha). Referred to in the literature as emergent farmers[1], these men seemed set to go back to the land in style. But if Zambia's remoter areas warmed to the idea of sufficiency in maize, their positive response was not caused by some collectively felt duty towards the nation-state. Enthusiasm in the countryside was primarily rooted in the growing need for cash. Maize cropping, moreover, helped solve the problem of seasonal labour shortages, as I shall presently show.

The knowledge that hybrid maize could provide some answer to problems related to cash and labour explains why outlying areas were (and still are) prepared to put up with many of the drawbacks that accrue to the adoption of marketable maize. The major problem is that the success of hybrid production depends upon the timely allocation of expensive inputs. To meet this crucial condition, Zambia's planners were asked to design an infrastructure appropriate for rural areas. It is in relation to the time factor that peripheral regions are most vulnerable. To date, Zambia's parastatal organizations - the National

Marketing Board (NAMBOARD) and various Cooperative Unions - have failed to provide an adequate, regular and timely service. The poor collection service and delayed payment for produce have in recent years undermined the position of 'emergent' farmers in outlying areas. As Wood explains:

Access to credit has become more difficult in recent years as government funding of AFC [Agricultural Finance Corporation] has not kept pace with the growing financial requirements of farmers, while in some cases the credit-worthiness of small-scale farmers had declined because late payment for their crops (as a result of government cash-flow problems) has prevented timely repayment of loans (Stollen 1983: 346) (Wood 1985: 144).

Many problems resulted directly from the 1974 slump in the price of copper, a disaster caused by global economic disturbances far beyond the control of Zambia's leaders. The fall in copper prices affected credit and marketing facilities and forced the production curve of SR-52 maize to take a decisively downward course. Modernization was not a unilinear progression. For the Mambwe area I take into account one further obstacle to the production of hybrid maize, namely the acidity of the soils in Northern Province (Chambers and Singer 1981; Dumont and Mottin 1983).

During the second half of the 1970s the production of commercial maize dropped sharply in all areas where maize had not been 'traditionally' grown, which is mostly in outlying areas. It would be a mistake, however, to interpret this decline in commercial sales from rural areas as signalling a lack of interest in maize. On the contrary, in spite of the many obstacles encountered by rural producers, their interest in maize production has not disappeared as such. While its significance for 'feeding the nation' became more marginal (GRZ 1977a), production itself retained a certain appeal. My fieldwork was instructive on this point. In Mambwe country, as elsewhere, sales were down by the late seventies; but maize production itself had clearly arrived to stay. This needs some explanation.

LAND, LABOUR, AND CROPS

When the hybrid programme was launched, Mambwe villagers had practical reasons for being enthusiastic about its introduction. Hybrid maize displaced 'traditional' millet, in part at least, and villagers welcomed the switch, particularly in the more densely populated areas. The part displacement of their traditional staple went unchallenged because cultivators found it increasingly difficult to meet labour requirements for millet. Causes of the displacement can be linked to labour shortages due to outmigration (a cause incompatible with the approach in *Tribal Cohesion*, but emphasized by Alder 1960) and to the ever-increasing pressure on the land. What made maize cultivation attractive, then, over and above the initial commercial appeal, was that the new crop was less labour-intensive under conditions of land scarcity, especially in terms of its weeding requirements. By the late 1970s millet production in Mambwe country had become very labour-intensive (see also Chapter 8).

Two related developments are equally important. First, fallow periods had been shortened due to population pressure; secondly, monocropping was introduced, allegedly because of a shortage of female labour! The latter point is specifically argued by Alder (Alder 1960, quoted in Willis 1966). When continuous monocropping and shorter fallow periods combine, cropping will activate the growth of weeds and will increase the demand for weeding – a task which falls on women. Under such circumstances, the growth of the allied weed *eleusine indica*, a weed hardly distinguishable from the millet plant itself (Watson 1958:13), gives cause for concern. Both processes - shorter fallows, continuous monocropping - were well developed by the late 1950s. And, if Alder's observations are correct, women's labour by that time was already in short supply.

It is intriguing that Watson warned of the dangers of monocropping, when he wrote, 'the soil is not rich and could not stand a continuous cereal crop' (1958: 24) and that Alder, who researched in the Fwambo Chieftaincy soon after Watson's departure, was able to confirm the existence of such a system of monocropping. Within two years of the publication of *Tribal Cohesion*, Alder argued that the practice of rotating millet and legumes had come to be replaced with 'monocropping of fingermillet with quite obviously decreasing periods of rest between cultivation sequences' (Alder 1960; cited in Willis 1966). Alder explained this transition as due to 'the fact that the adult man- and woman-power available to the Garden Family had decreased by 36% and 22% respectively *during the past eleven years*' (Alder 1960: no page reference given; emphasis added).[2]

Before hybrid maize was introduced, many Mambwe cultivators had adjusted to the new condition of shortage of land and labour by adopting cassava. Substitution of cassava, a crop which does not have any peak labour periods, occurred throughout the sixties. Substitution, according to Alder, came after a transition period during which the Northern Grassland system shed its emphasis on crop rotation in favour of millet monocropping (Alder 1960). The later date at which hybrid maize became available has led observers to describe the current system as semi-permanent and based on 'cassava, usually intercropped with maize or millet' (Mansfield *et al.* 1975a: 3).

The transition from a millet-based mounding system with grain/legume rotation (early fifties) to a strategy based on cassava, hybrid maize and use of ploughs (late sixties) passed through two distinct phases. In its first phase, as Alder argues for the later 1950s, outmigration of men *and women* reduced labour availability to the point where intercropping had to be dropped.[3] A simplified food production system then emerged (see also Chambers and Singer 1981:12). The second stage was reached soon after independence, when the Zambian policy of village regroupment restricted the movement of villages. This policy coincided with the virtual saturation of the industrial labour market (see Chapter 3). Villages could no longer move in the customary manner, which led to further relative shortages of land. The problem of land scarcity was compounded by the fact that would-be migrants were now cut off from the distant labour markets. Their answer to the cash crisis was to increase cultivation of marketable foodstuffs: hybrid maize (early-seventies) and later (mid-seventies) 'free market' haricot beans.

In an area long-known for its concentration of people (Willis 1966: 47), the increased importance of the land resource led to further reductions in fallows and, consequently, to extra demands on labour power. The introduction, first, of cassava and, later, of hybrid maize were advantageous from the point of view of eliminating seasonal peaks in the demand for labour. Labour needs for cassava can be spread out; while the requirements for hybrid maize, under conditions of land shortage, also compare favourably with the demands of the millet system (Bury 1983: 268-9).

The maize programme, to be sure, does imply certain long-term ecological risks - such as soil salinization, caused by repeated use of nitrates, and the risk of nutrient imbalance in the soil - but these problems are not immediately evident. The problems that were in evidence, by 1977-78, were those of the relative cost of the fertilizer requirements, and the poor supply situation. When I started research, the Aisa Mambwe had relegated millet to a subsidiary crop, whereas their neighbours north of the border with Tanzania (Mambwe, Fipa) had preserved the 'traditional' millet-based food system. The relegation had been made possible thanks to the ease with which Tanzanian millet could be imported. Southern Tanzania at that time was known to have substantial surpluses of 'black market' millet (Bury 1983:274). Differences in policy between the Zambian and Tanzanian national food strategies were crucial to the Mambwe economy at the time of my fieldwork (but see Chapter 9).

Even when the institutionalized framework for 'bringing development' to the countryside began to cough up fewer and fewer resources, in the wake of the mid-1970s economic downturn, Zambian policy remained strongly hybrid-orientated. To compensate for the inadequacies of a campaign originally designed to mobilize the entire nation, the Zambian leadership launched more specific, small-scale projects, while nevertheless preserving the emphasis on hybrid maize. All over Zambia, including Mambwe land, local settlement projects shot up. Such projects were often designed along the lines of the 'integrated development' approach and funded with external aid. From a planner's point of view, small settlements are easier to handle than a programme aiming to involve the country's entire rural population. Also, the neat physical lay-out of small projects has aesthetic appeal, and their potential for producing healthy-looking statistics never fails to impress the touring expert or the donor anxious for results.

Given the importance of 'modernization' and my focus on 'the money economy', it is essential that I set in perspective the role of the small settlement. This I shall do by way of a short account of the history of development priorities in Zambia, up to the late 1970s.

DEVELOPMENT PRIORITIES IN ZAMBIA

Watson's optimistic analysis of how Mambwe villages coped with migration in no way altered the facts that agricultural economies had remained underdeveloped and that the colonial administration had done next to nothing to promote income-earning opportunities in rural agriculture. When independence came, the Zambian state faced the gigantic task of having to build an infrastructure to meet the hopes raised by the political struggle. Facilities for credit, extension and marketing had to be designed, and implemented; a system of fair producer prices had to be worked out.

The history of planned effort to raise standards of living in rural Zambia has followed a course which alternated between spasmodic commitments to building socialism and painful calculations of their cost. In the immediate aftermath of legal independence, when the countryside awaited its reward for the struggle, Zambia's leadership attempted to implement the president's idealistic prescriptions for mobilizing rural producers. The leadership opted for a system of indiscriminate handouts under the auspices of the co-operative movement. But if political pragmatism ruled supreme in the early days of independence, the strategy never paved the way for a collectivized rural agriculture. After several years of administrative trial and error, President Kaunda finally admitted that his utopic vision of a collectivized countryside, united by the presumed zest for co-operative work, had proved unrealistic. The hoped-for conditioning for collective work was shown to have no base. Villagers had welcomed the loan scheme as their just reward for winning independence; not as a form of assistance to be repaid at some later date. Loans were spent on conspicuous consumption; not invested in agriculture. Decades of rural contact with capitalist forms of management, in the mines and on the commercial farms, had prepared rural Zambians for anything but a return to altruistic, collective efforts. The widespread enthusiasm for setting up cooperatives had been nothing more but one good way of making sure that the familiar system of migrant remittances did not disappear overnight.

The collapse of the movement for co-operative farming came in 1972. It had many causes, both organizational and financial (Quick 1978), but it was the low rate of loan repayments which made the winding up inevitable. Huge amounts of government money had been squandered. Planners needed to reconsider the course 'rural development' should take. The closure of the department of Co-operatives, coupled with the nation's first serious budget deficit, invited a radically different strategy, away from utopian visions, more in line with the spirit of capitalism and free enterprise. The Agricultural Finance Company (AFC) stepped in to salvage the remains of the movement and took 'merit' as its guiding principle.

AFC supported the strong, the upwardly mobile, the male farmer who could prove himself. It was a big step towards imposed differential treatment, not only within the rural communities, but also on a regional basis. The evidence about resource allocations by AFC, for the mid-seventies, reveals strong regional disparities, with outlying areas being denied a fair share of the funds. For instance, the four northernmost provinces (Northern, North-Western, Copperbelt and Luapula) - inhabited by nearly one third of Zambia's total population - received a mere 4% of all AFC funding in 1974 and 1975 (Elliott 1983: 170).

In addition to its policy of unequal funding, AFC suffered from ineffective liaison between the development bodies that existed at various levels of organization. A case in point is the information given by Due, who shows that not all of the allocated funds were taken up. Farmers whose applications had been successful, sometimes had second thoughts about picking up the inputs. Although Due's sample

was drawn from AFC lists of farmers who had been approved for a loan in 1975, it turned out that 24 and 35 percent of these farmers had not carried through and picked up the inputs in 1975 and 1976 respectively (Due 1980: 40).

The problem of Zambia's neglected rural sector is not just a matter of financial constraint at the centre or of farmers having second thoughts about borrowing. It is also a case of deficiency in centre-periphery communication – a deficiency caused by a clash of values. Value orientations at the centre continue to reflect neo-colonial interests or, if the term is preferred, urban bias. The birth of state capitalism, heralded by the 51 per cent takeover of the privately-owned mining companies, had never posed a threat to the entrenchment of urban-based interests. Shimwaayi Muntemba's argument that 'peasant agriculture was and is part of a market system regulated by the demands of the mining sector' (Muntemba 1977: 361) remains as true as ever.

The late 1970s programme for agricultural extension and for providing AFC credit favoured farmers who were already better off (Marter and Honeybone 1976; Klepper 1979: 140-43). This worked against peripheral rural areas. Klepper has stated in this respect that 'the smallest areas for which the AFC will make loans are frequently larger than the total area cultivated by the typical peasant household' (Klepper 1979:142). The statement applies to the majority of Mambwe villages in which I researched. With the exception of Kaka and Chele - two centres selected for Intensive Development Zone (IDZ) activity - I very rarely came across any serious village-based group interest either in AFC or in the extension service. It was not that subsistence farmers showed no interest *per se*. As will be illustrated in later chapters, it was rather that peasant opinion on the issue of 'guided' rural development continuously shifted between a feeling that the people were denied a share of official resources and the conviction that plausible survival strategies could only come from personal initiative, i.e. from deploying one's organizational capacity.

When criticism of the co-operative programme mounted, President Kaunda too conceived the idea that rural development should come from the people. Villagers, he thought, could organize themselves on the basis of their 'village councils'. He re-labelled the councils and called them: Village Productivity Committees (VPCs). Unfortunately, Kaunda once again misjudged, for the basic ideology of the VPC was 'alien both in concept and in doctrine' (Nelson Richards 1982: 154). On the other hand, the logic behind the decision of government was clear enough. By placing the initiative on the shoulders of the village community, the state could seek to revive the spirit of farming co-operatives and work-sharing without having to spend any of its dwindling public funds. The position of the Village Productivity Committees and the overarching development structures will be discussed in Chapters 5 and 6.

In spite of the post-1972 policy shift from agricultural collectivism to an explicit capitalistic approach, which was neccesary to keep the AFC alive, government still carried a heavy burden. Hybrid maize seeds and chemical inputs were subsidized at high cost, and vast amounts of fertilizer had to be made available throughout the nation (Dumont and Mottin 1983:46). Responsibility for the collection of maize surpluses also remained with government. The burden was too heavy for the government-controlled market organization. Inputs became more expensive in the second half of the seventies, their supply more erratic, collections and payments increasingly late. Peasants working in peripheral areas were soon starved of cash.

Government resources were also in short supply by the time I started fieldwork. Agricultural inputs were rising sharply in price; returns for commercial production stagnated. In a country shaken by inflation, peasant incomes were being reduced in real terms. I had anticipated some scarcity of land, scarcity of labour too, but the dearth of cash often struck me as the more severe handicap. The central agricultural administration in Lusaka responded to the ailing infrastructure by approving the drive for settlement schemes. Hedlund (1984) looked at the rationale beneath this 'new' idea:

The authorities were of the opinion that it was easier to administer and control a local project than to alter the government market organization and that there were greater possibilities of increasing [overall] maize production through a project than by influencing the Ministry of Finance into raising maize prices (Hedlund 1984: 243).

POLICY, SETTLEMENT, AND FOOD PRODUCTION

One such settlement project, supported by the parastatal IDZ (Intensive Development Zone) organization, has now made its mark on the physical and social landscape of the Mambwe grasslands. With its 'World Bank'-style

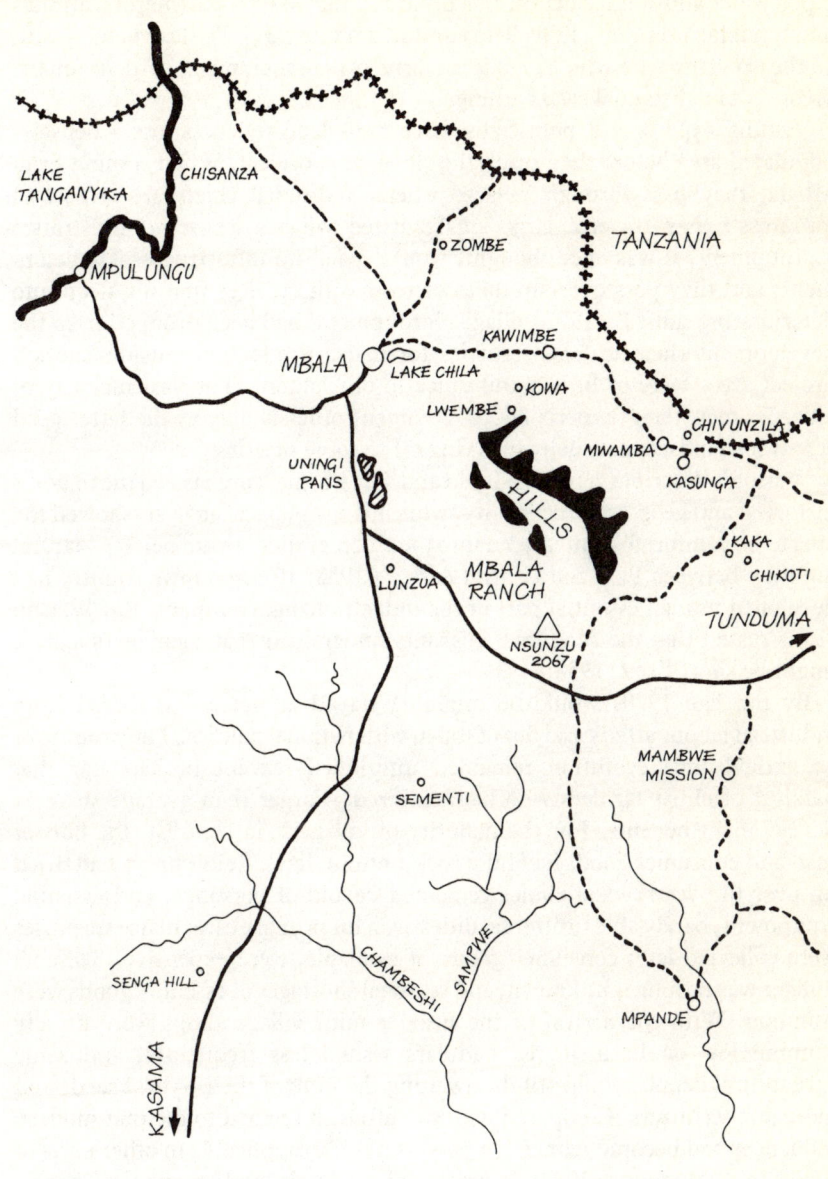

Map 1 Mbala district: Mambwe hinterland

houses and offices, neat rows of red-brick dwellings for farmers, scheme for piped water and storage depot, this project, situated in Kaka (map 1), attracts much public attention. Travellers comment on its carefully designed lay-out, on the expertise with which registered farmers plan their maize gardens, on the prospect of substantial cash earnings.

Visiting experts and politicians drive their land-rovers across a densely-populated area before they reach the site of this project. When coming from Mbala, they pass through villages where traditional chiefs are critical of 'progress'; they traverse large amalgamated villages whose administrative regroupment, it was once thought, would speed up infrastructural development; and they pass over stretches of road with crevices that dig deep into deteriorating soils. By 1977 'village regroupment' had been dropped from the development rhetoric, and statistics for maize production outside selected project areas were of little significance to officialdom. The vast majority of villagers met 'their' experts and government officials only as the latter sped across the landscape, usually hurrying off to some meeting.

Watson's description of 'The Land and The People' emphasized the region's historical and geographic centrality, while his sociological analysis showed the area to be comfortably integrated into the colonial state. From being a 'natural highway between East and Central Africa' (1958: 10), Mambwe country had developed into an essential part of the industrializing continent. But Watson also stressed that the Mambwe migrants understood that their involvement might be short-lived (1958:8).

By the late 1970s would-be migrants stayed at home – divorced from industrial labour affairs and out of touch with national politics. The promise of an agricultural revolution remained unfulfilled, except perhaps for that handful of elitist farmers who had acquired a larger than average share of development benefits. For the majority of villagers, in contrast, the flow of cash and consumer goods had hit a rock-bottom 'low'. Remittances had dried up over the years; local clinics remained devoid of personnel and essential equipment, barely able to offer facilities even for primary care; maize surpluses were collected late; consumer goods, if available, were expensive. Seasonal hunger was no longer unknown, and seasonal shortages of essential goods were common. With the arrival of the heavier rains village shops were usually running low on basic items, peddlars visited less frequently, and some agricultural depots would still be awaiting the bulk of their hybrid seeds and inorganic fertilizers. Compared with the fifties, it seemed to me that modern influences had become reduced, a perspective also applicable to other parts of Africa (e.g. Mendonsa 1982:75, writing about Sisala land, Northern Ghana).

What, then, remained of the natural beauty and grandeur which had moved Sir Harry Johnston to describe this region as a 'veritable paradise' (1958: 9)? Johnston's statement, which Watson recalls, reflected the lush scenery of the late-wet or early-dry seasons, as well as the agreeable Mediterranean-like climate brought about by the elevation of the plateau. I too found the climate delightful; I too enjoyed vistas of nature swelling with the promise of abundance. But climate and seasonal splendour belied those features of the physical landscape that were also known, even to the early travellers, to make the area bleak and desolate (Bury 1983: 24). Bury, the human geographer who shortly after my own fieldwork studied the soils and agricultural organization of a Tanzanian Ufipa village, stresses that pleasant temperatures on the plateau do not compensate for those features that make agriculture so very risky. The constraints that stand out in her assessment are the fairly uniform day length of twelve hours, evapotranspiration,[4] and the unreliability and paucity of rainfall receipts (Bury 1983: 47-51). Bury's calculations of rainfall distribution over a period of 35 years (1946-80) enable her to argue that the entire plateau should be thought of as located within Africa's semi-arid zone. She shows for Mwazye village, where she was based, that it is in the semi-arid zone 46 per cent of the time – a fact which farmers must incorporate into their agricultural production strategies (Bury 1983: 51-54; with reference to Porter 1979: 7).[5]

Watson's descriptions of the grassland fallow system and the woodland *citemene* technique, the two systems found in Mambwe land, are testimony of how cultivators on the plateau used to respond intelligently to the above-mentioned environmental constraints. The mounded grassland system, which normally combined crop rotation with adequate resting periods, ensured satisfying yields and full restoration of soil fertility (1958:24), while woodland cultivation produced maximum yields and lowered the requirements for weeding (1958:27-28). Watson also reported harmonious interaction with the environment and self-sufficiency at the level of the village community. Even under conditions of substantial outmigration for men and increasing population density, adequate food intake was still ensured.

The emphasis on village-level self-sufficiency would seem to clash with the emphasis, in the general literature, on plateau/valley systems of exchange. For indeed, the references to plateau/valley (or plateau/lakeside) interaction are sparse in Watson's account. He acknowledges the occurrence of regular visits to Mambwe villages by fish peddlars who travelled up from Lake Tanganyika (1958: 20), but there is no attempt (and perhaps there was no need for an attempt) to present this trading as an integral part of the continuous transaction between two complementary ecological zones. Whether such inter-zonal exchanges existed and whether they should have been presented as *the* mechanism which secured self-sufficiency at a wider level of organization, I cannot say. However, there is now historical evidence to argue that valley/plateau exchanges have pervaded the economy on the *Tanzanian* side of the Northern plateau for a very long time. Fish-for-grain exchanges, much in evidence during my own fieldwork, feature prominently in Wright's reconstruction of rural life in pre-colonial and early colonial Ufipa (Wright 1977). The strategies resemble those of the ecology-based systems of interdependence observed in other peripheral parts of East and Central Africa (Little 1983; Silberfein 1984; Pottier 1986a). Wright holds that the end of the nineteenth century was marked by the exchange of fingermillet produced on the plateau, for fish and cotton cloth produced in the Rukwa valley (Wright 1977:1; see also Willis 1966: 24). The fish-for-grain exchange 'allowed residents from one area to find refuge in another during times of environmental crisis or social upheaval' and continues today (Bury 1983: 43; referring to Wright 1977:2).

Notions of 'complementarity' and 'refuge' are still manifest on the plateau (see especially Chapters 3 and 7), but the underpinnings of the regional system today have more to do with geographical isolation and the proximity of the international border with Tanzania than with ecological complementarity in a 'natural' setting. The ecological dimension does exist, and is crucial to the Mambwe economy, but it has acquired strong political overtones. The new complementarity is the result of planned intervention, the result of styles in nation-building that have imposed diverse-but-intersecting agrarian policies. The complementarity I witnessed, from the Zambian side of the border, was a response to the displacement of fingermillet by cassava and hybrid maize, *a transition then not yet known in southern Tanzania*. Complementary transactions were also much determined by the dearth of essential consumer goods and cash, for shortages were felt on either side of the border. In an environment threatened by resource depletion and chronic shortages, adjacent peripheral regions pay much attention to how best they can develop their respective potential for interaction and mutual benefit.

I suspect that cross-border interaction during the 1950s revealed an equally strong interest in 'cashing in' on the supply-and-demand situation, but the overall picture in *Tribal Cohesion* is one where cross-border activities are dominated by the free flow of (male) migrant labour. The feasibility of a strong interest in cross-border activities during the colonial era will be taken up in the concluding chapter.

Recent decades have witnessed significant changes in respect of the border economy. These changes relate not only to the flow of goods, but also to the flow of migrant labour. The latter became more restricted with independence and the subsequent closure to foreign workers of Tanzanian labour centres. In addition, as later chapters will reveal, there exists a clear link between current developments within the local agrarian economy and those changes that have affected the recruitment of migrant labour. The link warrants an account of post-colonial migrant policies.

CHAPTER THREE

MIGRATION TODAY: THE VIEW FROM A RURAL DISTRICT TOWN

In part one of this chapter I examine the opportunity structure of Zambia's urban centres, by focusing upon the employment situation as it developed along the Line-of-Rail. That situation is then contrasted, in part two, with opportunities found in Mbala, the rural district town nearest to the Mambwe area. Developments in Line-of-Rail employment are assessed on the basis of secondary material; while the situation in Mbala is portrayed with the help of first-hand data. For Mbala I collected labour histories in three UNIP sections of Masaiti, the town's squatter settlement. These labour histories contain information about the nature of employment and social organization in the district town and also, importantly, about the nature of Mambwe return migration.

THE END OF CIRCULATORY MIGRATION?

The growth of peri-urban settlements after independence generated a demand for *informal* labour. This raises the question whether this demand could compensate for the stagnation in formal employment. The evidence to date is patchy and the answer far from obvious.

Zambia's difficulties with creating *formal* employment, in contrast, have been much better documented. The following statements describe the situation on the Copperbelt:

[in the mining industry] employment between 1960 and 1974 increased by just over 20 per cent or at an average rate of 1.8 per cent per annum or a little over 800 extra new jobs a year. This small increase was a result of a reduction in expatriate employment by 42 per cent and an increase in African employment by 41 per cent during this period.

...

The problem of stagnating employment is accentuated by the stabilisation of the labour force. ... the annual turnover among the African labour force fell from 30.2 per cent in 1960 to 7.6 per cent in 1973. As a result, employment opportunities to new-comers are not as often available now as they were a decade ago (ILO 1977: 108, 110).

Daniel put the situation into demographic perspective:

recorded employment declined, as a proportion of the Copperbelt population, from about 20.2 per cent in 1966 to 16.1 per cent in 1973 (Daniel 1979: 34).

Such broad generalizations have not yet been attempted with regard to the creation of informal opportunities. The paucity of first-hand evidence may well be responsible for this. Publications on informal sector economic activities in urban Zambia concentrate on trading in local markets, especially those found in Lusaka's low-income settlements. Sparse as the literature may be, the works of Nyirenda (1957), Miracle (1961, 1962) and more recently that of Oberschall (1972, 1973), Jules-Rosette (1982) and Hansen (1975, 1980) nevertheless provide us with a diachronic picture of informal opportunities for trading. The changes that have taken place are significant for establishing the current position of both long-term and would-be migrants. Changes in the overall pattern have only been documented for markets in Lusaka, but the findings also apply to the Copperbelt (Daniel 1979, below).

A summary of Oberschall's main conclusions is useful for grasping the position of aspirant Mambwe migrants today. By 1970 Lusaka's market vendors differed from those described by Nyirenda in two ways: firstly, vendors were on the whole more mature in age; secondly, people born in Northern and Eastern Province had come to replace the Lozi, Tonga, Lenje and Soli traders of a decade and a half earlier (Oberschall 1972: 119). These changes in the composition of Lusaka's trading population, Oberschall added, were 'more dramatic than the small corresponding changes in ethnic and regional composition of the Lusaka population as a whole' (*ibid*: 119).

Of Lusaka's many markets, one in particular (Mwaziona Compound, formerly Kapwepwe Compound) has attracted a higher proportion of Bemba and Mambwe speakers (Oberschall 1973: 488). This indicates that aspirant migrants from Mambwe country might still find a foothold in the capital. But how steady is this foothold? How do young rural Mambwe fit into the world of urban dwellers with whom they share an ethnic affiliation? Oberschall lists several aspects that are typical of Lusaka's trading communities. One of them is age:

The traders themselves tend to be long-term Lusaka residents, not recent migrants. Only 20 per cent have lived in Lusaka for less than five years. Their migration history prior to settling down in Lusaka shows that nearly all of them had been labour migrants on the Copperbelt, in Rhodesia, in South Africa, or some combination of these places. About 70 per cent are in their thirties and forties: they are typically middle-aged men (1973: 490; also 1972: 109).

Although there appears to be some room for younger traders, it emerges from Oberschall's data that the trading networks of Lusaka-based Mambwe lack the open character which would welcome young arrivals from the home district. He remarks explicitly that 'adolescents and young men are conspicuous by their absence from the market' (Oberschall 1972: 122). In view of the fact that the Mambwe traders of Mwaziona have firm urban roots and sizeable families (Oberschall 1973: 490), it is not too difficult to see why avenues in urban trading are now closed to newcomers. One Mambwe shopkeeper in Kabwata market, about whom Oberschall writes, exemplifies the point. Oberschall refers to his informant as Mr.M.

Suppose K90 is a reasonable estimate of M's monthly earnings, what becomes of that money? [K1=£0.66] All of it is used to maintain his family and dependants, leaving little working capital for the business. Of four sons, one is a clerk at the Ministry of Education, one is a messenger, one is a primary school teacher at Ndola, and the youngest one is still at school in Form III. Of the three daughters, two are married and one is divorced. His household consists of himself and his wife, his unemployed, divorced daughter and her child, his messenger son, who earns K22 a month, plus the son's wife and their three children. All these people live off his earnings. On top of that, for the last three years he has been supporting an unemployed brother, his wife and their eight children living in Chaisa Compound. He does not express any bitterness over this fact, and says that somebody has to help the family when it is in need (1973: 483-4).

This leaves Mr. M., a typical small businessman, with no money to expand his business. Most certainly he is unable to welcome distant nephews or nieces who might come down from Mambwe country to try their luck. To take on kin as business assistants, which is one possible solution, may also bring its problems. Miracle recorded the still common complaint that such assistants 'help themselves to stock or money as if it were their own' (Miracle 1961: 723).[1]

Small-scale trading absorbs seasonally unemployed, semi-skilled workers 'who choose rather to remain in town than return to their rural homes' (Mitchell 1957, in Nyirenda 1957: 31). Whether or not the term 'seasonal' still applies, rising unemployment during the seventies has now forced even established urban residents to be active in a variety of job situations (ILO 1977: 130). This development has reduced opportunities for newcomers to an absolute minimum. The large urban family base and the necessity to maintain ties of friendship with other established traders, who may be migrant friends of long standing, are factors that help create an inhospitable environment for the would-be migrant. The situation took a turn for the worse with the economic depression in the mid-seventies.

A major change in urban marketing is the reported increase in market women (Oberschall 1972: 120). The process whereby women came to dominate market places in Zambian towns had already set in by the late 1950s (Miracle 1962: 174), even on the Copperbelt (Miracle 1961: 713). Later increases occurred after the governmental decision to relax constraints on the movement of single women (Heisler 1974: 64). If we accept the suggestion that 'market women... [were] fairly satisfied with their lot' (Oberschall 1972: 114), we still need to bear in mind that 'operating a market stand ... [was] typically a wife's way of supplementing family earnings in low-income working class households' (*ibid*: 114), and that such a satisfying activity was denied to the majority of migrant women. The denial sometimes stemmed from the husband's disapproval of work outside the home for his wife.² At other times it resulted from 'the conditions created by the [administrative] world outside the township[s] which ... offered the married women very scarce work openings' (Hansen 1975: 798).

Such adverse conditions force women, particularly women for whom there is no place in the markets, to exploit economic avenues that outsiders have labelled 'illegal'. Women marketeers in urban Zambia, I infer from the literature, must be a relatively privileged but declining group, whose position is increasingly dependent on a permissive socio-economic environment (Hansen 1975: 798).³ The plight of the female migrant, then, is not a happy one that attracts a flow of newcomers. Nor does the position of the male trader offer any great security. Traders in Lusaka, male and female, were hardworking and probably quite content in the early seventies. More recently, they have been relegated to a low-income group with few legal rights and few avenues to explore. Oberschall foresaw this when he wrote:

> The immediate danger on the horizon is the slowdown of the Zambian economy, which is very dependent on the production and marketing of copper and on world copper prices. Tighter government budgets and a business downturn can be expected to decrease employment and purchasing power, and thus also the demand for goods by the African consumer (1973: 498).

This indeed is what happened. Low-income groups still contribute to the quality of urban life, as researchers and Commissions of Inquiry repeatedly point out (ILO 1977: 129-37; Simons 1976: 22-24; Van Velsen 1975: 296, 298), but they are precluded from developing their potential.

Small-scale trading is the dominant 'informal' activity throughout urban Zambia. It is fast being transformed into a system closed to new migrants. The development has also been observed on the Copperbelt. For Kitwe, Daniel suggests major restrictions in both the type and the location of 'informal' employment. He concludes:

> Whatever the way in which charcoal burning became the leading economic activity in squatter settlements, it is clear that the additional employment and income generation from the spread of informal activities in squatter settlements was limited.
> ...
> Whatever the limitations on the development of informal activities in squatter settlements, the Kitwe survey made it clear that informal activities tended to be concentrated in these settlements, rather than in authorised housing areas where restrictions were even greater.
> ...
> If there is, as we have argued, a strong association between unauthorized or squatter settlements and informal income opportunities, then the pattern of residential development in the Copperbelt suggests that the spread of the informal sector there was limited in comparison with its development in Lusaka (Daniel 1979: 42, 43, 47).

The depressing features of the urban informal sector are well understood by the Mambwe 'back home'. Would-be migrant men realize, as the details of their short-lived careers will show (Chapter 7), that they cannot rely upon their urban kin when searching for employment. It had always been difficult, even in the fifties (Watson 1958: 119-20). Likewise, women who wish to live and work in town know equally well how dependent they are, not necessarily on 'jealous' husbands who deny them an independent source of income,[4] but most certainly dependent on kin who cannot support them and on a politico-economic environment that does not stimulate work opportunity in the informal sector (Hansen 1980; Jules-Rosette 1982). In my experience of the Mambwe homeland, aspirant migrants prefer to comply with the reasoned thinking which Van Velsen found in squatter behaviour. He wrote: 'There is no evidence of squatter areas being overrun by rural migrants who keep flowing in irrespective of whether there are jobs for them' (Van Velsen 1975: 304).

At the urban end, however, where a first generation of urban-born adults has now emerged, the assumed rational behaviour of would-be migrants cannot be a sufficient guarantee for stability and progress in informal economies. As the ILO reported, 'given the slow growth of formal sector employment and the rapid increase of the labour force, particularly in urban areas, more and more people are having to seek income-generating opportunities in the informal sector in spite of its disadvantages' (ILO 1977: 130). Since there is no rural alternative for the urban-born, I expect urbanites will guard against any distantly-related newcomers who seek to join the urban ranks.

The repercussions caused by the saturation of urban labour markets can be seen in the recent growth of Zambia's provincial and district towns. It is for this reason that I now turn to a discussion of how Mbala, previously Abercorn, developed after independence.

MBALA: POPULATION GROWTH, SOCIAL GROUPINGS, ECONOMIC ACTIVITIES

During the earlier part of fieldwork I concentrated my research on Mbala's now legalized squatter settlement. The settlement, called Masaiti, did not exist at the time of Watson's study, so it was only natural to anticipate that it might have a role to play in the local economy, as a nucleus perhaps for town-country interaction. I spent some three months in Masaiti, observing daily life and collecting census data. I refrained from using a standard questionnaire, but worked through constructed interviews that covered topics from housing and employment to household composition and contacts with rural areas. I maintained a close link with the squatter settlement throughout my fieldwork.

At the time of fieldwork, Mbala's population was around 9,000. This compared with a total of nearly 3,500 in 1963, and 5,125 in 1969. An estimate in *Abercornucopia* (10 March 1964), the local weekly newsbulletin, set the figure for 1959 at 1,373. This included 132 Europeans. The numerical increase during the 1970s must not, however, be thought of as spectacular, since it was due in part to a change in the administrative terms of reference. The change had come in 1975, after President Kaunda announced the 'freedom of residence' resolution and relaxed the policy towards unofficial housing areas. The 1969 population survey, conducted before the resolution, did not, therefore, include the squatters. Nevertheless, in spite of the official recognition of Masaiti, a recent government document still stated that 'Mbala's town area supports about 5,282 people' (GRZ 1977b: 1). Its authors left Masaiti Compound, or 40% of the population, out of the picture. The omission reflected the attitude of politicians and civil servants who still felt embarassed about the settlement.

Official attitudes towards Masaiti have probably not changed all that much since the early days of independence. In those days, at a Board Meeting held on 22 January 1965,

The District Secretary reported that he was anxious to alleviate and, if possible, eradicate this housing problem as soon as possible. A detailed survey would be necessary, he said, but he understood that many of the occupants were employed, at least temporarily, by building contractors such as Messrs. Thomson and Piccioli. He suggested that some of these occupants be allowed to move into the High Density Area where they would be subject to Board jurisdiction and public health standards of sanitation and water supply, and an appropriate charge made to the contractor (*Abercornucopia*, 12 February 1965).

Even though 'eradication' was later dropped in favour of an 'upgrading' campaign, officials still seem annoyed with Masaiti's existence. It is still not clear to them, for instance, which proportion of the squatters are in formal employment, and they know that very few aspire to move up into the controlled housing area. There is also widespread ignorance about the settlement's internal organization, which means that officials do not attempt to mobilize Masaiti's workforce as part of the 'upgrading' campaign. Notwithstanding the reported successes with self-help projects in other parts of the country, Mbala's authorities prefer to contract labourers and to bring in workers from outside the district, when project work is undertaken. A poignant example, Masaiti's water scheme, was nearing completion in 1978. The situation contrasted with similar projects, for instance, in Lusaka's unauthorized settlements, where the local communities themselves had taken on the tasks with success (Muller 1976). In Mbala, the party channels of UNIP had helped convey the squatters' wish for improved sanitation, yet its leaders thought active local involvement in executing the water-scheme to be something of a risk. One leader who put it mildly said, 'we intend to serve the people in Masaiti by teaching them'.

The 1969 census figure of 5,125 excluded the inhabitants of Masaiti, which was then known as Misasa. In 1969 the squatters were registered at the Lunzua polling station, under the jurisdiction of Tafuna, the Lungu senior chief. They totalled some 2,500. For 1977-78, my own estimate sets the figure at about 3.500.[5] A survey carried out by Mbala Township Council, in June 1977, had suggested a total of 820 households (see GRZ 1977b: 89). Assuming the information is correct, my own survey from three UNIP sections, or 150 households, must have covered almost 20% of the entire settlement.

Mbala township is laid out following the pattern of income distribution. The town's high-income group, consisting mainly of high- and middle-ranking civil servants, occupies the centre of the town. Half encircling the centre stand the houses of government employees and workers who belong to the lower-level income group. Formal employment is a prerequisite for residence in that sector. To the west is Masaiti: a long stretch of spontaneously-built houses that accommodate a variety of social groupings. Masaiti counts many returning migrants, and nearly all its people are informally employed.

My major impression of Masaiti is that it should be viewed as a community of social groupings that have arrived at a crossroads. Whatever their reasons for coming to Mbala, residents in Masaiti are first and foremost a transient people – 'transient', not 'irrelevant' or 'disposable'. One major contribution is the role Masaiti people play in provisioning the town with foodstuffs and other scarce commodities.

The statistical evidence I collected strengthens the idea that the district-town squatter settlement does not attract residents on a permanent basis. My survey shows that some 80% of the adults who lived in Masaiti at the time had arrived after the 1969 census. Masaiti should not, therefore, be thought of as made up of an old established core with expanding peripheries, as Oberschall found to be the case in Lusaka. Mbala's squatters are essentially a people in transit.

Future trends in the pattern (or duration) of residence for each of the resident categories are difficult to predict. For one substratum of the population, the large group of female-headed households, residence may become more permanent in the future. But there are obstacles too, as I shall point out. For one other major category, the returning migrants, it is equally difficult to predict future tendencies regarding residence. Whatever changes the future may have in store, I must note that both categories – women household heads and returning male migrants – live in continuous contact with the surrounding village communities. This then is an important characteristic of district-town squatters.

WOMEN HOUSEHOLD HEADS

Most strikingly represented in Masaiti is the category of female household heads. The trend for divorcees or widows, and their dependants, to join the ranks of the urban poor is relatively new, and very likely still increasing. Households in Masaiti can be identified as Lungu, as Mambwe, or as mixed. The Mambwe/Lungu households in the surveyed UNIP sections can be broken down in the following types:

	MALE-HEADED			FEMALE-HEADED
	MONO-ETHNIC	MIXED	MIXED	
Mambwe	(M/M) 20	(M/non-M) 4	(non-M/M) 20	27
Lungu	(L/L) 23	(L/non-L) 12	(non-L/L) 8	21

Table 1: Marriage patterns for Mambwe and Lungu residents in Masaiti.

Note: polygynous unions count as two households - e.g. 5 Mambwe men married two wives each. This brings the total to 24 unions for 19 men. Ethnic origins have been bracketed, the man's ethnic group being stated first. For example, (M/non-M) refers to unions involving a Mambwe man and a woman of non-Mambwe origin; (non-L/L) refers to unions between Lungu women and men of non-Lungu origin.

The figures in Table 1 suggest that female-headed households, Mambwe and Lungu, account for nearly 33 per cent of the total number of households in my sample (27+21/150). The incidence of female-headed households for other ethnic groups (Nyamwanga, Bemba, Tabwa) is low, but sufficient to permit the generalization that one Masaiti household in three is headed by a woman. This is significant for the social development of a region traditionally marked by principles of patrilineal organization.

Not all single women who leave their natal village, the village of their ex-husband or the town where they resided with him, arrive in Mbala to become or remain the head of a household. Many, however, do remain independent. My sample includes 36 Mambwe women who were unmarried when coming to Mbala (of whom 32 arrived after 1970) and at least 23 unmarried Lungu women (of whom 18 arrived after 1970). Of the former group 13 became later involved in urban unions; of the latter only 5 married after their arrival. I use the term marriage in a loose sense here, since I recorded few unions where bridewealth had been transferred. The incidence of Mambwe women who live with non-Mambwe men (table 1) supports this idea.

The women of Masaiti cooperate with one another in many ways, and in a variety of activities. Some activities lead to cooperation with women from within the neighbourhood, others with relatives. The distinction, to be illustrated later on, could be typical of the social organization in Zambia's district towns. I note in this respect that Masaiti women have never experienced large-scale opposition by local authorities. Such opposition, reported by Hansen for Line of Rail women traders, has also been noted, for example, for Mathare Valley in Kenya, where it 'gave the whole Valley a great deal of social and political cohesion' (Nelson 1978: 92). In Masaiti, opposition from outside is on a limited scale. Before 1975, township councillors may have been opposed to the very existence of Masaiti, and they still sanction traders who flout market regulations (e.g. traders refusing to use scales), but their opposition never culminated in police raids or in mass arrests. Occasionally, scapegoats are found and fined, for instance for selling illegal crude gin (*cancine*), but Masaiti as a whole is not a systematic target for infiltration by the authorities. When opposition is experienced, the pressure is usually confined to the township markets. The sales of produce at home is not objected to, and the brewing and selling of maize beer (*katata*) is an accepted strategy for earning additional cash.

This comparatively moderate opposition to illegal or competitive economic activity must be seen in the context of Mbala's geographical isolation. The town has a poor grasp on the flow of consumer goods, especially in times of scarcity. To risk a caricature, many a civil servant, party leader and planning officer depends upon Masaiti residents for regular supplies of grains, fruits, vegetables, fish and *katata*. Town authorities understand perfectly well that they cannot do without the redistributive services of those who live by petty production and small-scale trading. So long as the nationwide distribution of consumer goods is taken care of by poorly organized parastatals (Chapter 5), so long the authorities will refrain from sanctioning Masaiti residents 'en masse'.

Katata brewing is always an additional means of income, never a full-time occupation. The connoisseur grades *katata* according to the amount of fingermillet that is mixed in with the maize. A high millet content gives the better quality. But millet has to be purchased in the countryside and becomes scarce towards the end of the rainy season. This is precisely the time when women prefer to stay at home rather than travel in search of marketable produce. Scarcity pushes the price of millet up, especially between January and March, when many women in Masaiti find it difficult to brew on a regular basis. Two or three times a month is considered a good average in the latter part of the rainy season. On the whole, though, profit levels remain too low to provide the extra income needed to alleviate the hunger. Many women in Masaiti anticipate the lean annual period by returning 'home' to a village they know will welcome them. Refuge during the hunger months is rationalized in terms of the cultivation needs of kin, but urban insecurity must not be dismissed as irrelevant. The case of Faides, described below, must be increasingly common.

Case Study 1: Changing Circumstances

Faides, a Lungu woman, lives in Masaiti. She has no children of her own, was divorced twice because of barrenness, and now lives in town with her half-brother's son, Njenje. The boy attends primary school. Faides deploys her labour on two fronts: as an active marketeer, Faides has recently developed an interest in cash cropping. This interest made her fairly unique at the time. But Faides is no different from the other women in her efforts to trade in minnow-sized herring (*kapenta*), a dry season activity, and in her interest in marketing storable produce and fresh vegetables.

Faides now exploits a small farm, with her mother and half-brother. The benefits are shared. This is no big enterprise, but the one bag of fingermillet (*malezi*) and the two bags of maize (*cisaka*) which Faides acquired as her share of the 1977 harvests were stored and later sold at her Masaiti home. By selling during the scarce season, she managed to make a net profit of K35, while keeping some of the produce for her own needs.

Faides's labour input was some six weeks of light clearing and planting at the onset of the rains, some four weeks for weeding, and another four to six weeks during harvest time. The end-product of her labour, in its cash form, was a welcome addition to the income derived from other sources, mainly beer brewing and vegetable marketing. Her home village being near the port of Mpulungu, the trips home were also occasions for acquiring goods that were in high demand in Mbala. Small quantities of *kapenta*, a few bottles of scarce cooking oil (*saladi*) smuggled in from Tanzania, and a few gallons of *cancine* all found their way to Faides's home.

The case of Faides highlights more than the transient nature of life in Masaiti. It is also relevant because Faides did not start farming in her half-brother's village until after some five years of urban residence, during which period she undertook no agricultural work whatsoever. Her 'sudden' interest in small-scale cash cropping was a safeguard against the risk of total impoverishment. Many more female household heads, I expect, will start supplementing their meagre incomes with farming 'at home'. Women like Faides, who in the early seventies derived much of their income from the local *kapenta* trade, have already had to find new means of maintaining standards of living. Growing storable crops with a view to hoarding is one answer to the restriction now imposed on the informal *kapenta* trade. (The restriction is discussed further down.)

Mbala's squatter area justifies its existence through contributing to the distribution of scarce goods and agricultural produce. Its internal organization is tuned to distributive activities that require the mobilization of extensive networks. The effective networks of active traders incorporate both neighbours and village-based contacts. Some of the latter live in Mambwe or Fipa villages across the Tanzanian border. Before I discuss Masaiti networks in depth, I must first outline the position of the other dominant social category in the settlement: the returning migrant.

MALE MIGRANTS IN MBALA: TYPES, ASPIRATIONS, HOME-TIES

When I arrived in the district I thought of Mbala as a rapidly growing rural town, capable of re-orientating migrant routes from the hinterland. I was influenced by Mansfield's reference to the 'chibuku' National Brewery, which he called an area of internal demand for maize (Mansfield 1975b: 17). (Chibuku means 'maize beer', in Cibemba.) The view proved ill-founded. As I gathered information about the development of the town I learned that labour opportunities had decreased compared with those available in the 1950s. The brewery itself employed only some twenty people. The most dramatic illustration of the decline in labour opportunities concerned the International Red Locust Control (IRLC).

Watson had stressed the importance of the IRLC, which then had permanent headquarters in the town. He wrote:

> Some local jobs in agriculture, domestic service and general labouring are ... provided by European farmers and traders. There are not enough of these to form an important market for the Mambwe. By far the largest private employer now is the International Red Locust Control. This organization's task is to control the breeding and swarming of the Red Locust in two areas, the Mweru marshes to the north and west of Abercorn and the Lake Rukwa valley in Tanganyika to the east. It maintains a large workshop to service its fleet of vehicles and special spraying equipment. This workshop employs some 130 Africans, many of them in semi-skilled work, as well as a body of about sixty African drivers. In addition, the administrative side of the organization employs clerks and messengers, and the European staff also employ Africans as domestic servants and gardeners. This organization therefore forms a considerable addition to the local wage market for Mambwe, both skilled and unskilled. It also serves to demonstrate the pull of a local market against the industrial market of the Copperbelt (1958: 49).

In addition to this, the IRLC recruited African workers on a temporary, casual basis (see table 4). Casual labourers cashed in on the money economy, while remaining available in their home villages during peak labour periods. Their recruitment, as it were, doubles the significance that Watson attributed to the IRLC. Watson's reference to nearly 200 African workshop personnel and drivers was really only half the picture.

Recruitment of IRLC casual labour remained high until about 1958, but declined in the years leading up to independence. By 1964 the IRLC had ceased to be an important source of local employment, not only in Mbala but in East Africa as a whole. Table 2 illustrates the decline in aggregate terms, referring to all IRLC stations. The figures deal with African staff only.

PERSONNEL	1953	'54	'55	'56	'57	'58	'59	'60	'61	'62	'63	'64
established	406	406	419	369	346	282	251	215	156	102	98	54
employed*	375	321	348	292	226	205	180	127	92	73	52	42

Table 2: Employment of African staff in all IRLC stations (1953-64).
Note: I compiled the information from the *Annual Reports of the Director*. (*The discrepancies between 'established' and 'employed' personnel reflect leave periods and vacancies.)

After 1964 the distinction between European and African staff was replaced by that between senior and junior staff. The latest figures available at the time of fieldwork were for December 1976. The breakdown of these figures, for Mbala, read:

Administration	10 (incl. 2 Tanzanians and 1 Ugandan)
Scientific Section	4 (incl. 3 Tanzanians)
Engineering Section	12 (incl. 1 Tanzanian and 1 Malawian)
Air Wing	6 (all foreign nationals; incl. 5 Tanzanians)
UNDP/FAO	1 (USA)

Table 3: IRLC employment in Mbala, December 1976.

The *Annual Report of the Director* (*ARD*) commented upon the reduction in the IRLC permanent labour force. The reduction in established personnel 'from 346 for 1957 to 282 for 1958' was attributed 'almost entirely (57) ... to the change in scouting methods and the use of swamp skippers on population assessment' (*ARD* 1958: 75). A subsequent 'reduction in the establishment of African employees from 215 in 1960 to 156 in 1961', was also caused by the introduction of new technology. It was 'due almost entirely to all scouting for locusts (except research) being done by aerial reconnaissance and maintenance in Rukwa ceasing to be the responsibility of the service' (*ARD* 1961: 34).

But equally important are the figures showing the decline in casual labour employment. The figures I obtained are for Mbala station and relate to the years of crucial change:

	FEBR.	MARCH	JUL.	DEC.
1958	231	200	135	79
1960	37	29	33	23
1962	10	12	19	16

Table 4: IRLC recruitment of casual labour, Mbala station. Compiled from *Council Minutes* kept at the IRLC library.

Casual labour opportunities were reduced because 'fewer men [were] working on buildings in Abercorn during 1959, and since hopper control no longer [claimed] any large number of labourers'. Further reductions were caused by the 'virtual completion of the scheme for making service houses "all-electric"' (*Council Minutes*, No.8, 1959). By 1962 the recruitment of casual labour had dropped to an insignificant level. Some fifteen years later, when I started fieldwork, the number of Zambians employed at the IRLC workshop was down to ten (Engineering Section, table 3). Among them was Chief Amos Kowa, who already worked there back in the 1950s (Watson 1958: 127). When I left Mbala district, Red Locust were planning to move their headquarters down to the provincial capital, Kasama. The move was prompted by the temporary closure of Mbala airport to all civilian activity.

One other employment sector had also virtually disappeared: the sector with 'local jobs in agriculture, domestic service and general labouring ... provided by European farmers and traders' (Watson 1958:49). Although much smaller in scale, this sector provided valuable experience in agriculture. I became impressed, for instance, with the number of Mambwe labourers who for longer or shorter periods had worked at the Lunzua Agricultural Station. In the late seventies, the disappearance of this kind of employment was felt by local job-seekers and by aspirant farmers. Another market on the verge of disappearance was the already referred to, and recently built, 'chibuku' brewery. This small establishment was also scheduled to be moved to Kasama, with the loss of twenty local jobs.

By 1978 the largest local employers were Mbala Township Council, Mbala Rural Council, Public Works Department and the Zambian Air Force base. I obtained detailed employment figures with respect to the former two (see Pottier 1981: 258). In terms of the prospect for creating more local jobs, these figures suggested strongly that no significant increases had taken place since Zambia gained independence.

The stagnant character of Mbala's formal labour market parallels the scene on the Copperbelt, but contrasts with the growth of its squatter settlement. No observer can help being intrigued by that contrast. Stagnation, however, is the key to understanding the position of that second category of Masaiti residents, i.e., the returning migrant men and their families. I focus on male migrants, not only because I want to link up with Watson's account, but also in order to highlight aspects of return migration. The latter is an understudied aspect of life in rural Zambia. This is not to say that female migration does not exist. On the contrary, as I shall show later on, female migration, and in particular return migration for women, has become most important for understanding the transformation of village structures (Chapter 4). Female migration exists in its own right, probably with a strong seasonal component (see the case of Faides, above), but it too remains understudied.

Since I have already written about the position of male residents who completed long-term migrant careers (Pottier 1983a: 11-13), I can restrict myself to a summary of the argument. Male migrants in Masaiti can be classified under three headings. For its 'returning migrants' (a first group), Mbala is the final step on the itinerary. Men in this first category invariably spent many years away from their villages, did in some cases return home in between jobs, and are now preparing for their retirement. They claim never to have doubted their return to Northern Province, but admit that the decision to resume *village life* after so many years in the towns is no easy matter. Such men want to hang on to an urban style of life, regardless of the cost, and many know that they would not be too welcome in the villages they left as young labourers. Although there are usually several residential options open to the returning migrant, a point developed in the next chapter, the actual return is postponed for as long as possible, or until an opportune moment arises. One good opportunity for resuming village life is when the returning migrant takes over as doyen (*cikolwe*) of a clan section.

Of the 60 Mambwe/Lungu adult men in my sample, I succeeded in meeting 44. In some cases there was just one extended interview, in many others we met on a more regular basis and also during leisure time. Of those I met only 15 belonged to the category of 'returning migrants'; 16 had never been to the distant labour centres; and 6 had been on one trip only, after which they had spent many years back in their fathers' villages. The remaining 7 were first-timers; young married men attracted to town life. Residents in the second category had moved to Mbala after their 'release' from village commitments (see "Released Farmers A", table 5), while men in the third category had returned to their villages to work the land and take part in social affairs, after just one trip to Tanzania or the Copperbelt. They 'released' themselves again at a later stage in the life cycle. The discharge from social and agricultural duties at home sometimes coincided with the death of the doyen of their lineage section and the dispersal of his children. Dispersal is common, especially in cases where doubts have been raised about the causes of the doyen's death.

The distinction between returning migrants and adult men who finally freed themselves from their villages is not locally perceived, yet it is useful for understanding attitudes towards the maintenance of rural gardens. 'Returning migrants' were conspicuous for their non-participation in village agriculture, whereas about half of the 'released farmers' kept an active interest. The breakdown was as follows:

MIGRANT CATEGORIES	MALE RESIDENTS TOTAL		CULTIVATING AT 'HOME'	
	Mambwe	Lungu	Mambwe	Lungu
(A) Returning migrants	7	8	0	0
(B) Released Farmers A	9	7	5	2
(C) Released Farmers B	1	5	0	4
(D) First-time migrants	2	5	0	2

Table 5: Migrant categories (Masaiti) and the maintenance of village gardens.

The table shows that fifty per cent (11 out of 22) of the 'released farmers' continued to maintain village gardens, whereas not one 'returning migrant' (out of 15) had started to cultivate in the 'home' village.

One other factor which (in theory at least) affects the maintenance of gardens 'at home' is distance from Mbala. Some 'returning migrants' with homes in Chief Mpande's area pointed out that they did not have rural gardens because of the distance at which Mpande is situated. Keeping gardens at home, they claimed, was acceptable for people from the grasslands. I checked their statements against my own data, only to find that four of the five Mambwe families with gardens at home were cultivating in the woodland zone. It seemed unlikely therefore that distance from the home village had much to do with keeping up an interest in rural gardens. Further inquiry revealed that in all four cases the migrants involved belonged to the 'released farmers' category. Some of them had male kin in those villages. Social distance, I concluded, was more of a key factor than physical distance.

The correlation between type of labour history and maintenance of village gardens also fits my data on Nyamwanga residents. Of the 13 Nyamwanga men with whom I could discuss the matter, only one stated that he had recently cleared a 4-acre plot near Isoka. The man, in his early sixties, intended to leave Masaiti shortly. As was the case with Mambwe and Lungu men who tended gardens in their villages of origin (a concept discussed in Chapter 4), this man too had been in close contact with home throughout his career as a migrant labourer. He had made just one trip, before his first marriage.

Nearly all of the 57 Mambwe, Lungu and Nyamwanga men whose labour histories I recorded expressed an emotional link with their home country (*kumwitu*). However, the migrant's concept of 'returning home' does not necessarily coincide with 'cultivating the land', an equation embedded in Watson's view on Mambwe return migration (Watson 1958: 135). For some migrants the homeland continues to be a truly rural environment; for others 'returning home' means extending an urban way of life in the district town nearest to a village one can call 'home'. Home-coming, as a concept, is moulded by the migrant's labour experience: the longer the period of absence, the greater the chance that 'home' is away from the village.

Cultivating the land, likewise, is no longer just a means of achieving security, since the home village is now also a place for raising cash crops. The table below shows the acreages of crops grown 'at home' by the male migrants who lived within my survey area. I also list their motivations for doing so. The table suggests correlations that could have wider applicability. Suggested is a link between type of labour history and the maintenance of rural gardens (with 'returning migrants' of course absent from the table); and a link between urban job insecurity (or advanced age) and the decision to resume village life. The information also confirms that rights in land do not lapse, not even after a long absence from the village (compare columns 'arrival Mbala' and 'gardens since').

A final category of Masaiti residents, to be added to the larger groups already considered (female-headed households; migrant households), groups the households of enterprising young men who chose Mbala for starting up a business. With formal job prospects lagging behind popular expectation, the ranks of this category are unlikely to swell in the near future.

ECONOMIC ACTIVITY AND THE NATURE OF URBAN-RURAL LINKS

One immediate outcome of the 'closure' of distant labour markets, formal and informal, has been the expansion of small-scale trading and petty production in the Mambwe homeland itself. The expansion of informal trading is not indicative of a flourishing economy, but rather epitomizes the region's worsening supply situation.

Masaiti, the hub of all informal activity, derives its importance from the proximity of other nation states (Zaire, Tanzania) and the lake that they share. The lake is a regular focus for debating regional development (GRZ 1977b). Since Mbala district borders on Lake Tanganyika, local people know that the lakeside town of Mpulungu has great potential for developing the region. Planners even believe that harbour activities in Mpulungu could expand, should the area be capable of producing 'a surplus to international requirements' (GRZ 1977b: 10). Such an expansion might mean that meat from the Mbala State ranch 'could find a market in the other lake countries', as could the products of a local manufacturing industry (*ibid*: 10). The boom would end a situation in which the role of Mpulungu, Zambia's only international port, remains confined to the handling of relatively small consignments of commercial fish - mainly *kapenta* - destined for the Line of Rail. However, local planners do understand that capital-intensive development, 'while benefiting the nation as a whole, will not bring marked change to the economic conditions of the people of the area' (*ibid*: 10). They have raised similar objections against the development of Mbala State Ranch, against schemes for large-scale commercial farming in the region, and against several other plans proposed in the TNDP (GRZ 1977b: 45-54).

Objections notwithstanding, state capitalism now controls the fish freezing plant at Mpulungu. The decision to part-nationalize was taken because of falling levels in the traffic of fish (GRZ 1977: 8-10). Placed under UNIP management, the fishing company, SOPELAC, offers competitive prices and more or less manages to buy up the bulk of the overall catch. The price incentive ensures that the high demand for fish in the country's urban areas can be satisfied, at least to some extent (GRZ 1977b: 13-14). But the monopoly of SOPELAC has had consequences for the local, informal economy. The impact of capital-intensive fishing is felt most strongly by petty traders in Masaiti.

ETHNIC ORIGIN	CAT.	ARRIVAL MBALA	VILLAGE GARDENS SINCE	ACRES GROWN	CROPS	MOTIVATIONS	AGE	PRESENT URBAN EMPLOYMENT
Mambwe	B	'73	'77	two	beans only	returning home	41	marketeer (lost job '76)
,,	B	'74	'72	two	cassava	security	38	cook ZAF
,,	B	'77	'75	four	maize only	commercial	24	shop assistant Namboard
,,	B	'70	'75	three	cassava, maize	security	33	occasional labourer
,,	B	'71	'77	two & a half	maize only	commercial + returning home	52	general worker P.W.D.
Lungu	C	'71	'48	nine	maize, beans, millet	commercial + security	62	watchman
,,	C	'69	'77	two	?	returning home	32	unemployed*
,,	C	'74	'73	three	cassava	commercial	48	occas. labourer
,,	C	'71	'77	two	millet, maize	commercial + returning home	63	unemployed
,,	B	'61	'31	nine	maize, beans, millet	commercial (+security)	65	marketeer
,,	B	'77	'69	twelve	everything	commercial (+security)	35	general worker N.C.U.
,,	D	'70	'75	six	maize, beans	commercial (+security)	29	cook ZAF
,,	D	'67	'76	eight	cassava	commercial	31	mechanic
,,	C	'54	'77	four	maize, beans, millet	returning home	63	unemployed

Table 6: Agricultural interests in the home village, relating to Mambwe/Lungu migrants in Mbala.
Note: *unemployed = not formally employed.

When labour migration ceased to be a viable source of income, many Mambwe looked out for alternative means of participating in the money economy. The need for such alternatives became accentuated when commercial maize farming, the alternative proposed by government, turned out to be constrained by the poor functioning of the parastatals in charge (see Chapters 2 and 5; also Pottier 1986b). The failure of the government option made it even more important that would-be migrants and their families succeeded in finding their own alternatives.

Before the fish freezing plant became part-nationalized, one popular alternative had been to take part in the *kapenta* trade. Masaiti households in particular had profited from this dry-season activity. The part-nationalization of SOPELAC, however, has now made it more difficult for small-scale traders to operate. By the late 1970s informal sales of *kapenta* had been declared illegal, while the official price was quite beyond the buying power of the average Masaiti entrepreneur.[6] Mpulungu now attracts the transport-owning long-distance trader, who knows that the trip 'up north' is well worth the effort. Not only does he control the fish market because of his strong buying power, he also knows that the district produces a considerable surplus of beans at approximately the same time that fishing levels reach their annual peaks.

In spite of the constraints, Masaiti traders still resort to *kapenta* selling and buying, since the trade is an effective means for raising their small profit margins. The *kapenta* they buy does not pass through the official checkpoints at SOPELAC. To circumvent the checkpoints Masaiti traders have contacts in lakeside villages where 'cheap' supplies of Tanzanian *kapenta* are regularly bought up. I shall now illustrate the importance of informal *kapenta* trading as a strategy for raising profits, and will discuss the span of the networks that are thus activated.

Case Study 2: The Petty Traders' Operational Field
Stage One: A Child Dies

Romance, a female Mambwe trader who resides in Masaiti, is the central figure in this series of events. One day in February she is called to the house of Melody, her husband's parallel cousin. Melody's younger sister's daughter has come from Kitwe with one of her children. The child is ill and needs medical treatment. A neighbour of Romance's provides remedial herbs upon diagnosing the illness, while other medicine is obtained from the divorced wife of Romance's husband's elder brother. The mother of the sick child intends to visit her husband's village in Tanzania. Sadly, the child's condition worsens and it dies.

The headman of the UNIP section where Melody lives is now approached to discuss the burial. In the absence of the child's father, who works on the Copperbelt, the headman decides that the father's brother must be contacted. He lives in the village of Mutula, in Tanzania. Neighbours and friends also agree that Romance will visit Mutula. At this juncture Romance calls upon one Nanyangwe, a relative. Nanyangwe and Romance visit Mutula regularly during their trading excursions. Their contact in Mutula is a daughter of Melody's.

It is at Mbala General Hospital, where Nanyangwe works with Irish nuns, that the trade route to Tanzania starts. It is at the hospital that Nanyangwe obtains children's clothes from the expatriate sisters. Such clothes, much appreciated across the border, are an ideal means of exchange. Besides the clothes, the two women also take a small amount of dried fish from Mpulungu. The fish belongs to a neighbour of Romance's. The trip to Mutula is partly by bus, up to the border post of Kaseshya, and then continues on foot. At Mutula the clothes and fish are exchanged for beans and some profitable tobacco. The 'father' of the deceased child is contacted and he agrees that the burial should take place in Mbala.

Stage Two: Relatives Express Their Sympathy

Meanwhile, news of the death has reached Chipanya's village. In Chipanya, which is near Kowa, lives the father of the bereaved woman. Romance's mother also lives there. Some of the villagers now leave for Mbala to express condolences. Among them is Lamek, a cross-cousin of Romance's father (see Diagram 1).

February is a time when fingermillet (*malezi*) is already in short supply, so Lamek takes with him the three bags of millet he had stored after the harvest. He asks Romance to sell the *malezi* on his behalf. She accepts, but decides against selling in Mbala. Instead, Romance travels to Kasama, a larger town, where Lake Moero and Luapula fish can be bought in the market. Romance also decides to travel in the company of her paternal uncle's wife, who lives in Masaiti, and whom she reckons to be trustworthy. The fingermillet is sold within a few days. Before the two women travel back to Mbala, they buy dried fish from Moero/Luapula.

Back home Romance first tries to sell the fish at the local market, where township regulations stipulate that fish must be sold according to weight. Realizing that profits will be low, Romance takes the fish back to the settlement, where she now sells privately, at prices of her own choice. This time, however, she faces the demands of neighbours who wish to buy on credit. Among them are the two women who provided medicine for the dying child. Not much fish is actually sold.

A few days later Romance takes the fish to the market place (read: bus stop) at Kawimbe, where fish is always in demand. Romance has little trouble selling her fish, for she has timed the visit well. Women in Kawimbe have already earned some cash from the sales of early beans. Enough money can now be put aside to pay Lamek. With her profits Romance buys rape, a tasty spinach-like vegetable grown in the waterlogged plains around Kawimbe (see Watson 1958: 9). She brings back to Masaiti a large quantity of rape, but sells few bundles. Although rape is scarce in Mbala, due to the unavailability of seeds at NAMBOARD stores, Romance takes her produce and boards the bus for Mpulungu. Her idea is to sell in the lakeside town and bring back a small quantity of *kapenta* from Chisanza, where Tanzanian fishermen or their Zambian contacts are ready for a deal.

On arrival the rape tastes bitter. Disaster has struck: Romance must lower the price of her inferior produce. Suddenly she sees the profits of her activities over the previous two weeks reduced to a minimum. Romance, nevertheless, proceeds as planned. Being at the lake, she approaches her husband's sister's grandson who lives in Chisanza. From the grandson Romance acquires *kapenta*, not as much as she had originally hoped for, and... on credit.

This case study documents not only the scale on which Masaiti traders habitually operate, it also suggests that trade partners are not necessarily recruited from within the Masaiti settlement. The latter point must now be developed.

Romance's trade partners fall into three categories (see Diagram 3). The first and most frequently mobilized category is made up of immediate neighbours,

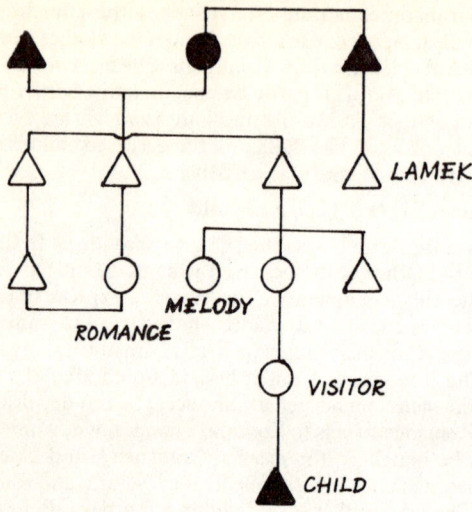

Diagram 1 Romance's effective network

several of whom, like Romance herself, originate from villages near Kawimbe. Romance is also related to some of her neighbours (e.g. M-03 and M-09 in Diagram 2). She usually chooses a travel companion from within that group. Members of a neighbourhood-based trading network have common contacts among the village producers, advance one another small sums of money, and sometimes place group orders. Reconnaissance trips into Tanzania are often undertaken by individual women who then place orders for themselves and for other members of the network. Since optimum safety measures need to be taken during such cross-border trips, traders find it practical to choose only close friends: well-informed women whom they meet regularly. Such friends do not always live in the neighbourhood, as the case study has made clear, but they are always part of the trader's social drinking network. Information relevant for trading is passed on during bouts of *katata* drinking. Selection from within the *katata* network ensures that trading partners are well-informed about security, sources of marketable food and other aspects of trading. One further aspect of cross-border trade is that small operational networks tend to form around residents, like Melody, who have kin or affines living in Tanzanian border villages.

The second category of trade partners includes rural kin and affines who have a right to the trader's labour. Rural family members turn up on occasion and receive help with the marketing of whatever produce needs selling. There are no immediate rewards for this service, though a token sum is sometimes paid. Payment does not, in this case, indicate the end of the transaction. There are two reasons for this. Firstly, the service which Masaiti residents provide must be seen in the light of the ongoing dialogue between Masaiti and nearby villages. Everyone in Masaiti is involved in that dialogue, returning male migrants as well as female household heads. Everyone is involved because life in the squatter settlement is insecure and may come to an end at any time (see the case of Bornwell S., in Pottier 1983a: 12). So, refusal to cooperate with visiting relatives could jeopardize the squatter's chances of a smooth return to village life, should conditions in town necessitate such a return. Secondly, the Masaiti trader who accepts to make a deal on behalf of visiting kin is usually given time to use the proceeds of the transaction for personal investment. Romance, for example, sold Lamek's millet in the provincial capital, acquired fish in her own name, and could thus hope to obtain some kind of tangible reward. The financial leeway that is allowed and the 'credit' one earns towards a happier village retirement offset that touch of exploitation that many deals between Masaiti traders and country folk appear to have.

Finally, trading activities that carry high financial responsibility or risk demand a different mode of recruitment. In such cases the trader will rely upon kin or affinal contacts who are particularly trustworthy. She may even be instructed to do so by the villager who initiates the transaction. Of course, family links are no guarantee for honest behaviour. People who have only recently taken up long(er)-distance trading, like Romance, may therefore decide to switch to another member of the extended family, should the first choice be found to be less trustworthy than had been expected.

Neighbourhood networks within this small district town do not assume the exclusive significance which they may do in larger towns. To recast Nelson's conceptualization of female networks in Mathare, the effective network of the Masaiti trader is by no means synonymous with the resident cluster (Nelson 1978: 87). The effective network is primarily made up of neighbours, but among the neighbours are lifetime friends and relatives from the area of origin. Diagram 2 illustrates the high incidence of kin and affines in Romance's urban neighbourhood. Moreover, friends, relatives or affines from outside the neighbourhood may also be key figures within the effective network. The comparatively open character of the effective network of small-scale traders could be typical of the economic organization in small urban towns throughout Zambia.

OTHER INCOME-EARNING ACTIVITIES

It is difficult to estimate real incomes from activities such as brewing and selling beer. There is seasonal variation in the amount of brewing that can be undertaken, beer may go off, and profits are usually reinvested into some form of trade. Given the economic importance of the *katata* networks, Masaiti is a good illustration of the view that 'it is not a question of whether these urban

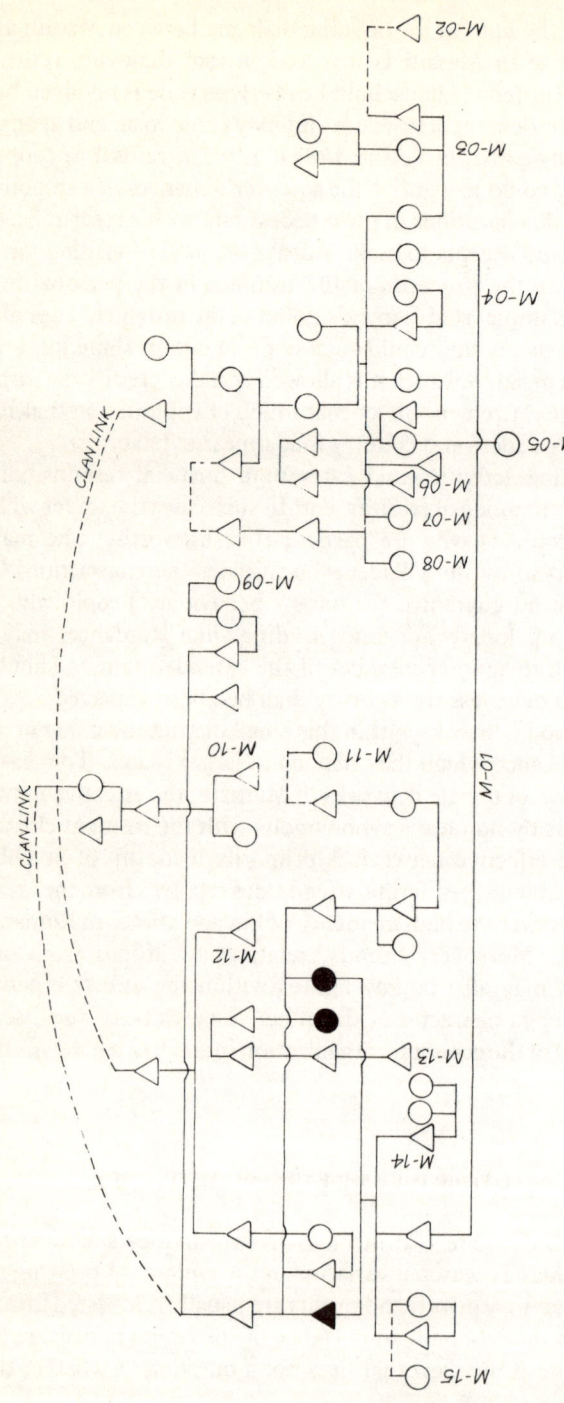

Diagram 2 Kinship and affinal links of M-01 (Romance) within the three UNIP sections surveyed

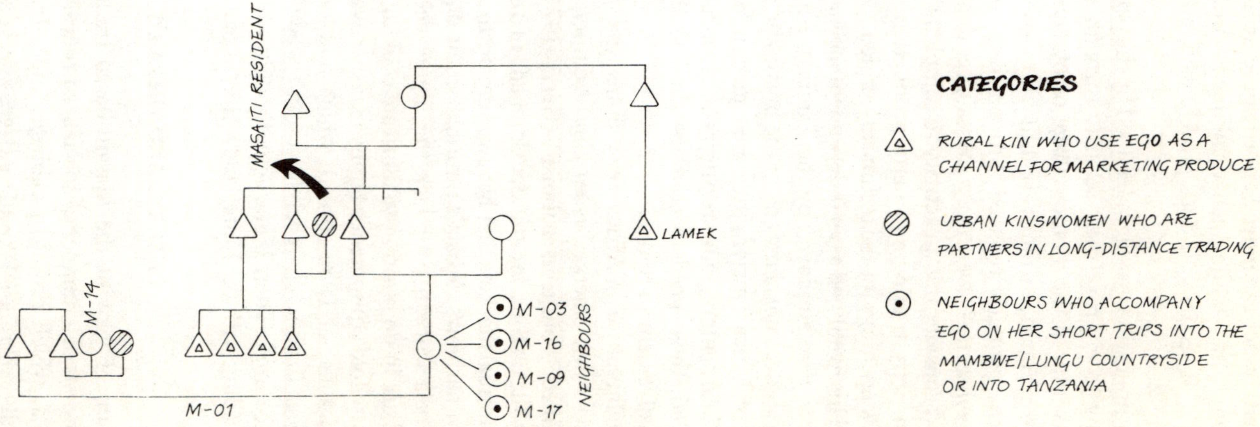

CATEGORIES

△ RURAL KIN WHO USE EGO AS A CHANNEL FOR MARKETING PRODUCE

◍ URBAN KINSWOMEN WHO ARE PARTNERS IN LONG-DISTANCE TRADING

⊙ NEIGHBOURS WHO ACCOMPANY EGO ON HER SHORT TRIPS INTO THE MAMBWE/LUNGU COUNTRYSIDE OR INTO TANZANIA

Diagram 3 Trade Partners of M-01 (Romance)

poor ... can afford to drink but whether they can afford not to' (Lomnitz 1974; cited in Lloyd 1979: 181). Being so dependent on receiving accurate and timely information - about the availability of produce, the reliability of rural contacts, etc. - no Masaiti trader can indeed afford not to drink. But it is true, as Lloyd also points out, that 'while such drinking is functional in maintaining a minimum level of security, it does prevent saving for other purposes' (*ibid*: 181).

The latter implication is well understood by the people of Masaiti, and many are now trying to improve their security through food production – either through cultivating in the 'home' village or by laying on vegetable gardens within the town. Again, earnings are difficult to assess, for the plots are small and the returns regularly reduced through theft, bad seeds, poor soil, and destruction by insects. Nevertheless, Masaiti residents are attempting to grow vegetables and consider this an activity to complement trading.

Apart from petty trading and petty production, Mbala's informal sector shows very few openings for the technically skilled. Only one young man in my survey earned his livelihood as an independent mechanic; while nearly all other skilled workers were employed by the Zambian Air Force. Masaiti, and the town in general, does not show any of the hustle and bustle that mark the low-income areas of Africa's major cities. Few men in Masaiti are able to work as self-employed carpenters, radio-repairers or car-mechanics. And of those who have succeeded, most need to combine their skilled work with at least a minimum involvement in trade.

Against the literature on Africa's city slums, the squatter settlement of this remote district town emerges as an almost empty stage, devoid of what is sometimes called 'bourgeois rubbish' (Gerry 1977: 6). Rural districts in Zambia offer little scope for the development of recuperation or recycling. Unlike the informal markets that have sprung up around Africa's capital cities and important harbours, Mbala's informal sector does not deal with recycled materials. Mbala's urban poor lack the inputs needed for artisanal metal-founding and are in no position to fabricate cooking utensils or garden tools. Whatever household equipment a family may own was once imported from the industrialized zone, or from abroad, which nowadays often means China.[7] Except for beer drums, charcoal stoves and wooden utensils, very little is locally manufactured. There is one item, though, which is made in Masaiti, for use in bean trading with the hinterland – the tin pail.

OF BEANS AND TIN PAILS

From the point of view of the Masaiti-based trader, the Mambwe/Lungu hinterland consists of a number of specialized zones. A first zone is the Kowa-Kawimbe area, which produces cabbage, rape, Irish potatoes and various fruits. Secondly, there are lakeside villages specializing in the fishing trade.

The importance of both these zones has already been illustrated. Thirdly, there is Mwamba, the area known for its surplus of beans.

I now turn to the interest in beans, as viewed from Masaiti. Not unlike the trade in fish and vegetables, bean trading too is a seasonal activity. The difference, however, is that bean traders ultimately aim to reach the Line of Rail markets, whereas the vegetables and fish traded by locals is mainly for distribution within South Rukwa. A related fact is that bean trading in Masaiti is almost exclusively in the hands of men. How they operate is shown in the case study that now follows. The man who provided the information, one Mr Simbeya (pseudonym), did not own any means of transport. His story is typical of the Masaiti-based male marketeer.

Small-scale cash crop traders like Simbeya depend upon more successful entrepreneurs for transport. The entrepreneurs are said to charge high fees. As a result, the cash crop trader from Masaiti finds it unprofitable to use cash in the villages. He will invest whatever savings he has in items that can be used for exchange. Cooking pots and colourful pails made from 4-gallon paraffin tins are among the more popular items. Many marketeers make their own pails.

Case Study 3: Beans and Exchange

Mr Simbeya explained his strategy in the following terms: 'The tin pails I make myself during the rainy season. Of all the different types I prefer to make medium-sized pots. The cost of manufacturing is about K3,50. When the pots are ready I take them to my rural contacts, who live in villages near Mwamba. Local women fill these pots with beans until approximately three quarters full. I get the beans, they get my pots.'

A quick count tells me that one medium-sized tin pail is exchanged for about $3^{3}/_{4}$ gallons of beans, or roughly K9,50. It appears therefore that the bean producer pays dearly for the pail she receives. But how does the transaction look from Simbeya's point of view? Transportation costs are as follows. Between Mwamba and Mbala he pays K1,50 to the lorry-owning entrepreneur for every bag of beans transported. For the subsequent journey to the Copperbelt or Lusaka, Simbeya pays K5,50 per bag. Simbeya himself gets a free ride. There are two entrepreneurs whom Simbeya can contact. One owns a popular bar in Mbala; the other a well-stocked store in Mpulungu. The K1,50 cost for regional transport is also the fee charged by UBZ, the national bus company. Simbeya prefers to use public transport, but the bus service had become most unreliable in the latter part of the seventies.

It takes the contents of six 4-gallon tins to fill one bag of beans. Receiving about $3^{3}/_{4}$ gallons for every tin pail, Simbeya fills a bag after 6,4 transactions. One bag therefore costs him roughly K22,40 (K3,50 x 6,4). Adding the cost of transportation, the amount Simbeya pays per bag rises to about K30. The price at which he sells in Lusaka or on the Copperbelt is fixed at K85. This means a net profit of K55. An average bean season yields between 15 and 20 bags, or a profit in the region of K1000. (This was £660 at the official exchange rate.) Simbeya does not usually make more than one such trip a year.

Once Simbeya has decided on a particular market, he works there for about three weeks, living in a makeshift tent. He never leaves the produce alone. Every bag is sold at the standard K85. Before returning to Mbala, Simbeya reinvests the profits and purchases some 20 bags of groundnuts (*mbalala*). Groundnuts along the Line of Rail cost K45 a bag. How much the transport costs amount to, and how much profit can be made from selling one bag of *mbalala* at home, remains a guess. But considering the scarcity of groundnuts in the region (see Chapter 8), I have reason to believe that profits could more or less have equalled those made on beans.[8]

Simbeya's house is one of the more miserable in Masaiti. The household often goes hungry. In spite of the apparently high returns for his labour, the money made from bean and groundnut trading remains far below Simbeya's needs. Part of the explanation lies in the fact that Simbeya has teenage children from various marriages. These children, some of whom attend secondary schools, are a constant drain on his income. (In 1978, K50 for a pair of good trendy shoes was considered a normal price.) Of course, Simbeya also has to reward his village contacts. I could not find out exactly how many middlemen were involved, but one contact, Simbeya's younger brother, was more important than the others. Being a junior, however, the young man received only a token commission for his help.

Simbeya's labour history is also significant. His migrant experiences are spread over some 17 years. He worked in Lusaka, Kabwe and Ndola, mostly as a bricklayer. He returned home in 1961 to a village near Mwamba, where he stayed until 1972, at which time he was buying up cattle for 'his' butchery in Mbala. Simbeya claims that his wealth was a cut above the average, and that social pressure and accusations of sorcery soon began to intensify. In the end, Simbeya had little option but to leave for the district town.

The Simbeya case study sheds further light on the articulation between the urban poor and the impoverished villagers. Basically, their mutual interactions are marked by solidarity and conflict. Hoarding millet for retailing in times of scarcity is no sign of solidarity with the squatter settlement; nor is it a gesture of sympathy when urban petty traders tour villages and sell their scarce goods (tin pails, paraffin, salt, soap, sugar,...) at exaggerated prices. It is my contention, however, that many of the observed instances of apparent exploitation through overcharging are eventually cancelled out because of the advantages that accrue to maintaining amicable relations. Thus the Masaiti marketeer values village contacts, since they constitute a resource pool that can be activated for many desired ends. Such contacts are important because of the ultimate security they provide, and because they are indispensible in the organization of trade - e.g. as providers of specialized foodstuffs or when overnight accommodation is needed (see also Case Study 2). Villagers, for their part, value Masaiti as a place to turn to when they need to stay in town or want to raise some instant cash. The latter point was brought out in the words of a woman I once met by the roadside. She was on her way to Mbala, and explained:

The money I earned after selling my beans is already spent. I always have debts to settle. Now I wish to go and visit my daughter in Tanga [Tanzania], and I am short of cash. I am taking this bag of fingermillet to my sister in Mbala. She will brew *katata* and I will be able to travel.

In the overall pattern of relationships between the villagers and the urban poor, their interdependence stands out as dominant. The world of small-scale trading is marked by petty conflict (maximizing a bit here and losing out a bit there), but the two sides are conscious of the benefits that accrue to mutual cooperation. At the same time, no-one can afford to take too many risks, for all struggle to make ends meet.

The main arguments in this chapter can now be recapitulated. Mbala has not developed into a town capable of absorbing young, would-be migrants. Compared with the fifties, both formal and informal employment opportunities have stagnated. This small district town provides outlets for informal trading, mainly of agricultural produce, but few residents can find a solid foothold. Residents in Masaiti are a transient people. Some have returned from long migrant careers, others use the district town as a possible 'second chance' in life.

Most households maintain active links with villages in the hinterland, through trading or agriculture. The field over which the Masaiti traders operate spans the entire Northern plateau, which includes the international border area, as well as the Tanganyika lakeside region. The trading field is unified by culture and by networks of kinship and affinity, but separated by international politics and differential pricing mechanisms. This separation is conducive to economic complementarity. Shortages of essential consumer goods exist on either side of the border. They are explored and exploited by mobile traders who operate independently (in the case of men) or in groups (in the case of women). Traders make ends meet, but only just. Occasional superprofits are quickly dissipated through social drinking and obligations towards grown-up children or village-based residents with whom the marketeer needs to remain on friendly terms.

Successful returning migrants delay their homecoming by staying on in Mbala for as long as is possible. Life in the district town is not very secure though, since profit margins are low and trade avenues may become restricted, as happened in the case of informal *kapenta* trading. This insecurity prompts the Masaiti resident to plan towards his or her retirement.

Notwithstanding the constraints, Masaiti marketeers work hard to make the most of every opportunity coming their way and have earned themselves a central position in the economic life of the district town and beyond. The district relies on them to ensure that scarce goods and foodstuffs in demand do get distributed against the odds. Increasingly cut off from previously existing labour and consumer markets, many would-be migrants now concentrate their activities in the district itself, within which Mbala township is conveniently situated.

CHAPTER FOUR

COHESION TODAY: KOWA REVISITED

This chapter explores three basic themes. Anticipating later discussions on the chances of socio-economic survival for Mambwe country (Chapters 7 and 9), I shall first examine developments within the structure of villages. This I shall do through reconstructing the pattern of residence for Kowa, described in *Tribal Cohesion* (1958: 123-130), as it developed between 1952 and 1978. Developments in Kowa will confirm the political character of marriages with the dominant Siuluta clan and the importance of cognation. Watson stressed both these aspects. In addition, the data will reveal structural aspects that do not conform to Watson's emphasis on residential permanency for men. The new evidence points to a preponderance of flexible residential arrangements which suggest that affinal relationships have become just as important in establishing residence as were agnatic, patrilocal connections during the 1950s.

The second theme is return migration. Here I shall pay attention to the impact made by those who returned to their village of origin after relatively long periods of absence. Kowa remains the venue for this inquiry. My third theme is the current pattern of wage migration and formal employment, which I discuss with reference to Mbala and the Line of Rail towns. Looking in particular at Kowa's position vis-à-vis the job market in Mbala, I shall examine the consequences of wage employment for relations on the land and will consider their meaning for social cohesion today.

Anyone interested in 'measuring' the incidence of labour absenteeism from villages in Central or Southern Africa will appreciate that the Mambwe village today no longer shows up any clear pattern of either clan dominance or interclan linkages. There is accelerated proliferation of clans, as will also be seen in later chapters, and there is regular movement between villages. These developments are significant for 'measuring' rates of absenteeism, a problem compounded by the fact that many women who joined their migrant husbands after independence have by now returned to the countryside. The presence of clusters of agnatically related women results in part from this home-coming, and also from the growing preference for uxorilocal marriage. Such clusters are significant for understanding present-day features of the Mambwe economy, since they help ensure the area's continued participation in the cash economy.

In this chapter I allow myself a detailed look at developments in Kowa, a village known for its enthusiastic response to the 1950s labour market. To link up with Watson's account I have produced an updated genealogy of Kowa, using round brackets to refer to Watson's generalogy (reproduced as Diagram 4) and square ones for reference to my own (Diagram 5). Lest this approach becomes all too confusing, I shall first recall the main features of Kowa's village as Watson described it.

KOWA: DEMOGRAPHIC COMPOSITION, 1952

Chief Kowa's village, situated some seven miles from Mbala, is on the border between Mambwe and Lungu territory. Chief Kowa is head of the Siuluta clan and recognizes the political sovereignity of the royal Sichula clan (1958: 124). Chief Fwambo, the royal representative nearest to Kowa's village, and Nsokolo, the senior royal chief, are politically superior to Chief Kowa. These relative positions have not significantly changed since the early 1950s.

The political tie between Kowa and Nsokolo was expressed through marriage. Generations of succeeding Kowas had married royal princesses from Nsokolo's family. At the time of Watson's fieldwork, the reigning chief Kowa had 'inherited his elder brother's wife, who was a daughter of the [then] Chief Nsokolo's father' (1958: 124).

Interestingly, the kinship structure of Kowa's village revealed an *internal* parallel that bound the two main residential groups: a succession of marital ties between members of Kowa's own Siuluta lineage and members of one Simpungwe clan. Of the latter Watson wrote:

The senior living member of the Simpungwe, Nsyazye (C7), blind and deaf with age, is Kowa's father's sister's son, but addresses Kowa as mother's brother. He stands in a perpetual relationship of sister's son - mother's brother to the reigning chief. *This relationship has been renewed in generation D* [see diagram 4], for Nsyazye's brother's son (D18) has married a daughter of Kowa, thus reaffirming the link between the two groups in this generation' (1958: 124-126; emphasis added).

Two other adult men living in the village were also cognates to the ruling Siuluta. Another three (C8, D22, D24) were linked to the Simpungwe lineage by marriage. One of the three, Stone Sichiliango (D22), went on to strengthen his position as an important cognate. With fourteen Siuluta men, four cognates to the Siuluta and three to the Simpungwe (out of a total of twenty-two men over eighteen years of age), Chief Kowa's village appeared extremely cohesive. Watson attributed the material success of Kowa's village to the solidarity of its kin group (1958: 129).

KOWA: DEMOGRAPHIC CHANGES, 1952-78

Two issues are important in this section: first, Watson's notion of a fixed village allegiance, secondly, the nature of the structural links that give the Mambwe village its coherence and continuity. Data towards an historical account of how Kowa developed between 1952 and 1978 are here examined in the light of Watson's theory that Mambwe men have a fixed allegiance to the paternal village (1958: 113).

The evidence I collected on the demographic composition of Kowa illustrates the problem of how labour migration from villages can be 'measured'. This methodological problem is rooted not only in the residential choices of returning migrants, choices that are never straightforward (see Chapter 3), but also in manifestations of inherent residential flexibility. In this respect I intend to show that significant sections of Kowa today resided in the village prior to Watson's study, although they were absent in the early 1950s. They were absent not as a result of wage employment, but because they lived elsewhere in the grasslands.

A central characteristic of Kowa in 1952 concerned the politics of marriage. As already indicated, Watson observed that the 'marriage between the first Kowa chief and Nsokolo's daughter [had] been repeated by each generation of succeeding Kowas' (1958: 124). The continuity of the marriage tie between Nsokolo and Kowa has now been broken. The present (1978) wife of Chief Amos Kowa, the first wife he married, is a daughter of Chief Fwambo. Of the two other women Amos married later, one has died and the other has been divorced. Neither came from Nsokolo.

The importance of this break with tradition is not that the uni-directional wife-giving link between Nsokolo and Kowa has been discontinued, though this in itself may be significant, but that the strategy of building alliances through marriage was never restricted to marriages between political centres. This is a new gloss on Watson's perspective. As my reconstructions indicate, alliance-building in the fifties also occurred between Kowa and neighbouring villages. Thus I shall show for the central Siuluta-Simpungwe alliance that the connection was not restricted to marriages within Kowa.

In this context I must note that the Siuluta core identified by Watson has been modified as a result of fission and fusion. One very important member of modern Kowa is Henry Kalandanya Siuluta. As headman of a village that merged with Kowa sometime after Watson's departure Kalandanya is of course omitted from the genealogy in *Tribal Cohesion*. But Kalandanya and even more so his deceased brother played emminent roles in the structuring of inter-clan relations in Kowa today. Up to 1976 four of Kalandanya's brother's children resided in the village: one daughter, who became the third wife of Stone Sichiliango, and three sons. The sons set themselves up as progressive farmers at some distance from the 'old' village (map 2), but one of them later

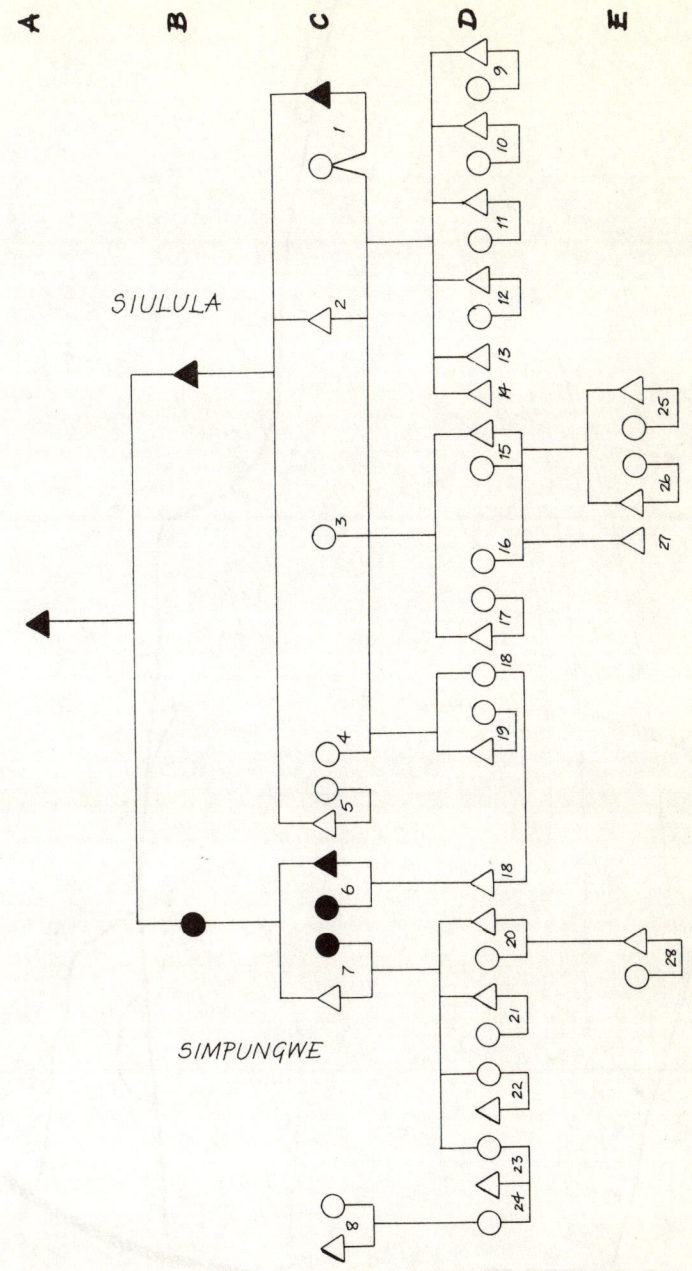

Diagram 4 Kowa 1950s taken from *Tribal Cohesion* (page 125).

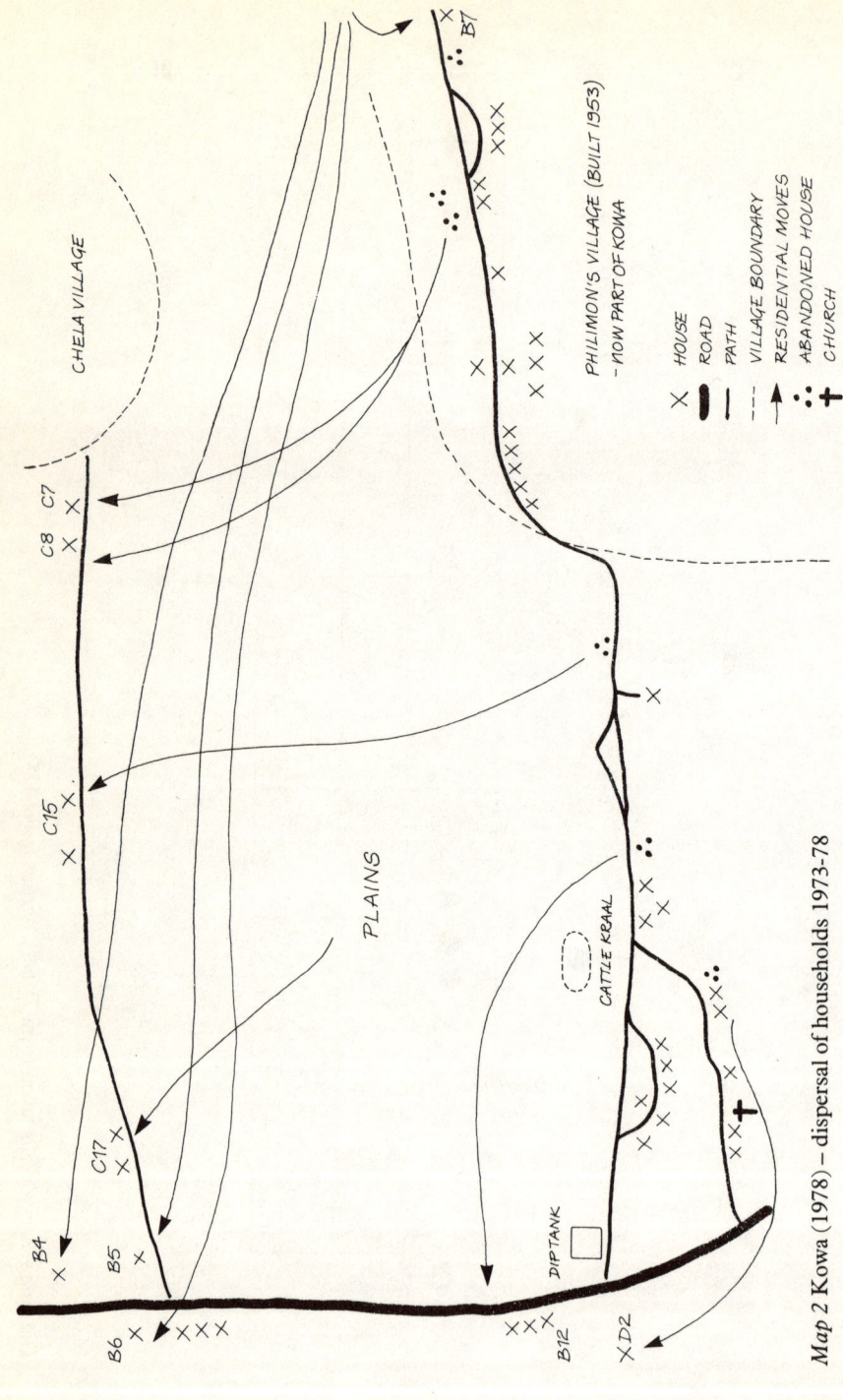

Map 2 Kowa (1978) – dispersal of households 1973-78

left after a period of bitter quarrels and fighting. Some of their neighbours are Sichiliango.

The Siuluta continue to be the dominant group in Kowa, but many other clans have now secured a foothold or strengthened their position. The Sichiliango, for instance, have gained prominence through the marriages of Stone [C17]. Stone Sichiliango's three wives, who all live in Kowa, represent connections with the two groups Watson referred to as dominant. Stone first married one of Nsyazye's (C7) daughters, then married Enika Nauluta (daughter of Jason Siuluta, D17) and has more recently married a divorced daughter of Philimon Siuluta. Spear Kavuzya Sichiliango [C4], Stone's brother, has also set up a polygynous household. He married two parallel cousins from the Sikate clan. At least one of the cousins is a grandchild of Kaputula Simpungwe [A3]. At the time of my fieldwork Kaputula was the senior living member of his clan. He had taken over from Nsyazye (C7).

It was one of Watson's arguments that social cohesion at village level was created and strengthened through strategic marriages. The plural unions of Stone and Spear Kavuzya subscribe to the thesis. Within a framework of alliance-building, the women involved can be thought of as lynch-pins within Kowa's social fabric. The view is somewhat attractive. On the other hand, it is not clear whether and to what extent these women, some of whom are returning divorcees, have been able to control decisions surrounding their secondary marriages. If they have had no or very little control in the matter of re-marriage, these women could indeed be regarded as pawns in a game. (To avoid any misunderstanding, I did not research on choice of marital partners.) But I do not favour such a view. I must point out, for example, that many returning divorcees quite openly state, as I often heard in Chivunzila (Chapter 7), that should they marry again, they will have no desire to leave their father's home and take up residence in their husband's village. This attitude alludes to a measure of autonomy for women in respect of their later marriages.

Regarding the composition of Mambwe villages today, it is one of the more fascinating findings that their structural cohesion cannot be 'measured' solely on the basis of the number of male residents and the connections between them. The Simpungwe are a case in point, as the information on clan membership and inter-clan connections so very clearly indicates. To provide data for a debate on cohesion today, it is necessary to first give detailed information on marriage and residence and to establish how the new data relate to Watson's observations.

SIMPUNGWE-SIULUTA

In his genealogy Watson suggested one (then) recent union between the Simpungwe and the Siuluta clans. The marriage was between Agnes Nauluta (D18, Lamek Siuluta's sister) and Gilos Simpungwe, nicknamed Mpulungu.

COHESION TODAY

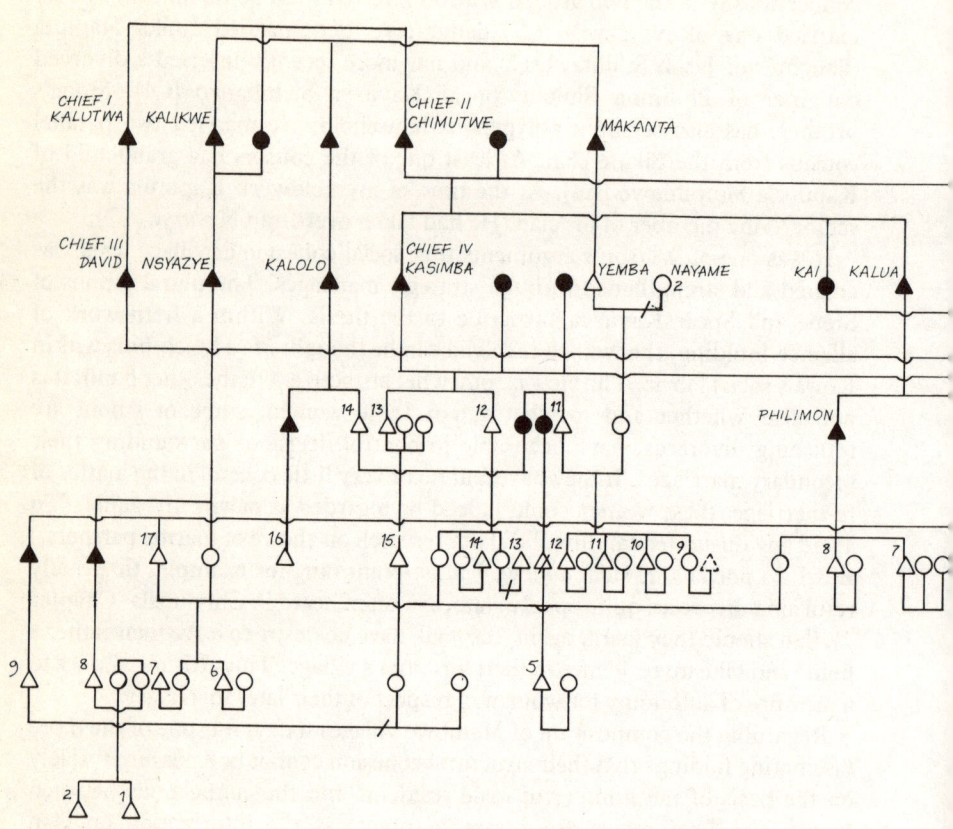

Diagram 5 Skeleton genealogy of Kowa Village 1978

MIGRANTS NO MORE

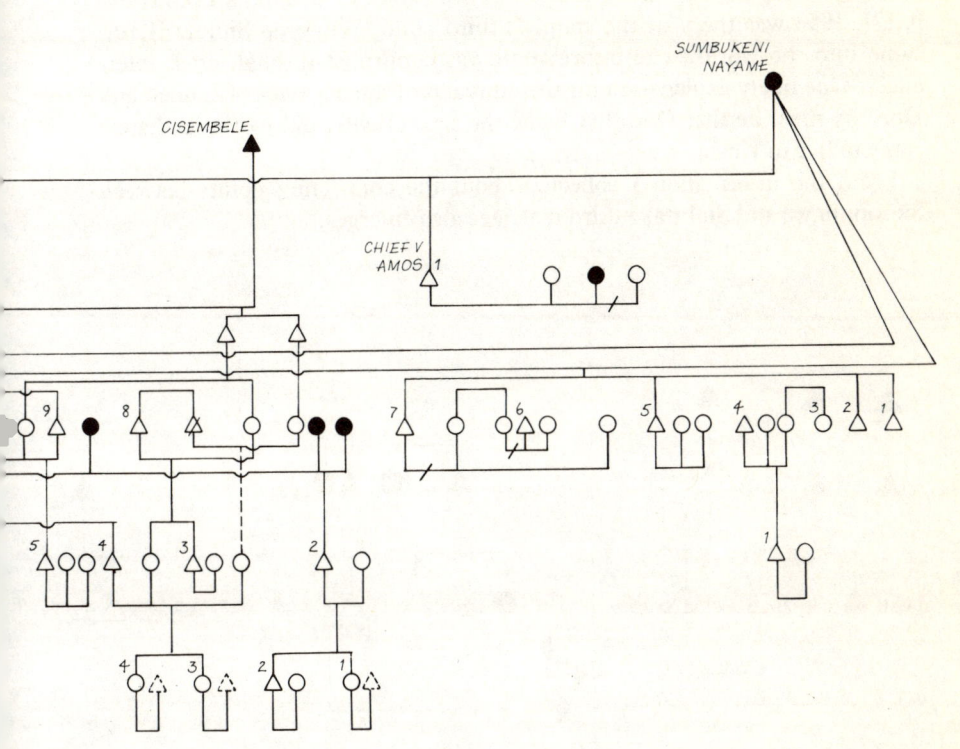

The information I obtained suggests that this marriage was only one of several similar inter-clan unions. To illustrate the recurrence of the Siuluta-Simpungwe link, Lamek Siuluta himself (D19, [B11]) also married a Nampungwe. Lamek is shown to be married in Watson's genealogy, but not to a Nampungwe. This might be because Lamek at that time was married to a different woman. However, at least two of the children Lamek Siuluta and Dorothy Nampungwe had together were born before 1953. They are [C11] and [C12]. 1953 was the year the couple's third child, Whiteson Siuluta [C10], came into the world. The information was confirmed through cross-references. One likely explanation for the omission of the marriage of Lamek and Dorothy must be that Dorothy, being the second wife, did not immediately come to live in Kowa.

From the information I collected about the connecting points between Siumpungwe and Siuluta, a third marriage also emerges:

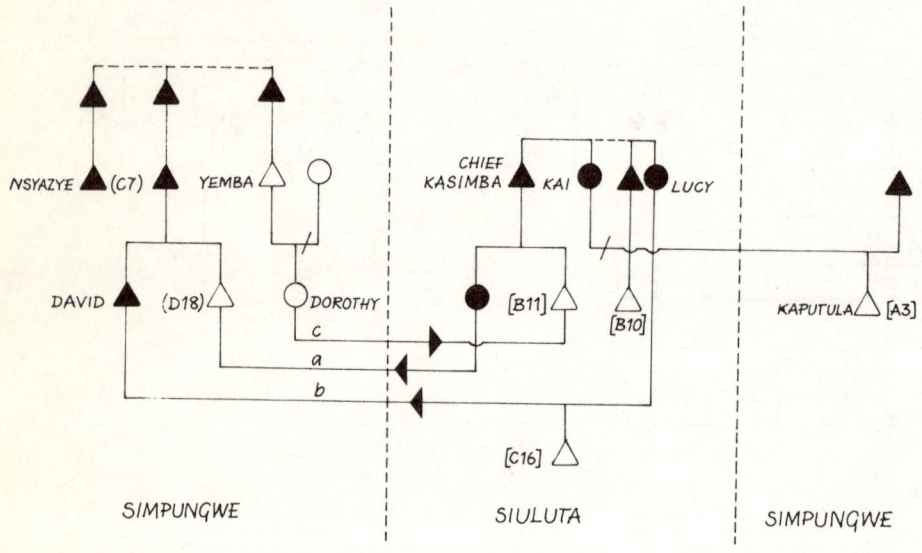

Diagram 6 Linkages between Siuluta and Simpungwe in Kowa.

This third union, between Lucy Nauluta and David Simpungwe, involved two people who both lived outside Kowa in the early fifties. They lived to the east of Kowa, in Sinyangwe's village (see map 3), with which Kowa later merged.[1] The relationship between Sinyangwe's village and Kowa is discussed.

Watson made an important point when he showed that the marriage between Nsyazye's brother's son, Gilos (D18) and Agnes Nauluta (daughter of Chief Kasimba Kowa) reaffirmed the link between Simpungwe and Siuluta (1958: 124-5). The two marriages were structurally and politically important. Yet when the field of observation is widened, as I was able to do because of the post-1952 amalgamation of Kowa and Sinyangwe's village, then it becomes clear that the importance of the union between Agnes Nauluta and David Simpungwe was more than its being a replica of a marriage from the previous generation. As I show in diagram 6, the marriage of Gilos and Agnes was no once-in-a-generation affair, but part of a system of marital exchanges in which other *villages* participated. Indeed, going back further in time, a fourth Siuluta-Simpungwe tie can be added. This is the marriage of Kai Nayame, sister of Chief Kasimba, and Cisembele Simpungwe. Kaputula Simpungwe [A3] was born from that marriage. Although raised in Mpande village, under Chief Fwambo, Kaputula later came to live in his mother's home village. Kaputula, I must emphasize, does not belong to the Nsyazye (C11) branch of Simpungwe.

Watson emphasized that the internal cohesion of Kowa resulted from agnatic, cognatic and even fictitious links. It is difficult to comment upon the current importance of fictitious links, since I knew of only one case where lineage manipulation might have taken place. In this particular case, the link between a woman and her daughter did not seem very straightforward, but I had no evidence to argue that the link was faked, that the daughter had been adopted perhaps (see dotted line in Diagram 5). Agnatic and cognatic ties, in contrast, remain paramount, with cognation quite clearly gaining in importance. Here I also recognize a new phenomenon, which combines cognation with return migration for women who separated from their urban husbands. Over the years this combination has led to the emergence of clusters of agnatically related women. I shall discuss the potentially cohesive quality of such clusters after presenting the genealogical evidence.

Other inter-clan linkages in modern Kowa are also worth mentioning. The Simpungwe are cognates to the Siuluta, as Watson pointed out, but this fact must not obscure the growing significance of cognation in general. To complete the record on marriage some further unions of political importance should be added. Significantly, such unions do not always involve Siuluta.

SIKATE-SIMPUNGWE

Just as the Simpungwe stand in a cognatic relation to the Siuluta, so the Sikate have become cognates of the Simpungwe (Kaputula branch). The Sikate in Kowa number only two adult men and two Nakate parallel cousins. There is no direct link with the Siuluta. As a lineage segment the Sikate are rather negligible, but they are important as members within Kaputula Simpungwe's following. The older Sikate [B8] is Kaputula's son-in-law.

SICHILIANGO - SIULUTA/SIKATE

The fourth residential group - members of the Sichiliango clan - has emerged more forcefully. Stone Sichiliango (D22/[C17]) married two Nauluta women, daughters of important Siuluta elders, while the link was repeated in the next generation with the marriage of Peter Sichiliango [D9] and the granddaughter of another Siuluta. Although Peter's marriage ended in divorce, its occurrence endorses Watson's argument that affinal links are sometimes repeated in later generations. Prior to his marriages to the two Nauluta sisters, Stone had married into the Simpungwe clan (1958: 126).

Spear Kavuzya, another prominent Sichiliango [C4], is a brother of Stone, and heads the local Church of God.[2] Spear married the parallel cousins from the Sikate clan. Through their marriages the two brothers have contributed significantly to the structural cohesion within Kowa. The marriages of Stone link the Sichiliango firmly to the established Siuluta core; while Spear's religious services bring together many of the younger village members.

Watson mentions the Sichiliango as an important group in the *stockaded* village before 1930 (1958: 124). This might indicate that more affinal links between Siuluta and Sichiliango could be found in the past. I did not pursue such an inquiry, but the probability is intriguing, since the position of the Sichiliango could have developed in a fashion which copies the cases of 'cyclical residence' described in the next section. It is interesting in this regard that Watson mentions Stone Sichiliango's siblings, of whom he says that they 'had long gone off to live elsewhere' (1958: 126). One of those siblings, Spear Kavuzya, has since returned to Kowa.

SICHIMBA - SIMPUNGWE

As with the Simpungwe-Sikate link, this one too involves only Simpungwe from Fwambo (as opposed to the Simpungwe mentioned in *Tribal Cohesion*). The cast is as follows. Mwanaboy Kaulwe Sichimba [B9] is married to Kaputula Simpungwe's first daughter. This elder Sichimba accompanied Kaputula when the latter left Fwambo to take up residence in Kowa.[3] The affinal link between Kaputula and Mwanaboy Kaulwe is expressed in residential proximity.

The Sichimba and the two Sikate men mentioned are cognates to the Simpungwe from Fwambo. Neither clan established affinal links with the Kowa family. Only Damson Sichimba [C2] married a Nauluta, but this woman is from Fwambo, not Kowa. But of course, when we remember that Chief Kowa's wife is a daughter of Fwambo, the whole picture begins to change, since marriage into the same clan creates special bonds.

The marital history of the Sikate clan is somewhat like that of Sichimba. The one Sikate-Siuluta link, between Fridah Nayame and Kennedy Sikate [C3], is again a union with the royal lineage of Fwambo. Therefore, if Sichimba and

Sikate have not forged affinal links with the Siuluta Kowa, it is clear that two members at least, one from each clan, have married into Fwambo, and by doing so have copied Chief Kowa's own first marriage! The act of marrying into the same clan creates strong bonds between men (see also Chapter 7). Rather than conform to the pattern Watson found to be normal practice, i.e. internal alliances with the core group, younger Sikate and Sichimba men have married women from Fwambo. Kaputula's following may reside in Kowa, which is the village from where Kaputula's mother originated, but the younger generation of cognates have yet to marry within Kowa. This fact underscores the inherent flexibility of village residence (which is contrary to Watson's claim), yet marriages are patterned, and duplicated as time goes on (which confirms a different claim).

Young men in Kowa readily acknowledge that home is not just a question of one's place of birth. When they reflect on the idea of a possibly fixed village allegiance, these men bring out that several factors must be considered. Damson Sichimba's thoughts on 'where home is' make this clear. Damson [C2] came to Kowa as a young boy, leaving several brothers behind. They now live in Mwambezi, a Lungu village under Chief Zombe. The link with Mwambezi is kept alive, as I witnessed when one of Kaputula's great-granddaughters married someone from there. It was on the occasion of the wedding that Damson commented on the link with that village. Having been chosen to lead the wedding-party to Mwambezi, Damson remarked that the trip had been 'a bit like going home'. He later told me that 'home' could mean any of three places – Kowa, where his parents had settled; Mwambezi, where his brothers lived; and Mpande in Fwambo territory, where his father was born and from where he and others in Kaputula's following had married wives.

The practice of taking up residence in one's mother's village (especially for an older man) and the related practice for younger men (especially in the next generation) to marry women from their fathers' village suggest in effect that many Mambwe men acknowledge two homes of origin instead of one. These are the village of residence and the paternal home. In the case of Lungu settlers, a third reference is then added: the ancestral Lungu village. Returning migrants may choose to go back to any of these two or three possible places. The decision, sometimes a difficult one, is often delayed through prolonged residence in Mbala (Chapter 3). Moreover, younger men today may well decide to follow an altogether different course by choosing to live with their in-laws.[4] The latter practice, uxorilocal residence, depends in part on the groom's need for good land, which may not be available in the parental village. The decision is also influenced by the labour needs of the groom's family and those of his in-laws, by the bride's view on residence (women starting secondary marriages prefer to stay in the parental village), and by the amount of bridewealth the groom is able to amass.

Although Watson resorted to the idea of residential permanency for men when explaining the 'success' of the Mambwe reserve, he implicitly supported the notion of inherent flexibility. For example, he wrote:

> Many Mambwe are born, live and die in their father's village, *particularly* members of the royal clan and of those commoner clans whose head holds a chieftaincy (1958: 113; emphasis added).

The statement allows for numerous exceptions. The qualification Watson added in the above passage and the case material he collected are compatible with the notion that regular movement between villages occurred. Residential flexibility is certainly not new: it did exist in the fifties.

Watson's account of the composition of Kasunga village, for instance, shows very clearly how unrealistic it would be to view that village as organized on the principle of fixed allegiances. Of course, the make-up of Kasunga fitted Watson's argument that the village core was stable: the royal Sichula lineage was dominant, and the headman's title of Kasunga, which was linked to the Kasunga estate, stood in a perpetual 'relationship of son to father to the title of Kela' (1958: 150-1). The permanence of the title and its being linked to a specific estate both suggested stability. Beyond that, however, every suggestion of residential permanency failed to hold. Samson Sinzumwa (D41), who headed the Sinzumwa section, had come to the village during the reign of the then acting headman. Being the son of headman Kasunga's mother's brother, Samson had been 'accepted ... into [the] village without demur' (1958: 88). (As with Kaputula, I note here too the importance of links traced via the mother.) Kari Sinyangwe (D19), another man-on-the-move, had arrived during Watson's fieldwork. He was welcomed because of his large following, yet it was known that he 'had moved from village to village throughout his life [and] seemed unable to live peaceably anywhere' (1958: 88). Taking all this evidence into account, Watson concluded:

> The permanent residential group in this village ... was the segment of the royal clan which held the title Kasunga, and its associated estate Mwansa. The village site had often been moved within the bounds of the estate which formed the cultivating area round the village. The other groups were less stable, residentially. Apart from Elliam Sinyangwe (D25), who was born in the village and whose father too had lived there, the other groups had a history of movement between villages before coming to Kasunga (1958: 89-90).

When one realizes that 'the other groups' comprised no less than two-thirds of the adult men who lived in Kasunga at the time, it becomes extremely difficult to accept, *in the context of out-migration or return migration*, that the permanency of the core group can be generalized to include all villagers. The overall conclusion Watson reached about the composition of Kasunga casts doubt upon the legitimacy of his general argument that Mambwe people adjusted to wage labour migration thanks to the permanency of their villages; a permanency ascribed to the principles of patrilineal organization and the practice of virilocal residence. In the debate on migration, Watson considered 'residential stability', through virilocal residence in marriage, to be a major coping mechanism (1958: 225). The idea does not do justice to the evidence so painstakingly pieced together throughout *Tribal Cohesion*.[5]

My own data on demographic developments within Kowa and on the residential histories of individual groupings back the view that residence, while not haphazard, is nevertheless not patterned on fixed allegiances. On the contrary, the majority of Mambwe villagers excel in their ability to move on from village to village.

A HISTORY OF MOVEMENT BETWEEN VILLAGES: KOWA (1952-78)

Evidence against the notion of a 'fixed allegiance', even in the fifties, can also be derived from reconstructing the history of residential groups within Kowa. In order to understand the composition of modern Kowa I must first go back to the 1930s.

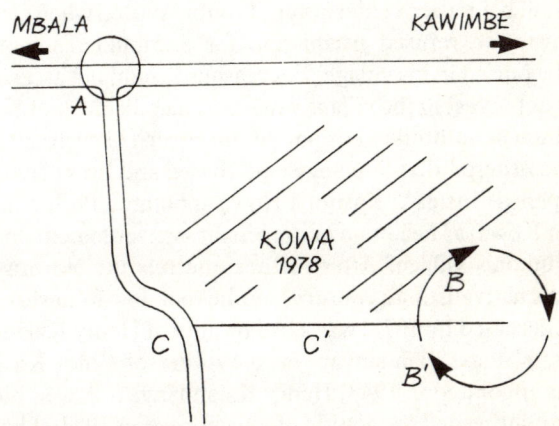

Map 3 Kowa 1935-78

In his discussion of Lwembe village, which he contrasted with Kowa, Watson mentioned that Lwembe was made up of many diverse elements. It included people of Lungu and Nyamwanga origin (1958: 129). In several respects, Lwembe was a settlement for refugees. But Kowa too, in its earlier history, had played host to the uprooted. In 1935, after their land had been alienated by a European farmer, three villages of Lungu origin were moved into Chief Kowa's area (1958: 124). One of the villages re-settled in the vicinity of Kowa. The settlement, called Sinyangwe's, included members of the already mentioned Sichimba clan. The Sichimba too were Lungu, even though the group had lived in Fwambo before moving on to one of the three farming areas (Lunzua) alienated in 1935.[6]

The refugees from Lunzua were first resettled near the junction with the Mbala-Kawimbe main road (map 3: position A). Soon after their arrival, one Mr Duncan, European manager of the cattle ranch west of Chele (Chapter 6), claimed the area and had the village move again. Position B was occupied for about a decade, whereupon headman Chikango Sinyangwe made the village move in the circular fashion typical of swidden cultivators. Shortly after Watson's fieldwork, the Sinyangwe settlement and Kowa moved their sites simultaneously, and for the last time. Kowa moved from point C to C', Sinyangwe village moved to B'. Before the final move to adjacent sites, Sinyangwe had already been placed under the jurisdiction of the Siuluta. (This is explained below.) Other important moves occurred after 1953 (see map 2), but these were made by individual households, and within the boundary of Kowa.

Chikango Sinyangwe's successor, Philipo Sinyangwe lived on cordial terms with the Kowa family. The climax of their 'entente' was the marriage of Philipo himself and Sarah Nauluta, daughter of Jason Siuluta (D17). The happy days came to an end following the death of Chenda Sumbukeni's mother (*amayo yakalamba*), i.e. her father's elder sister. Trouble started when acting headman Malinda Sinyangwe refused permission for Sumbukeni's mother, a royal princess, to be buried in his village. For reasons I could not ascertain, the royal princess was not to rest in the village where she had died. Chief Kasimba, head of Kowa and son of Sumbukeni, reported this breach of custom to senior Chief Nsokolo, who ordered that Sinyangwe be chased and his village burnt down. Neither happened. Instead, Kasimba Kowa appointed Philimon Kalandanya Siuluta (from Kowa) as headman of the Sinyangwe settlement and changed its name to Philimon's village. After further quarrels the old Sinyangwe head returned to his native Lungu country, but he took few followers.

Philimon, deceased by 1978, was a real brother of Henry Kalandanya [B10]. Their father, Kalua Kalandanya, was a brother of Chief Kasimba. When Philimon was appointed in 1943, Henry Kalandanya followed him to the new village. Henry succeeded to the title of village head in 1954. The Kalandanya lineage is absent from Watson's genealogy, because Philimon's village was then quite separate from Kowa. Today the two villages have merged. There were several marriages between the settlements, while internal residential moves completed the fusion. The marital alliances that bound the people of Kowa have meaning for understanding how the structure of the Mambwe village has developed.

The marriage between Philipo Sinyangwe and Sarah Nauluta was not the only link of political importance. Two other prominent Siuluta, Henry Kalandanya himself and David Sitbet Kowa (D10/[B7]) also married Nanyangwe women from Sinyangwe's village. David's first wife was headman Philipo Katundulu's brother's daughter; Henry married her sister. The Simpungwe mentioned by Watson also established marital ties. At least two of

Nsyazye Simpungwe's daughters married men from Sinyangwe's village, and Nsyazye's second wife is said to have been a niece of Chikango Sinyangwe. Nsyazye's second marriage and those of his daughters could be thought of as illustrations of delayed exchange, comparable to the Siuluta-Simpungwe marriages shown in Diagram 6.

The above information confirms the political significance of Siuluta-centred marriages. What Watson argued about the relationship between the major clans in Kowa, namely that they were linked through cognation, can also be read in the data about how Kowa developed after 1953. The developments, however, led to the emergence of a new group of cognates, the Sinyangwe, who gradually displaced the previously important Nsyazye branch of Simpungwe. So, although the principle of cognation is still strong, the durability of such links must now be open to question. What Watson, on the basis of his information, rightly described as a 'perpetual relationship'(1958: 124) has failed the test of time. This is not to say that the old order has totally vanished. The particular alliance came to an end, but cognation itself survived.

A further qualification is necessary. If internal alliance building with the dominant lineage (or core group) continues in Kowa, such practice has become a thing of the past in many other villages. This can be seen in the build-up of those villages that resemble chains-of-affinity, like Chikoti (Chapter 8), which is an increasingly common pattern. The data from Kowa suggest that marriage may retain its political character, but modern Kowa is the exception, not the rule. This is evident too in the village of Chivunzila, the largest amalgamated village I worked in (Chapter 7). Chivunzila has a core of nine Siame (Siuluta) men, which is considerable, but only two of these men established unions with women from other residential clans. Likewise, only two Nayame women had married within Chivunzila. This total of four marriages is a poor score for such a large royal segment. The principle of structural cohesion through cognation with a dominant core has lost much of its significance; except perhaps in villages like Kowa, where the village head is also doyen of a clan.

In spite of these erosive developments, I am still not suggesting that village cohesion today would be weaker than in the fifties. If anything, the premium now put on uxorilocal residence has strengthened co-operation, especially within some sectors of the economy. The new trend for women to return to and remain in their fathers' villages (e.g. in the event of a secondary marriage) effectively means that such villages now retain whole clusters of agnatically related women. From an economic point of view, these clusters have become valuable resources for the organization of trade and agriculture, and their activities may enhance the survival chances of the Mambwe village. The noted absence of marital links into the village core group or the proliferation of clans must not, therefore, be thought of as signs of 'cohesion undermined'. If the proliferation of clans coincides with a greater incidence of clusters of agnatically related women, then we have every reason to believe that such clusters could contribute to the economic well-being and cohesion of the Mambwe village. At this stage of analysis the possibility must remain theoretical, but a later chapter will confirm that clusters of agnatically related women are indispensible for successful trading, and therefore invaluable in the quest for continued participation in the money economy (Chapter 7). Such clusters also enhance the likelihood that adequate labour power is always at hand.

I shall document the increased incidence of women agnates who reside in their fathers' villages when I discuss the importance of cross-border trading, which has become a major alternative strategy in the quest for cash. Kowa, however, also provides supportive evidence in this respect, since Kaputula Simpungwe's following included no fewer than five married daughters and granddaughters, and two great-granddaughters whose prospective husbands were negotiating to take up residence in the village. Kaputula is important from a simplistic political point of view (i.e. 'men doing politics') because his faction contains the households of two sons-in-law and two grandsons. From the point of view of village economics, however, Kaputula's faction is powerful because it is made up of a large number of agnatically related women who have drawn in several men from outside the village. The importance of the cluster must be acknowledged. We can no longer justify a conception of structural cohesion which is entirely in terms of agnatic linkages traced through men. The occurrence of agnatically related women-in-residence is a significant change in the structure of the contemporary Mambwe village.

Large clusters of agnatically related women were not in evidence in the 1950s. The development is a by-product of the drift back to the countryside of women for whom life in the towns had become unbearable. Many women had also become estranged from their husbands. Increasingly, such women prefer to stay on in the parental village in the event of a new marriage. The reason for this preference relates to the difficulties women experience when they try to obtain a divorce certificate from the local courts. Since it is the husband who must initiate divorce procedures, divorce is often delayed or made impossible, which pushes women into concubinage. This situation provides little security and is best coped with when the support of relatives, male and female, is available. Hence the preference for staying on in the parental village or in a village where siblings live. The new preference adds further complexity to the question of what constitutes village allegiance.

The reintegration of agnatically-related women contrasts with the older practice whereby men negotiated a new place of residence at regular intervals. The old practice, illustrated in Watson's analysis of Kasunga (see above), is also quite central in the story of how Kaputula Simpungwe came to live in Kowa.

The details I obtained about Kaputula's residential record strengthen the perspective that village residence is far from automatic. The movements of

Kaputula Simpungwe [A3] and Blackson Sikate [B8] illustrate a process of fission and fusion, which suggests that Mambwe villages may well be evolving in circular fashion. Kaputula and Blackson both lived in Kowa during the mid-1940s. In 1947, however, Mr Martin, successor to the European cattle farmer mentioned earlier, threatened to extend his farm up to Kowa. The expansion meant that the traditional Kowa/Zombe boundary would be overstepped. For the first time in the colonial history of Kowa, its land was threatened with alienation. The people of Kowa disputed that Martin could legitimately claim any part of their village, since the ranch was situated on land belonging to Chief Zombe. When they were unable to reverse the decision, several people from Kowa decided to leave. Among them were Kaputula and his son-in-law, Blackson Sikate. A good two decades later, I found them again living in Kowa, side by side.

People's wanderings from village to village often occur following accusations or fears of sorcery. Movements also take place after norms have allegedly been breached. Upon leaving Kowa in the late 1940s, Kaputula and Blackson settled in Chipongoma, the village of origin of Blackson's first wife. All went well for Kaputula until his spouse became ill in 1966. I recall the events in Kaputula's own words:

Case Study 4: A Cycle of Residential Movements (I)

'Samuel Kashiyete bewitched my wife. It happened like this. One day my wife fell ill. I took her out of the village and built a temporary house near to where my gardens were situated. I spent one week there with her. One day Kashiyete passed by and he said, '*mulale uli?*', 'how are you, sick one?' I told him the condition of my wife was improving. As soon as Kashiyete had left, my wife became critically sick. I carried her on my back, to Chipongoma, where many people gathered. But there was no sign of Kashiyete. In the morning I took my wife to hospital. People came to the house with bicycles for transport. At the hospial in Kawimbe my wife became better.

When we were back in Chipongoma, Kashiyete repeated his treacherous act. The wife fell ill, was not taken to hospital, and died. Then I started to fear for my own life and decided to leave the village. I left for Mulangua, where I spent two years with my [new] wife's kin. People there became jealous because my harvests were good, and they accused me of 'knowing much' (*kumanya ivingi pa yalozi*). So, I decided to settle in Chipundu, the village where my son John lived. There my later wife died after we had both been very ill. I feared something was going to happen to me as well, so I thought of building a house near the Kawimbe leprosarium. When the Rev. Minister Leonard Ndawa heard of my intention, he refused to grant building permission. I then returned to Kowa.'

The story of Kaputula's departure from Chipongoma is quite different when told by his grandson, Kennedy Sikate [C3]. According to Kennedy, the reasons for the move from Chipongoma were not different from those that made Kaputula leave Mulangua. Kennedy recalls how Kaputula's rich harvests earned him many accusations of being a sorcerer (*mulozi*). One day a touring witch-finder (*muchape*) was called in.[7] This *muchape* discovered the source of Kaputula's success, which was due to his being a master practitioner of *mwankole*.[8] Kaputula's medicine bag was seized and destroyed, and Kaputula himself took the cleansing *muchape* drink, a mixture believed to neutralize control over the supernatural. It was either the fear of other people's sorcery or accusations that he himself was a *mulozi* which caused Kaputula to look for new accommodation at various times in his life. Even during my fieldwork, people in Kowa 'knew' that Kaputula had caused one of the wives of Henry Kalandanya [B10] to grow very thin indeed. Henry's beautiful gardens and his interest in farming commercial maize had roused much envy in the village.

Case Study 5: A Cycle of Residential Movements (II)
Not only Kaputula, but Blackson Sikate too was chased from Chipongoma. Blackson left not as a result of sorcery allegations, but because of an alleged breach of conduct. In 1970, after his first wife had died in childbirth, Sikate was accused of having had extra-marital relations. This accusation was within the local idiom of disease aetiology. Blackson arranged for the body to be ritually disposed of, met the expenses, but continued to deny adultery. The constant denial made Sikate's presence in the village a source of frustration and anger. Eviction followed. About that time, Kaputula too had his problems in Kawimbe. Aware of each other's difficulties, the two men decided to return to Kowa, a place where at least one of them had known better days.

That people return to a given village, after residence in a number of other places, has already been suggested in the case of Stone Sichiliango's brother. The wanderings of Kaputula and Blackson confirm that residential arrangements are not fixed, but constantly negotiated, even to the point of a second negotiation at some future time.[9] Although several decades may lapse before a group returns to a previous place of residence, the practice is common. And of course, it adds complexity to the analytic 'measuring' of village-level rates of absenteeism.

But the story of Kaputula's departure from Kowa in 1947 is not finished. That he left Kowa because of the threat of land alienation is Kaputula's own version; it is not shared by many. While it is true that the expansion of the ranch led to a small exodus from Kowa and from neighbouring villages, cross-checking showed that the expansion of the farm and Kaputula's departure were mere coincidence. The many moves Kaputula made in his life, including the 1947 move from Kowa, all took place after serious accusations of sorcery had been aimed at the man. Cross-checking confirmed Kennedy's interpretation.

The circumstances of Kaputula's dismissal from Kowa are meaningful for a discussion of how attitudes towards wealth (or modernization) have changed over time. As I shall indicate later in the chapter, the villagers' stand towards Kaputula (in 1947) is in stark contrast to their handling of a comparable case, some twenty-five years later, when a returning migrant was accused of having poisoned a kinsman. First I must give details of Kaputula's departure from Kowa.

I collected the story about Kaputula's 1947 eviction from Blackson Sikate, his son-in-law. Blackson recalled:

'It is true that Kaputula is a *mulozi*. He often goes into gardens to collect plants that are growing there. These plants are then mixed, at home, with other roots. When the owner of the garden harvests, he cannot harvest much. The people of Kowa, where Kaputula had been living for a long time, uncovered his deeds. This happened shortly after the Great War. Chief Kowa then brewed beer, and called the villagers and Kaputula together to talk about the case. The chief said: "Kaputula, we know that you are bewitching us." Then, people became angry with Kaputula, telling him: "We shall kill you, and that fat cow which you have, we shall also kill it at your funeral. You are no good. You have not got much land, but you have more grain storage bins (*zyantanta*) than we have." Kaputula, frightened, left the village for Chipongoma, taking his seventy-two cows with him.'

Inappropriate wealth and the envy such wealth causes were important elements in Kaputula's accusation. The theme of wealth and envy will reappear in the trial of Wosheni Siuluta (1972), described below, when this returned migrant too was accused of being a sorcerer. But here the similarity ends. In the case of Wosheni, the mode of the trial differed quite radically.

Before I proceed with Kowa's record of current occupations and return migration, it is useful to summarize the argument so far. My re-analysis of the composition of Kowa suggests that Mambwe villages have become structurally more complex than some three decades ago. Watson conceptualized the Mambwe village as a 'segment of an agnatic lineage ... round [which] are grouped a number of men of other clans linked to the core by various ties of kinship and marriage' (1958:18). The presentation remains valid in its elementary form, as developments in Kowa indicate. However, we also find (for Kowa) that dominant groups of cognates (in this case, the Simpungwe of the Nsyazye line) do not necessarily keep their position. Watson thought the major coalition in Kowa to be 'perpetual' (1958: 124). Secondly, linkages to the Siuluta core have become less frequent. They still exist in Kowa to some extent, especially between Siuluta and Sinyangwe, but I found them to be absent in other places. This does not mean that cognation itself is less important today. Ties of marriage remain structurally meaningful, although their character has changed. This can be seen, for example, in the relationships within Kaputula Simpungwe's following. Almost all of the men in Kaputula's entourage relate to him through marriage, but the backbone of this following consists of seven adult women who relate to Kaputula as daughters, granddaughters or great-granddaughters. The emergence of clusters of agnatically related women and the practice of uxorilocal marriage are notable features of the new village structure. Finally, I have evidence to argue that the notion of a fixed village allegiance must be increasingly suspect.

RETURN MIGRATION TO KOWA

The changing structure of the Mambwe village, and my claim that the notion of fixed allegiances is suspect, should have implications for the record of return migration. How does the evidence regarding return migration to Kowa reflect on the new perspective?

In this section I first examine the employment situation of Kowa men, current residents as well as absentees. Many men who lived in Kowa in the late 1970s were returning migrants; some had become migrants well after Watson's field trips; some had yet to return. From the discussion of residential moves we already know that any attempt to assess return migration at the level of the village is likely to be hampered by the absence of fixed allegiances. Kowa, however, is an exception, since it has the advantage that its chief is doyen of the Siuluta clan. The Kowa Siuluta therefore see Kowa as their 'real' home. They are more likely to return to it at the end of a migrant career. So, for the Kowa Siuluta at least, an accurate picture of return migration may be obtainable. A related issue, also discussed, is whether the re-integration of returning migrants poses any serious problems.

RETURN MIGRATION (1952-1970) AND LOCAL EMPLOYMENT

Mbala's nearby labour market provided formal jobs for nine Kowa men. Twenty-five years after Watson's fieldwork, Chief Amos Kowa (D9) was still employed as a mechanic at the International Red Locust Control (IRLC). He cycled to and from Mbala every working day of the week. Of his so-called brothers[10], Nkolo (=Wangwe, D11) and William (=Nedi, D12) were also still employed as wage-workers in Mbala. But only Nkolo cycled daily. William lived in town, a necessity really, since he was employed as a hospital driver.

Nkolo made only one labour trip. He left for Kitwe in 1958, immediately after David Sitbet (D10, [B7]) returned from his final stint on the Copperbelt. Nkolo returned in 1960, from which time on he had worked in Mbala as a plumber. David Sitbet also took up employment in Mbala, still had a job there, and he too cycled daily. Kwenlengula (D13) and his brother Yasula (D14) had not yet returned. Kwenlengula was still on the Copperbelt, and visited Kowa on occasion. Yasula, an IRLC employee in Tanzania in the early 1950s (Watson 1958: 127), still lived in Tanzania. He had almost no contact with Kowa, but the villagers thought a return still possible.

Two other wage-earners, both working in Mbala, were semi-residents. One Mr Simuyemba [D7], driver for Zesco (the Zambian Electricity Supply Company), had a house in Kowa, but lived with his family in town during half the year. Mrs Simuyemba and the children moved to Kowa during the wet season to cultivate the land, while Mr Simuyemba then commuted between the two places. The household of Gilbert Sikazwe [E2], a PWD (Public Works Department) labourer in Mbala, also changed residence at the onset of the rains. Sikazwe acquired land in Kowa through his brother Dennison [E1], an in-law of the Sichiliango. William Kowa [B4] and Benson Sikate [B8] also had homes in town, but they kept gardens in Kowa. These gardens provided food security and occasional surpluses for trading. Benson's gardens were managed by his second wife, a daughter of Jason Siuluta. This daughter (who had been married before) lived permanently in Kowa, unlike Benson, who spent most of his time in Mbala with his first wife. Benson's elder brother [B8] too lived in the village.

The list of commuting wage workers further included: Spear Kavuzye Sichiliango [C4], a gardener at the Zambian Air Force base (ZAF); Kamfondo Sichilima [B6], employee at the Public Works Department; and J.K.H. Simukonda, a Nyamwanga office orderly at the veterinary department. Simukonda had been posted to Kowa prior to his appointment in Mbala. Like many others, he too kept one foot in the village economy.

Although rural employment was hard to obtain, some residents did manage to become so employed. Gentile Siuluta (E25/[C15]) was a diptank foreman (*kapitao*) in Nsangu village, where he had a second wife and children. The others were Stone Sichiliango [C17], part-time veterinary assistant for Kowa, and Field Sichiliango [D6], son of Spear Kavuzya, who had a temporary job in Kawimbe with the Department of Water Affairs.

This gave a total of 14 wage-earners, or well over a third of all male household heads (thirty-five). Three of these wage-earners, however, were semi-residents, two had minimum contact with the village, and two of the remaining nine were employed temporarily or part-time.

RETURN MIGRATION: THE 1970s

Although the Kowas did not think that Yasula, aged 45, would come back to settle, they did know of unexpected returns. Wosheni Siuluta [C8], for instance, son of Philimon, made a surprise return shortly before my stay in Kowa. In 1952 Wosheni had left for Dar-es-Salaam, where he worked as a self-employed carpenter for over twenty years. Only twice did he come home. In 1975, after his first-born child was denied entry into secondary school, Wosheni informed his brother Whiteson [C7] of his intention to return. Wosheni sent money to enable Whiteson to buy banana trees and start a small plantation. Whiteson also hired a labourer. Awaiting his brother's return, Whiteson vacated his own premises and moved across the plains (see map 2). The land he had previously cultivated was now reserved for the returning Wosheni. Not much land was transferred, mere kitchen gardens (*ivizule*), but the arrangement made the home-coming smooth. The arrangement, moreover, was temporary. In the second year of his return, Wosheni had a house built near Whiteson's. When I lived in their village, Wosheni and Whiteson developed extensive tracts of land, and were keenly interested in commercial maize farming. Both households derived their incomes mainly from selling surplus.

The table below lists all migrants who returned to Kowa between 1970 and 1978. For those who were in their twenties, the decision to stay in the village was perhaps not a firm one. On the other hand, as I was often told, numerous young men were forced to stay at home, because life in the towns was expensive and jobs scarce (Chapter 3; see also Scudder 1985: 53 for a similar view from the Gwembe Valley). When the evidence in table 7 is compared with the overall record for absenteeism from Kowa (table 8), then it becomes clear that few long-term migrants returned to Kowa over the eight year period.

REFS.	AGE	YEAR RETURNED	MIGRANT CAREER
[D9]	27	1972	National Service (18 mths); Mbala (6 mths)
[D2]	27	1973	Kasama (3 years of 'piecework')
[E1]	28	1977	Mbala (6 months)
[C8]	41	1975	Tanzania (23 years/2 visits home)
[D6]	28	1976	Lusaka (1 year)
[C5]	53	1976	Lusaka (12 years/regular visits home)
[C1]	26	1975	Isoka (1 month)
[C3]	24	1975	Mbala (16 months); Kafue (4 months)
[D5]	31	1970	Lusaka (2 years); Kabwe (1 mth); Lusaka (3 mths)
[C6]	25	1976	Mbala (1 month)

Table 7: Return Migration to Kowa, 1970-1978. [11]

The central feature of return migration to Kowa during the 1970s was the high number of residents who returned after extremely short and unsuccessful labour trips. This included some younger people who went out in search of work after completing several years of secondary education. In contrast, between 1970 and 1978 only two migrants [C8 and C5] returned to the village after more successful, long-term careers. The two, Wosheni being one of them, differed markedly in how they adapted to living in 'modern' Kowa. Their respective experiences will be discussed shortly.

NON-RESIDENTS

Given the methodological problem that 'measuring' outmigration is difficult in the absence of fixed village allegiances, I can do little more than attempt a rough sketch of the Kowa villagers away at work. The number of absentees and their destinations are stated below. Towns that appear in roman script indicate that the absentee was studying; place names that are italicised are villages where potential Kowa residents were living. Some day they may still decide to come and live in Kowa. All other destinations are labour centres. (I have not indicated the nature of employment; Appendix 2 contains some relevant data.) The information seems complete, and is broken down per clan.

Findings about the position of absentees are necessarily biased, because of the absence of clear-cut, fixed village allegiances. Except for the Kowa Siuluta, it cannot be said that Kowa is the one-and-only possible home of residence. In this respect I have already presented the views of Damson Sichimba and noted the absence of the Nsyazye Simpungwe section, whose presence Watson assumed to be permanent. In 1978 the section had only one grandson of Nsyazye's living in Kowa, while five of his six brothers were on the Copperbelt. They would stay there as long as conditions allowed.

Siuluta:	[C15]:	2 sons (Kitwe x2);
	[B12]:	2 sons (Lusaka, Ndola);
	[B4]:	1 son (Kitwe);
	[C7]:	2 brothers (*Kalekwa, Washama*);
	[B10]:	5 sons (Lusaka x2, Serenje, Kafue, Mongi);
	[B13]:	5 sons (Chingola, Mporokoso, Kasama, Mbala, *Chela*);
	[B11]:	1 son (Kapiri Mposhi);
	[B7]:	2 brothers (Ndola, Tanzania). They are D13 and D14 in Watson's geneology. Also 8 sons (Copperbelt x3, Lusaka, and four in secondary schools).
	[A1]:	9 sons (Copperbelt x4, Copperbelt, Lusaka, Lusaka x2. Mbala).
Sikazwe:	[E1]:	3 brothers (*Mbala, Washama, Saul's Village*).
Simpungwe:	[D8]:	6 brothers (Lusaka x3, Luanshya x2, *Lukumpa's village*);
	[C16]:	1 son (Kitwe);
	[A3]:	1 son (Lusaka).
Sikate:	[B8]:	3 brothers (Mbala, Kafue, *Chipongoma*).
Sichimba:	[C5]:	3 sons (Lusaka x2, Serenje);
	[C2]:	1 son (Mbala);
	[B9]:	1 son (Chingola).
Simukonda (Nyamwanga):	[n.a.]:	2 sons (Lusaka, Mbala).
Sichiliango:	[C4]:	1 son (Lusaka); 2 brothers (Tanzania, *Mbukila*).
Simwanza:	[D5]:	3 brothers (*Chipanya* x3).

Table 8: Outmigration from Kowa.

This gives the following totals:

Note: i) Adult men in distant labour centres: 40 (including 3 in Mbala). 24 absentees are Siuluta; 6 Simpungwe.
ii) Young men in education: 13 (incl. 10 Siuluta).
iii) Adult men living in other, mostly nearby villages: 11.

The inquiry into absenteeism from Kowa is also biased in the sense that I collected data on the assumption, valid in the fifties, that return migration was an affair of men. As my fieldwork progressed, I became aware that homecomings have a gender aspect too. By the late seventies return migration was as much an affair of women who independently returned 'home' as it was the preoccupation of migrant men. This implies the data in tables 7 and 8 give some idea of the history and scale of outmigration, but that migration cannot be gauged by simply concentrating on the home-coming of male migrants. In Kowa few women had returned on their own after periods of residence away in the labour centres, but numbers in other villages were usually more substantial (see for example Chapter 7).

The re-appearance in the village of one Simpungwe-from-Fwambo elder, his 'daughters' and his cognatic following, underscores that wage labour absenteeism can really only be discussed at higher levels of aggregation. I have attempted an aggregate sketch elsewhere (Pottier 1983a), on the basis of survey work in eight villages, but cannot say with certainty how meaningful such information is. My fear is that the emerging pattern does not highlight the incidence of outmigration today. Most people who are recorded 'absent' left some time ago. What the aggregate information does reveal, on the other hand, is that many rural Mambwe have close relatives living in urban centres, both in the district and along the Line of Rail. That information remains relevant, since such contacts are useful for establishing trade outlets.

Having identified the Mambwe village as continuously affected by processes of lineage dispersal and movement between villages, it must now be clear why it is unrealistic to want to assess rates of absenteeism for any particular village. Only for younger would-be migrants is the trend unmistakable at the level of individual villages: the scarcity of jobs, formal and informal, has caused a virtual standstill in outmigration.

One major objective of the Mambwe re-study was to clarify the position of the present generation of migrants. Against my expectations, the evidence revealed that the Mambwe area has a growing number of young people who are (in their opinion) denied access to the rewards of Zambia's independence. The 'problem' they face is not how to re-adjust to village life, but how village life itself will adjust to the decline in formal labour opportunities and to the ensuing reduction of cash flows. The intrigue in this respect is the contradiction between the generally agreed need for cash on the one hand (shortages are felt by everyone) and, on the other, the widespread apprehension towards people who resort to commercial farming for raising that cash. The need for cash is agreed by all; the means to achieve it are not. Somehow, beautiful gardens continue to stir up suspicion.

The problems of the returning migrant have much to do with the fact that no consensus exists about what constitutes proper adaptation. This can be read into the events that marked the return of Wosheni Siuluta. His story reveals the up-hill struggle of the ambitious returning migrant. It also points to changes in the local value system. Whereas individual success is still frowned upon, the individualized nature of social relationships has become much more recognized.

Case Study 6: Wosheni's Return

(The story of Wosheni Siuluta was told by a group of people gathered round a pot of millet beer.)

'Whilst in Tanzania, Wosheni had much contact with several sorcerers (*yalozi*; sing. *mulozi*). He obtained many medicines. One *mulozi* told him: "When you go back home you will earn lots of money. It is better for you to kill a relative - father or mother or a younger brother of yours." Wosheni came back and built new houses. These are the ruins near David Kowa's house. One day, it was 1974 or 1975, people were drinking *cipumu* (millet beer). Mr Temba Siuluta, the younger brother of Philimon Kalandanya (Wosheni's deceased father), attended the beer party. So did Wosheni. Wosheni used his medicines that day and put some poison inside one of the drinking straws. Temba used that straw and then disposed of it. Wosheni and Temba went on drinking for a while, but Wosheni left before Temba did. That night Temba failed to reach home. He died on the way.

Wosheni visited the dead body during the night. He placed a pestle (*munsi*) on one side of the body, and on the other side one [unspecified] tree branch and a cassava stick. Wosheni returned to his house. In the morning people went to look for Temba. They found him, and knew Wosheni was guilty. When Mbala police were contacted, they took Temba's body to the hospital for a post-mortem. It was "discovered" that the heart had been taken out without surgical intervention. Wosheni, people said, had taken the heart to his *mulozi* in Tanzania.

From then on nothing could stop Wosheni from making big gardens and earning lots of money. The police never arrested him, but we people, we knew.

Then the villagers started to accuse Wosheni. Angered, Wosheni burnt down the property of the main accuser, his brother Similyeni. To settle the dispute Chief Kowa called a private meeting, at which Lamek Siuluta and David Kowa acted as councillors. They advised Similyeni to leave the village. And so he did.

Some time before burning the houses, Wosheni had told his brother: 'you are the remaining one' (*wewe wa shiala*). The brother had kept his cool (*wasozile*), but his house was nevertheless destroyed. When Similyeni consulted Chief Amos and his councillors in private, the chief said: "Well, it is your brother, I do not care." Later on, after Similyeni had called the police, he received a similar reply: "What do you expect from us? The one who burnt your house was your elder brother."

This short case study shows that affairs between brothers are no longer invariably the concern of the whole village. Unlike Kaputula's trial a good twenty years earlier, the incidents surrounding Wosheni did not call for public inquiry. The meeting was private. Moreover, Wosheni was allowed to stay on, despite his dangerous powers and offensive wealth. I believe that Wosheni won the case because of the intervention of David Kowa, his uncle, since David too aspires to be a successful farmer. Social relations in Kowa have become dyadic. This change, the product of decades of wage labour migration and contract work, now permeates the entire agricultural sector.

The individualized, contractual nature of many agricultural activities is discussed in the final section of this chapter. Kinship obligations are still honoured, but mutual labour agreements (e.g. between plough-owners) and payments in cash are now on a par with work-sharing based on ties of kinship and affinity. The village has ceased to be a place where food was communally produced and consumed (Watson 1959: 42). A few men in Kowa, including

Wosheni Siuluta and David Kowa, have become members of the 'progressive' Village Productivity Unit (VPU) in the nearby village of Chela. Villagers in Chela welcome people from Kowa, since, as they rightly say, Chief Kowa is not interested in commercial farming.

Wosheni's problematic return contrasts with the return of Anuel Sichimba [C5], the other long-term migrant who returned between 1970 and 1978. Anuel too produces maize surpluses, but his industriousness is not for personal profit alone. During the time he was absent, some eight years in all, the polygamous Anuel always had one wife staying on in Kowa! Anuel himself visited Kowa every other year. Unlike Wosheni, Anuel was no stranger when he ended his migrant days: he was indebted to many villagers for their help with maintaining the family gardens. Because one wife had always remained in Kowa, Anuel's household had never ceased to be an active unit in the village. Anuel encountered few problems upon returning and his interest in commercial maize growing was not challenged. As he explained, part of the surplus the household now produces is used to reward those to whom it is indebted. Anuel and those who listened to his story may have idealized the situation, but many agreed that Anuel compensated for past services: through distributing some of the food surplus, by providing a free drink, by offering his own labour. In spite of his ambition to be a registered farmer who could meet cash needs through hybrid cropping, Anuel had remained 'one of us'.

RELATIONS ON THE LAND: KOWA MONETIZED

An account of labour recruitments within Kowa may help to put the debate on cohesion in perspective.

When new land is cleared work-parties with hoes are no longer the dominant organizational mode. Work-parties recruited on the basis of reciprocity are still popular, but very rarely do they become occasions that mobilize the entire village. Reciprocity now depends on ownership: plough-owners team up with other plough-owners; hoe-cultivators make their own arrangements and reciprocate amongst themselves. At the same time, working for a reward, in cash or in kind, has become more widespread, as has the formation of small gatherings recruited from within the extended family.

While in Kowa I kept a day-to-day record of 'paid' agricultural activities. Having previously mapped all land in the village, my knowledge of who owned which plots was a great help in establishing cases of 'employed' labour. I covered a period of three busy weeks during the month of April, when the major agricultural tasks consisted of mounding, done by men, and weeding millet gardens, done by women. The scene was a far cry from the customary rule that heavy fieldwork was performed through the system of cooperative labour (1958:106). The only sizable parties I observed were staged by young men of the Church of God choir, who cooperated every other day. They made mounds on church land, worked the gardens of fellow members who were incapacitated, and also hired themselves out as a work-party.

Unless women had joined from within the extended family, weeding parties rarely brought more than three women together. In the final week of observation, when the weeding period was nearly over, all paid labour was undertaken by women who worked on their own. The reward in cash was 60 *ngwee* per woman per day, or its equivalent in fingermillet or bananas. Cash payments predominated. The reward for making mounds (*ntumba*) was always K1 (1 *Kwacha*) per man per day, while the Church of God Choir received a K2 lump sum. Employed men always worked alone. Some banana gardens too were being weeded at the time, but this work was taken on by young men and did not pay very well.

In all I recorded thirty-seven instances of labour recruitment, paid in cash or rewarded in kind. In twenty-six of these the employer (man or woman) belonged to the Siuluta clan. Non-Siuluta who hired labour were nearly always men who had jobs. Women who employed other women, for weeding, were often married to wage-earners. They would usually make the point though that the money they used was their own – it was money made from trading or brewing.

Paid agricultural work is now common in Kowa. The bulk of the labour, however, is still borne by small groups of women who are related through kinship or affinity. This mode of recruitment is linked to the increase in uxorilocal residence after marriage, to which I referred earlier on. The groups of family labourers I met during the weeding period were much smaller than in the past, but they regularly consisted of adult women who under conditions of virilocal residence would almost certainly have lived well apart from one another. Small family groups often consisted of older women with grown-up daughters who had 'distant' husbands and children of their own.

The increase in paid labour exposes the facts of social differentiation. 'Cohesion' in Kowa now exists on a reduced scale, due to polarization. It would be difficult to deny this. Wage-earners and long-term (or returning) migrants lay on extensive fields and recruit the unwaged for casual labour. Such arrangements may be long-lasting. The important consequence, however, is that selling labour delays production tasks in the family gardens of those who are contracted. This can have disastrous effects, especially when the poor who sell their labour use hybrid maize in their own fields. As I understood the scene in Kowa, the delays did not have too bad an effect on production, since households engaged in casual labour still tended to grow traditional maize. But should hybrid maize become more widely available, as it has in the areas described in the next chapter, then I expect that resource-poor households will be moving closer towards a self-perpetuating cycle of poverty.

CHAPTER FIVE

FOOD SECURITY, FOOD TRADING AND LOCAL ADMINISTRATION

Population growth and environmental bankruptcy are major determinants of Africa's poor performance in agriculture. The present 'low' in food production threatens the survival chances of many communities. Given the magnitude of this crisis, it is only fitting that I now examine the future of Mambwe villages in terms of their potential for achieving food security. The chapters that follow all deal with the broad theme of food security, each one looking into a different aspect. Food production, the environment, food trading and the impact of local administration are among the topics discussed.

The issue of survival for rural Africa has not always been looked at from the angle of its food security record. Anthropologists working in the 1940s and 1950s, for example, sometimes held different views on what constituted survival. *Tribal Cohesion* is an instructive example, as the following quotations make clear. Watson wrote:

> The striking stability of Mambwe villages, which are the residential units of their society, raises the question whether patrilineal societies are better *fitted* than matrilineal societies *to survive* in conditions of rapid economic and social change. Read and Richards have both suggested that patrilineal peoples adjust themselves more readily than matrilineal peoples to the absence of large numbers of men. Read compares the patrilineal Nyasaland Ngoni with the matrilineal Cewa, and comes to the conclusion that the Ngoni show a far *greater stability in family and village life* and more care for the upbringing of children' (Watson 1958: 226; emphasis added).

For Watson to suggest consensus was superficial, since Read had also written:

> when [the Ngoni migrants] return to their villages, they do not achieve a uniform change in their surrounding. *The standard of food has not gone up to the same degree as that of housing and clothing* (Read 1942: 627; emphasis added).

Watson labelled a migrant community as benefitting from wage labour when institutional cohesion – family stability and political cohesion – was maintained, when consumption of imported goods increased (1958: 220), and when subsistence production was not disrupted (*ibid*: 222). Choosing political integrity, family cohesion and consumption of imports as the prime indicators of *survival*, Watson overlooked one most important variable, that is, the community's capacity to ensure an adequate, balanced diet *for future generations*. Today survival in Mambwe villages is about ensuring adequate access to land and labour (Chapter 6), about reversing the process of ecological degradation (Chapter 8) and about maintaining cash flows.

In this chapter I shall outline the national strategy for rural economic survival, its social and political dimensions, and how it is perceived by Mambwe villagers. First, I examine the ways in which the government-approved structures for development interact among themselves in the context of a community targeted for project-induced technological and organizational change. The discussion exposes problems of coordination and communication. Kaka is the venue for this debate. Later in the chapter I shall look at Zambia's strategy for mobilizing the rural masses. The structures designed for mobilization will be examined on the basis of case studies recorded during local-level public meetings in Mwamba, which is the seat of a traditional chieftaincy. My major concern here will be to assess how cultivators who do *not* benefit from the resources made available by government view the development strategies open to them. I shall address the question whether the bureaucratic structures that have resulted from state intervention have awoken any participatory enthusiasm beyond the boundaries of specific target groups. The local responses described will enable reflection on the quality of the Zambian strategy for instigating rural development and on the 'problem' of rural poverty. Broadly speaking, the government programme for hybrid maize production was (and still is) the major 'civilized' activity through which this cash-starved ex-reserve can make money in a legally approved manner.

I set my analysis against the economic recession that has plagued Zambia since the mid-seventies, against the national need to step up food production for feeding urban areas, and against the party programme for political penetration. The overall framework for raising living standards in rural Zambia has not perceptibly changed since the introduction of the Village Productivity Committees, during the early seventies (Chapter 2).

My argument in this chapter has less to do with aspects of food production than with the political and administrative structures that underlie attempts to induce development. The link between the efficiency of the structures and the local drive for adequate levels of production will be taken up in the next chapter. My immediate interest is with the pattern of interaction between civil servants, emergent farmers, agricultural extension workers and local-level party cadres. I shall consider how these interactions are perceived by cultivators – the majority – who do not make use of the development package provided. Government assistance comes in the form of the familiar package of credit, inputs and technical advice for raising hybrid maize crops. Planners believe the package to be an invitation open to all rural Zambians.

The discussion also refers to current academic attempts to evaluate the merits of alternative marketing structures, notably, 'state controlled' versus 'free market'. This issue, for which I provide a village perspective, has been taken up in recent publications on market intervention in agrarian Africa (e.g. Bates 1981; T.Schultz 1976; Shivji 1976; von Freyhold 1979; World Bank 1981). Some in this debate have advanced the view that government-controlled agricultural markets depress commodity prices and nip food production efforts in the bud. One notorious consequence of government monopoly over the purchasing and retailing of food staples, disclosed by the Berg Report (World Bank 1981), is that public sector organization tends to become seriously overburdened. The report states:

The central problem in marketing and input strategy is the very general tendency to give too large a set of responsibilities to public sector institutions, and too few to other agents - individual traders, private companies and farmers' cooperatives (World Bank 1981: 58).

A related line of thought is now emerging in the work of development anthropologists who react against deterministic views on the nature of social change (see Chapter 1). With regard to state intervention I accept that the state imposes restrictions on how the public sector operates and that government control over food prices may indeed curtail production, but wish to stress that state intervention itself is not locally experienced in any passive or uniform manner. Individuals and social classes respond to processes of intervention (Long 1984: 7) and it is with their responses that I am concerned. What I present in this chapter supports Long's position, although my data should also be read as an anecdotal commentary on Berg's implicit prophecy that the 'free market' mechanism (in the Mambwe case: the marketing of cash crops through Watch Tower channels) could provide that magic 'fix' which will help Africa out of its food production impasse.

My overall assessment of the ecological situation in Northern Zambia, stated briefly at the end of this chapter (and developed in Chapter 8), will make me argue that reservations about the benefits of free market trading must be taken seriously. I shall nevertheless endorse the view that the process of policy implementation is never passively accepted by local populations. In the Mambwe economy, policy transformations occur both at the micro- and at the middle-level. The administrators, politicians and traders involved at the middle-level do not follow national directives in blindfolded, euphoric fashion. There is scope for manoeuvres. The underlying rationale has to do with the fact that middle- and lower-level actors play multiplex roles and experience multiplex, sometimes conflicting, allegiances. The existence of multiplex roles cautions against accepting unilineal, deterministic approaches to development. Local-level responses to the 'state-controlled' versus 'free market' alternative are marked, as I shall show, by role ambiguities that can only be understood in terms of the local political arena.

GOVERNMENTAL AND PROJECT STRUCTURES: TWO MODES OF ASSISTANCE

The Mambwe area 'benefits' from two approaches to agricultural development. First, there is the grid of participatory institutions, from the Village Productivity Committees (VPCs) upwards to the Central Committee in Lusaka. Villagers interested in commercial maize farming - which in Zambia is (still) equated with rural development - need to be on good terms with the chairman of their VPC, for the chairman's signature is essential when applying for seasonal loans to the Agricultural Finance Company (AFC). In practice, interested villagers are often themselves VPC members. After obtaining approval by the VPC chairman, the applicant then seeks the support of his local Ward Council representative or contacts the Ward Councillor in person. Approval at this higher level means that the application will be considered and endorsed by the local Agricultural Assistant, when the full Ward Committee meets.

The second type of assistance relates to the Intensive Development Zone (IDZ) programme, for which a number of Mambwe villages had been selected. Such villages received assistance with improved farming. Being a parastatal, IDZ draws from external and government resources, and relies on the organizational capacity of the official framework for local-level participation in development. I shall assess the organizational capacity of both modes of assistance.

LOCAL-LEVEL INSTITUTIONS FOR PARTICIPATORY DEMOCRACY

The contradiction between the well-publicized principles of Zambian Humanism and the regional biases built into the national programme for rural development, for instance in AFC budgeting (Chapter 2), fosters in the fieldworker an interest in peasant attitudes towards implemented support structures: VPC, the Ward, the Party.

At a first glance the United National Independence Party (UNIP) has successfully penetrated even the most remote parts of rural Zambia. This is an illusion. On further reflection it transpires that the proliferation of registered branches is not synonymous with large-scale membership (Chikulo 1979: 209). The party is still completing the build-up of a suitable politico-administrative infrastructure, especially at the local level. After the One-Party state was declared in 1972, the process of penetration aimed 'not only to consolidate the hold of the state on [the] ethnically and linguistically diverse periphery but to increase and spread development benefits that had not reached the countryside under colonial rule' (Bratton 1980a: 33). The task proved difficult, since the colonial authorities had left an 'institutional vacuum' at district level and below. As a result, Zambia's development front became a patchwork organization of government, party and traditional institutions (*ibid*: 40-41). Planners attempted to fill the vacuum through the imposition of a multi-level grid of development committees. The framework was to provide horizontal linkages among all government agencies at lower levels of organization and vertical linkages between the national centre and peripheries farther afield (*ibid*: 33-41).

Bratton's approach to the administrative problems that bedevilled implementation of the chosen strategy focused on what he called the 'local social structure'. Rather than view the process of top-down development from the perspective of its internal organization, as others had done before him (Gertzel 1972; Kapteyn and Emery 1972; Kaindu 1973), Bratton chose to focus on the development of alliances between the memberships of local development institutions. These consisted mainly of elements from party and state bureaucracies and from petty bourgeois trade and agriculture (Bratton 1980a: 38-41). Local-level institutions, he argued, represented the interests of an emergent class alliance. The composition of this alliance was not fixed; nor was there any 'evidence that rural social strata had evolved into conscious social classes' (*ibid*: 277). Peasants were unable to influence the distribution of central resources, but their being 'frozen out' did not result in greater solidarity. Peasants had become differentiated among themselves (*ibid*: 277).

Bratton concluded his field observations on VPC activities in Kasama district by suggesting that traditional leaders were disinclined to promote changes that undermined their own positions of authority (Bratton 1980a: 80). This suggested a low organizational capacity on the part of the state:

In choosing chiefs and headmen as its grass roots allies, the Zambian state acknowledged a low capacity to replace even severely weakened traditional institutions, and accepted the likelihood of minimal village-level socio-economic transformation (Bratton 1980a: 80).

My data confirm the patchwork character of local-level development organization. However, unlike the social field observed by Bratton, the 'local social structure' for development in the Mwamba constituency did not have a privileged traditional leader. The Mwamba Case Studies, with which I conclude the chapter, illustrate Chief Mwamba's position.

THE IDZ PROGRAMME

One form of planned assistance for the Mambwe area is through the Intensive Development Zone (IDZ). The history of the IDZ programme for Northern Province was examined in an article by Gertzel (Gertzel 1980: 248-57). It is not necessary to repeat Gertzel's argument. On the other hand, I need to point out that the IDZ activities here described relate to a period when similar projects in other parts of the country had already come to a halt. Gertzel explains this paradox:

By the end of 1975 the IDZs had been largely abandoned, although the strategy of concentrating investment and services in selected areas of relatively high agricultural production potential once again received government support with the term 'rural growth areas' being employed in the Third National Development Plan (Gertzel 1980: 257).

Kaka, a woodland village in the 1950s, became the rural growth area *par excellence* when the Tazara Railway project promised to open up Zambia's northern regions (Hall and Peyman 1976: 178-9).

The IDZ 'Work Programme 1978' specified for the Mambwe area that

'accelerated development is being brought about by:
(a) The introduction of improved farming and cattle keeping systems.
(b) An increase in the quantity and values of agricultural products.
(c) The development of effective distribution and marketing systems.
(d) Improvement of access to basic infrastructure, water supplies, roads and general service' (GRZ 1978: 7).

Kaka is a resettlement. It has attracted an unusually high number of successful, experienced, returning migrants. Facing the usual residential dilemma at the end of their careers (Chapter 3), several returning migrants came to settle in the 'promised land' of Kaka, hub of the Mambwe IDZ project. Kaka's location near the grassland-woodland boundary means that this centre is within the Kasama sphere of influence, where IDZ has its regional headquarters. The relative proximity of Kasama facilitates contact with the larger towns. Kaka has also become the 'modern' counterpart of the old Mwamba chieftaincy. As a showpiece for medium-scale mechanized agriculture, it has an important role to play in the political penetration of Mambwe country.

The IDZ Mambwe work programme report stated that 1977 had been a year of good progress: 'Most of the targets within agricultural production, building of houses, marketing sheds and diptanks, extension and so on [had] been reached' (*ibid*: 2). The report warned, however, that 1977 had also been

a year of many and increasing difficulties. IDZ is supposed to have its work done through other departments, but in an increasing number of cases, those departments have not been able to perform the work. ... With regard to transport there have been big difficulties, and this has caused delay or even set-back to some projects (GRZ 1978: 2).

'Other departments' is a reference to various government departments based in Mbala, and above all to the Northern Co-operative Union (NCU), the parastatal responsible for the collection of maize surpluses. Since NCU did not own any significant number of transport vehicles, its policy was to make use of locally-hired, private transport. In practice this meant that businessmen based in Mbala were asked to render a public service. Unfortunately, compensation was low, and the service was required precisely when the businessmen were making huge profits by sending truckloads of beans down to the Copperbelt and Lusaka. The *Annual Report (1976-77)* issued by the department of

Agriculture in Mbala mentioned for 1977 that NCU had been troubled by the 'lack of a full week of about 17 lorries of businessmen' [sic] (GRZ 1977a: 28). NCU also failed on a wider regional level. This was dramatically conveyed when the *Zambian Daily Mail* reported in mid-November, after the rains had set in, that NCU had collected about half of the 85.000 bags awaiting collection in Kasama district (18 November 1978). Figures for Mbala district showed that a similar problem had arisen in the previous year:

The seasonal result [for maize] was going to be a favourable one, but the marketing of the crop was started very late. And delivery of empty sacks has been very poor. To date [mid-November] only 24.000 bags of maize ... have been collected from farmers to Namboard depot in Mbala. The saleable target would be 42.000 (GRZ 1977a:8)

The annual report for Mbala district blamed the late collection on the late arrival of sacks imported from India and on NCU's inability to secure the assistance of private truck owners. The latter had declined to help out despite a last-minute offer by the NCU district manager to raise compensation from 15 *ngwee* per kilometre to 24 *ngwee*. In Mbala district NCU collects, but sells to NAMBOARD as soon as the lorries return to the town.

Although reliance on private traders is not typical of Zambia's marketing co-operatives as a whole, the practice in Mbala exposes a recurring flaw in the national effort to promote maize cropping. Year after year the effort of Zambia's small-scale rural producers is frustrated by the bureaucrats' inability to liaise between regional-level development institutions. NCU's reliance on private transport may have been exceptional, but the lack of co-ordination between components of the 'official' machinery still occurs nationwide. It is the same problem of which the IDZ Work Programme warned.

The IDZ strategy proceeds along lines in keeping with the conventional wisdom of integrated development (Gertzel 1980: 251). IDZ seeks the services of the Department of Agriculture and, in the case of Kaka, also those of NCU. The Kaka-based Agricultural Assistant had received a Honda motorbike out of IDZ funds, while the IDZ-built marketing shed was handed over to NCU upon its completion in August 1978. It was to no avail. The motorbike was soon out of order and the NCU shed became the focus of a furious row after the arrival of 400 bags of refined maize flour. NCU thought it necessary that the flour should be imported from the Copperbelt; IDZ argued back that such importation was against the spirit of self-reliance (details in Pottier 1983b). NCU and IDZ, the two institutions that matter most to the emergent farmers in Kaka, rarely see eye to eye.

The IDZ programme also suffers the effect of major cracks in the 'official' development apparatus. When Gertzel listed the structural weaknesses that eventually led to the winding up of IDZ in other parts of the country, she deplored the chronic shortage of transport, the low organizational capacity of the village and ward committees, and the impotence of the party to mobilize at the grass-roots level (Gertzel 1980: 253). Notwithstanding the growing support for decentralizing all administrative structures, the lowest levels were clearly ill-equipped for the task. The case material I collected highlights the organizational (in)capacity of branch-level party cadres, VPCs and ward committees.

CASE MATERIAL

KAKA CAMP: THE FARMER-BUREAUCRAT NON-ALLIANCE

The thinking behind Zambia's rural development effort can now be elucidated for the village of Kaka.

The political rivalry between 'modern' Kaka and 'traditional' Mwamba is most clearly visible in the contrast provided by their respective market orientations. The orientation of Mwamba and its surrounding villages is both regional (based on transactions with peri-urban Mbala and with the economy of Tanzanian border villages) and national, in that this area produces and channels vast amounts of free-market beans towards the Line of Rail. Kaka's registered farmers differ in this respect, by catering exclusively for the larger urban areas. Kaka has few trade links with Mbala. Its outlets, whether for beans or for NCU-handled produce (maize, wheat), run directly to Kasama. The farmers in Kaka expect to make substantial cash profits and want to tune into the national distribution of consumer goods.[1] The money they earn is not invested in contraband commerce – a practice common in the northern part of the grasslands. In Kaka most cash is spent at the local NCU-managed store. This emphasizes the self-contained nature of project Kaka.

Some of Kaka's achievements are impressive, especially the construction and provision of a regular water supply. The housing scheme too has been successful, a fine combination of self-help and aid. In 1978 Kaka already boasted a dozen neatly-aligned brick houses, roofed with corrugated iron sheets. The re-housed families, all of them headed by registered male farmers, had contributed local building materials (sand, rafters, bricks,...) in addition to their labour. Technical assistance and more sophisticated materials (cement, pipes, windlasses, glassplanes,...) were provided by IDZ through the Department of Community Development. For the manufacturing of doorframes, windowframes and doors, the resident Community Development Assistant (CDA) contacted local carpenters and paid them from IDZ funds. I found that the re-housed families were pleased with the project. The standard of housing matched the returning migrants' expectations, and the women and children had nothing but praise for the pipeline that brought water right up to their doorsteps.

But the transport problem mentioned in the work programme affected the delivery of construction materials, cement in particular. It also affected the collection of the more popular marketable crops, hybrid maize and wheat, and reduced the mobility of IDZ personnel. In addition, the transport problem was used as a dubious excuse for delaying the much publicized 'sheep scheme'. Kaka's registered farmers had responded enthusiastically when the scheme was launched in 1977, with prompt payment of first instalments. However, the first sheep had still to arrive in Kaka as late as November 1978. Experts claimed that the sheep had arrived in Kasama, but said they could not be delivered because the IDZ lorry had broken down. Another story told that the sheep were kept in quarantine. And to add to the confusion, the IDZ 'Work Programme 1978' expressed an altogether different point of view, depressing but credible: demand had outstripped availability. The programme revealed that out of the provincial total of 279 enthusiastic farmers only twelve had received sheep in the earlier part of 1978: 'it was not possible to buy more in the province' (GRZ 1978:8).

The tensions surrounding the ill-fated sheep scheme pointed to a lack of communication between the institutions involved, and between field staff and farmers. The scheme seemed to have been unrealistic from the start. The better I came to know the extension workers in Kaka, the more I realized that poor communication was rife, as was the workers' evasiveness about the feasibility of sub-projects. This was due to social cleavages: rifts within the group of extension workers, as well as between the workers (as a group) and the registered farmers. The latter cleavage was pronounced, and much in evidence on the day International Literacy Day was celebrated.

Case Study 7: International Literacy Day
Since it took place in the heart of the IDZ domain, the celebration in Kaka brought together extension workers and a small group of registered, so-called 'emergent' farmers.[2] Contrary to my expectations, the two groups kept to themselves throughout the day. A day filled with speeches, ethnic dancing and a demonstration of writing skills during which women 'brought shame' on men. Farmers and extension staff gathered in opposite corners of the assembly room when the evening meal drew to its close.

After some campaigning UNIP electoral candidates had made an appearance, albeit briefly (1978 being a year of local elections), the Mbala-based District Community Development Officer (DCDO) decided to address the Kaka extension staff. The farmers did not take part in this exchange of ideas. Instead, they turned to their IDZ representative, who had come from Kasama, to complain bitterly about the deterioration of the feeder road system.

The extension staff too voiced a complaint about the threat of geographical isolation, but this concerned the expansion of postal and public transport services. The progressive farmers may have been aware that the two conversations, which went on simultaneously, touched upon similar issues. What they did not know (I later discovered) was that the 'solutions' proposed to the two groups varied considerably.

The DCDO urged the extension staff to press on with their request for making Kaka a priority area, and suggested that the UBZ depot (United Bus company of Zambia) and the post office in Mbala be contacted at once. The IDZ representative, addressing the farmers, dismissed the idea that outside help should be sought. His answer to the farmers' request that the IDZ road grader be sent back to their village was to say that 'IDZ policy [was] based on the concept of self-help'. He clarified that the grader, which had been at the farmers' disposal during the first phase of the project, was now in the Nakonde area, adding that it was 'up to the community here to see to road maintenance'. The contrast was clear enough. Whereas the farmers were told to lower their expectations about external help, the extension workers, in their discussion, were told it was reasonable to request more help from outside.

Farmers and extension workers refrained from socializing on the night of the celebration. Some four years after the inception of project Kaka, cooperation between farmers and extension staff - a potential alliance - was being subjected to considerable strain. Tension peaked with the realization that some of the project's targets might never materialize. Not only did the sheep scheme look a non-starter, it was by then also known that Zambia would not manage to import the required quantities of chemical fertilizer for the 1978-79 agricultural year. Fertilizer deficiency was expected, and occurred, as a result of the Presidential ruling to close the country's southern border with what was then 'rebel Rhodesia'.

The potential alliance between farmers and project personnel had all the trappings of a 'patronage machine' (Bratton 1980b: 225), but it was ill-defined and dormant during the latter half of 1978. As far as the farmers' relationship with IDZ was concerned, it was the very first time that farmers had been confronted, in an unpleasant way, with the policy principle of self-help. The confrontation signalled an all-time low in the relationship between the bureaucratic patrons and their rural clients.

There were also signs of tension between the IDZ representative and the field personnel based in Kaka. The tension was brought into the open some time after Literacy Day, when the district co-ordinator for IDZ, Mr P.M. Katenda, attacked Kaka's extension workers in a strongly worded letter. Katenda wrote: 'I have seen some of you have no idea on what projects are in your camp area, e.g. ox training, demonstration plots, etc. As a result these projects are not supervised and therefore I receive no reports about them.'

The major social division that surfaced on International Literacy Day, between emergent farmers and field-level civil servants, was symptomatic of funds running low and of an administrative laxity aggravated by geographical and political isolation. Kaka may be fertile and important for district politics, but the Mambwe area itself remains peripheral to the national economy. Kaka's actual location adds to the handicap. During the weeks of heavy rainfall (Jan.-Feb.) the project site is very hard to reach by road. It is common, then, for the wooden bridges across the Saisi tributaries (Mbala-Kaka road) or those of the Chambeshi/Sampwe (Senga Hill - Kaka road) to be submerged or even swept away. Whenever a motor vehicle does reach the village during such times, field staff and farmers compete with each other for lifts. In 1978 competition between the two groups extended well into the dry season. The reason, initially, was the breakdown of the UBZ rural service. But later that year, when so much marketable surplus remained uncollected by NCU, farmers turned restless and attempted to contact urban-based administrators in person, thus trying to overcome Kaka's dependence on 'other departments'. Regarding the collection of maize surpluses, 1978 will be remembered as the year when late collections and late payments began to affect the whole of rural Zambia (Dumont and Mottin 1983: 43, 50).

The spatial separation observed on Literacy Day reflected low morale and an absence of honest dialogue, both rooted in the scarcity of public and private resources. The separation also reflected Kaka's failure to link up with regional trade avenues. Catering almost exclusively for a national market, farming households in Kaka experienced their isolation to the full when problems arose over the 1978 collection of surpluses. NCU's reliance on precarious transport arrangements resulted not only in the late collection of maize, but affected even the newly introduced wheat crop. The latter problem was an embarassment to all who were involved in administering the project.

The failure to link project Kaka with regional trade avenues became exacerbated with the reduced mobility of its adult population. The lack of mobility, a theme I shall turn to in Chapter 6, relates to a general constraint on the time budgets of households. The constraint affects households from the 'farming' and from the 'subsistence' sector.

MWAMBA: WARD STRUCTURES

The failure of the Kaka administration has raised questions about the efficacy of the nationwide programme for maize cash-cropping. I now propose to examine the situation for areas not 'targeted' for assistance. The focus in the present section is on how political and developmental structures interrelate outside the setting of a project and on how the quality of the interactions is viewed by the masses who work and live at the so-called subsistence level. In order to achieve this, it is useful to present further ideas about the development machinery.

The nature and duties of local-level committee structures is set out in the pocket manual, *Village Productivity and Ward Development Committees* (GRZ 1971). Their functions can be summarized with the help of short extracts from the manual. The VPC is an elected body which makes 'day-to-day decisions and supervises the administration of Village affairs' (GRZ 1971: 9). Village headmen are committee members by virtue of their traditional status; all others, usually including one or two senior women, are elected. VPC registration had started in 1972, under the auspices of the Registration and Development of Villages Act (1971), when registration teams, comprising the local chief, the ward councillor, regional party officials and sometimes students from the University of Zambia, toured the nation to organize the campaign. For many chiefs this became the occasion for recouping some of the prestige and judicial powers lost under the British or after independence. Many chiefs welcomed their involvement in VPC registration, since it amounted to an official recognition of their *de facto* powers, for example as arbitrators in land disputes.

The next step up the hierachy is the Ward Council, to which each village is expected to send two representatives. 'The Ward Council is a policy-making body and [should] meet at least twice a year to formulate and review development programmes and also to approve future plans for economic and social improvement of the ward' (GRZ 1971: 4-5). Its coordinator is the Ward Councillor, who (like the constituency chairman) is appointed through formal elections.

A third structure, the Ward Development Committee (WDC), is responsible for raising productivity in the ward (GRZ 1971: 23). It assembles WC members and field-based civil servants. Its major task is 'to plan and organise the ... utilisation of natural and human resources within the framework of the Government's overall development programme for the Ward' (*ibid*: 23). In reality this programme boils down to the promotion of hybrid maize.

The WC/WDC programme in Mwamba was simplified in more ways than one. This is common in many rural areas. The Ward Council met only once a year, and this solely for the allocation of AFC seasonal loans and for planning the annual agricultural show. A proper Ward Development Committee meeting, the ward councillor admitted, had still to be organized in Mwamba. The situation in Mwamba had something of the 'cold front' I witnessed during the International Literacy Day in Kaka. The yet-to-be-organized WDC signalled that extension workers and farmers (for WC members are farmers) do not make full use of the facilities that could stimulate an alliance between them. Moreover, as the diagram (p.105) shows, villages are not each represented by two people. It is rather the other way round, with one WC member representing two villages, or even three.

The main characteristics of the party-cum-development administration in Mwamba ward are the narrow scope of its programme and the narrow basis on which its members are recruited. Not only is the ward programme unduly confined to the annual show and to reiterating loan decisions taken beforehand, the annual assembly (as a Ward Council) also contains fewer members than stipulated in the government manual. This can be seen in the make-up of the UNIP Branch to which Kasunga (Watson 1958: Chapter 5) belongs. (The diagram is incorporated in case study 10). The six villages of the branch send only two representatives to the annual Ward Council meeting.

Some extension staff stationed in Mwamba do attend the Ward Council meeting, the local Agricultural Assistant for instance, but their presence does not usually culminate in a discussion of 'development in all its aspects.' The Ward Council in Mwamba operates with a restricted number of participants and fails to mobilize those who are supposed to be mobilizers themselves. Except for organizing the annual agricultural show, the WC has no programme other than to pass on information on loan decisions already taken. In this respect both Winel S. and Donald S. are explicit that the Agricultural Assistant at the Ward Council meeting merely endorses the decisions on loans for fertilizer and seeds which individual Council members take, in their respective sections, in the weeks preceding the meeting. Donald S. commented upon the low profile the Agricultural Assistant adopts at the meeting, saying: 'Really, the Assistant fears our Ward Councillor. He has little power, for he cannot secure the services of the Mechanization Unit in Mbala. Only the Ward Councillor can arrange for a tractor to come to our area. The Agricultural Assistant in powerless.' [3]

Restricted participation at Ward level is symptomatic of the widespread opposition to the government-backed Village Productivity Committee (VPC) idea. This opposition usually centres on the proviso that 'each Village Productivity Committee shall have not less than six and not more than ten members' (GRZ 1971: 4). One village headman I interviewed expressed strong public feeling when he said: 'Why should there be a VPC in my village, if we only meet to settle marital disputes or to arrange for compensation when cattle destroy crops? Why should we have a set number of people discussing what is the concern of all the people living here? Why should I exclude certain people from helping to achieve agreement in a dispute just because they are not on my VPC list? That would be against our custom. Here everyone is free to join in a dispute.' He later added, 'unsteady marriages and destroyed crops have been the only real concern of my VPC ever since we have had to have such a committee.'[4]

What applies to VPC membership also applies to UNIP representation at branch level: membership exists mainly on paper. The Ward / Party structures and activities (the two must not be analytically separated!) are not geared towards raising the low income levels of the rural masses, not even in the long run, and local villagers, including branch leaders, are aware of this. At the grass-roots, the only visible expression of so-called mobilization is in the form of financial contributions per family head, towards public functions and party membership dues. As the final case study will show, it costs rather than pays for the masses to be politically involved.

I conclude that neither the VPC nor the assembly of VPC chairmen and their secretaries (the Ward Council) has anything to do with the 'P' that stands for productivity. As a penetrative structure the Ward Council lacks a programme for increasing productivity because development resources are restricted; and the village shows no interest in having a formal committee because its members consider casual meetings more democratic. In addition, some villagers ignore the formal structures because they believe that existing production levels, in combination with the windfalls of cross-border trade and free market transactions (Chapter 7), are the best they can hope for under the present economic circumstances. Development structures and party strategies for long-term planning (GRZ 1971) are ignored in favour of self-help strategies that combine bean cash-cropping with intensified cross-border trading. The self-help strategies may have long-term pitfalls, since they reduce regional self-reliance and encourage monocropping, which affects the diet adversely. But these drawbacks are masked by the fact that free trade provides instant cash and, therefore, some instant relief.

The importance of cash (see also Chapter 6) and of free-trade enterprise runs through all three of the Mwamba case studies.

THREE MWAMBA CASE STUDIES

The case studies that follow were recorded at the time the 1978 Mwamba Agricultural Show was being prepared. In the discussion I shall refer to role playing by 'modern' and 'traditional' office bearers. The terms 'modern' and 'traditional' have been retained in spite of their inadequacies, because they were used by the participants themselves. The anecdotes reveal the extent to which political roles are intertwined and show which roles take precedence in the event of a dilemma. The contextual intertwining of roles has implications for the debate on 'free' versus 'state-controlled' marketing alternatives, since it provides clues about how local producers view the choice.

The sketches enable us to understand that those who occupy key positions in branch politics and ward organization remain in the first instance *village* members. Low-level party leaders may enjoy advantages through their having more direct access to departmental officials and resources, but they have by no means become immune to the problem of erratic supplies (goods and cash) or to moisture stress in fields or to pressure from village communities.

The first anecdote shows how the party machinery fails to reach the masses. It exposes the depressing fact that when people do take initiatives towards improving their living standards, they may have all aspirations and hopes shattered because they ultimately lack control over the decision-making process. The self-interest of certain initiatives taken by the party may be one good reason why UNIP has thus far failed to secure a firm foothold in Mambwe country.

Case Study 8: The Rural Image of UNIP

The Kaka Constituency leaders called a meeting, one Saturday in September, to inform the masses of the results of the Mulungushi Conference and of the spirit in which it had been held.[5] The place of this meeting was the primary school ground in Mwamba.

People had gathered in a circle. Slightly inside the circle were seated the Chiefs Mwamba and Penza, while party representatives took their seats at a table which formed part of the circle. The seating arrangement symbolized that the chiefs' position was one of respect and of isolation.

The crowd was some sixty men to start with and later increased to about eighty-five, including five women. The majority had come to represent their villages: names were taken down. Damson Simfukwe, chairman of the Kaka constituency, led the UNIP delegation. Damson is a local employee of the veterinary department and, by local standards, a very successful farmer. His secretary (one Mr Bwalya, Bemba teacher in a village near Kaka) and the chairman of the Mwamba branch sat beside him. A priest of the United Church of Zambia joined the panel. He opened the meeting with a long prayer in which the names of President Kaunda and Chief Mwamba were frequently cited.

The main purpose of taking the Mulungushi meeting to the masses was to denounce the former leader of the banned United Progressive Party (UPP), Simon Mwansa Kapwepwe, the politician from Northern Province who aspired to oppose Kaunda at the forthcoming presidential elections.[6] Kapwepwe, who had only recently rejoined UNIP (Mwangilwa 1986: 181), saw his candidature declared void after a hasty, unorthodox amendment to the constitution (*ibid*: 172-176). The people of Mwamba were told to express contempt for Kaunda's rival with the slogan, 'Who can choose Kapwepwe? ... Kapwepwe, *Awe!* [=No], Shame!' The slogan fell on deaf ears; the audience managed only a faint mumble. The slogan did little to improve UNIP's poor local image. If the anti-Kapwepwe campaign achieved anything at all that day, it was to strengthen the villagers' belief that Kapwepwe was still a politician of some repute.

The audience focused its attention not on politics but on the wooden spoons and sieves that circulated. Some people had obviously come to do business. The actual meeting was low key. Only one attendant, the headmaster of Mwamba Primary, showed genuine interest. Although he spoke in English, his sharp comments and pragmatic questions caused considerable embarassment. The teacher detailed the malfunctioning of the party machine and its failure to do something for the rural masses. He was more than a match for the constituency leaders. Much of what he said was missed by the crowd, but the intervention paved the way for a later discussion about the payment of party dues.

Findings of the Mulungushi Conference were easily summed up: first, give president Kaunda a massive 'yes' vote on 12 December 1978; secondly, no-one will be entitled to vote when not in possession of a valid party card. The constituency chairman then asked for a hands-up count of all who had paid their dues for the current year. Fifteen hands went up. This was less than twenty per cent of an audience that included many headmen.

The crowd awoke when the rally ended with a new song in praise of Zambia's President, the leader of UNIP. The constituency chairman and secretary started to sing in CiBemba, then danced in front of the crowd, inviting everyone to join in. The crowd, offended, started jeering. Their militant mood invited Chief Mwamba to speak. Mwamba, who till then had kept an air of indifference about him, rose and addressed the party officials, with the words: 'There are only two things my people want. Number one, we want our clinic (*chipatala*) to be built now. It is long ago since the people of Mwamba contributed their money. Number two, we want water (*manzi*) here in the village. The dry season is wearing us out.' The chief referred indirectly to the permanent water supply installed in Kaka.

The constituency secretary, scholar and non-Mambwe, with his trendy trousers, fashion shoes and slim-fit Mulungushi T-shirt, failed to answer the chief's call for an explanation about the clinic. When he started to beat about the bush, the people interrupted, shouting 'Our money has been stolen'. The people also accused representatives of the Rural Council and their own Ward Councillor, Mr Evans Fungo. All were blamed for 'not caring about a clinic here.' It embarassed the constituency leaders that the building of a government-sponsored clinic had recently started in Kaka, their own headquarters. Kaka had never been asked to donate money to the scheme! In an attempt to restore order, the secretary made a note of the chief's complaint. It was not clear to whom the note would be taken.

Order was not to be restored yet. Next on the agenda came the distribution of party cards. Some attendants who had paid dues said they were still waiting for their stamps. This time the panels did have an explanation, for 'foreigners' had infiltrated the rural areas. Allegedly, these 'foreigners' collected party dues, at the normal fee of K1,50, but gave out faked receipts. Anyone who complained about not receiving stamps had fallen victim to conmen. The chairman added that the intruders would be found and punished. He further disclosed how the party now planned to expand its network of offices, 'through donations from the people'. The scheme would enable the people of Mwamba to pay for their stamps and collect them at their constituency office. This would end the present problem of having to rely on the regional office in Mbala.

Commotion followed this announcement. The farce was complete. The constituency leaders prepared for a speedy retreat; back to Kaka in their landrover. Further debate was pointless. As the crowd dispersed, several headmen expressed their sympathy with Chief Mwamba and assured him of their continued support.

There are several comments to be made. 'More donations to make us pay even more...' is how Chief Mwamba summed up the meeting. His comment hinted how the party programme presents itself to the people of rural Mbala. For a people who value cash investments that pay off quickly, the existing party programme is not worthy of any serious thought. To fuel anti-UNIP feelings, the party had now failed to answer the charge that money had been 'stolen' from the people of Mwamba. How could UNIP hope to regain the people's trust?

The widespread absence of a grass-roots interest in the party programme for rural development reflects the everyday hardships of the rural rank-and-file, leaders and led. The majority of branch-level leaders, and the traditional authority, waste no time with vague promises or long-term strategies. Instead they join the masses in their search for an immediate solution to the impoverishment of rural Zambia; an impoverishment which they view primarily in terms of their being starved of cash. As a result, low-level politicians wholeheartedly support an activity such as bean cropping, which gives higher profit margins than hybrid maize, and they consent or turn a blind eye to trading with villages across the border. Whatever criticisms outsiders (like me) may have about the ultimate viability of a survival strategy based on free-marketing and contraband commerce, one result stands out: the strategy is able to bring some relief, instantly.

Grass-roots (i.e. branch-level) leaders and led share a common perception as to what constitutes the best attack on the impoverishment of the area. With few government resources to be distributed, peasant households do not so much feel 'frozen out' as angry about the fact that the party intervenes when it is unable to deliver. Mambwe peasants know very well that constituency leaders and ward councillors have larger-than-average farms; and they sometimes resent such relative affluence. But stronger than this resentment is the notion that they themselves can raise some money, through trading, through their own efforts, and that this money is required to continue participation in the money economy. The flow of cash and of consumer goods is less voluminous than during the heyday of circulatory migration, but the Mambwe have no wish to live outside the cash economy. They know they must work hard and mobilize all their resources, natural and organizational, if they are to carry on as before. The Mambwe cultivator, man or woman, does not believe that allegiance to the party will reverse the trend of dwindling finances. From their point of view, all the party and the development committees are capable of is extracting money from an already cash-starved population. Only through personal hard work, and trading, can something of the flow of money and goods, something of the glory days of the migrant, still be ensured.

The second of the Mwamba situational sketches reinforces the idea that building personal contacts is more important than turning up for political rallies. Once again the occasion is International Literacy Day. This time, however, the celebration clashes with a local wedding.

Case Study 9: Literacy Day Boycott

International Literacy Day celebration in Mwamba (22 September, 1978) was organized by the Area Functional Literacy Committee. Its main purpose was the presentation of certificates to peasant-students of the 1976-77 literacy class. All had completed with satisfaction. Although bureaucrats in Mbala were informed of the celebration at very short notice, their response had been swift. Departments were represented by Mr B. Phiri (District Community Development Officer) and by one Mr Bwalya, assistant to the District Agricultural Officer (DAO). IDZ was represented by its Kasama-based coordinator, Mr Katenda. One other prominent figure was Mr Kazia, Mwamba chairman of the Literacy Committee. Mr Kazia was also the local UNIP constituency vice-chairman and a candidate in the forthcoming regional election. He owned the only record shop in Mbala. But the ward councillor, Mr Evans Fungo of Eliya's village, was absent due to illness – diplomatic, it was rumoured.

The headmaster of Mwamba Primary opened the festivities with a long and studiously prepared speech, in English, on literacy. Mr Katenda translated *ad hoc*, in CiBemba, with an enthusiasm to match that of the speaker. The keynote address brimmed over with threats to the illiterate, misunderstood and badly formulated slogans, and dubious principles about development. The teacher aimed to impress fellow intellectuals; he made no attempt to look at literacy in terms of the living conditions of his audience. Few understood. No-one was offended. Moreover, the attending crowd was about twenty local people. There was no sign of the chief. And worse, no sign of the literacy class!

As the celebration neared its end, with a poorly conducted display of traditional dancing, a UNIP vehicle arrived at the scene. From the vehicle emerged the Regional Party Secretary and the Youth Regional Secretary. Without delay the Party Secretary made for the platform to deliver his speech. He too spoke in CiBemba. This time the audience did take exception at being spoken to in a language not their own. A handful of peasants began shouting halfway through the speech. The Regional Secretary carried on, unperturbed.

Later that day, the Party 'Top Two' did air their disappointment, but not during the public part of the celebration. Having just returned from the eighth Mulungushi Conference, the Top Two presented the new electoral slogan 'Dr Kenneth Kaunda - no change! no change!'. By then, the number of attending locals had risen to some forty-five. There still was no sign of any students. The students, nearly all from the same village, were attending a wedding in their own village, a mere three kilometres from Mwamba. Eventually their headman did turn up. Not in the least embarassed about the absence of his people, the headman shook hands with the Regional Party Secretary at every presentation. Twenty successful candidates, twenty certificates, twenty handshakes, twenty broad smiles. It was most entertaining.

The Party Top Two had been at a rally in a Lungu village earlier than morning, when they were informed about the Mwamba Literacy Celebration. Expecting to meet an enthusiastic crowd of potential voters, they had rushed off to Mwamba, knowing they would be late. When they arrived, which was something of a surprise, they were shocked by the absence of the crowd and, especially, the now literate peasants.

When the VIPs later gathered to consume beer, food, and more beer, a scapegoat had to be found. That was not too difficult. During the drinking hours, the blame went from Mr Kazia, the Committee Chairman whose bad cold had prevented him from giving a speech, to the committee's secretary, young Musonda (pseudonym), who had only recently arrived as Mwamba's new Community Development Assistant (CDA). The young man had failed to awaken the people's interest! Worse still, he had stopped the Committee Chairman from 'mobilizing' support for the occasion.

The CDA accepted the blame without demur. But 'mobilizing', he objected, was not the right word. 'Canvassing' was more appropriate. Eager to make his mark at the start of his career, Musonda offered to explain his position. Chairman Kazia, he agreed, had indeed attempted 'to organize the people', just as he had done in previous years, when people had attended in their hundreds. Kazia's strategy, also this time, had been to visit all villages of the Mwamba constituency. There he had asked for money, with the promise of a 'free beer for all' on the day. Musonda clarified: 'That is the only way you can make people move these days! But I, as CDA, I objected to this. I wanted it to be a celebration for our literacy students, and prepared by them. This is why I stopped Kazia collecting money. I wanted the villagers to be informed about the celebration so that they could come out of interest and not because of the beer. As CDA I told Kazia to stop collecting and to return whatever money he already had in his possession. Kazia with his 'free beer' was only trying to make himself popular in view of the forthcoming elections. Kazia toured the villages *not* as Committee Chairman but as an electoral candidate. And so, no free beer finally meant no audience.'

The incident disclosed some contrasting views about modes of political mobilization. Kazia, prominent local UNIP figure and chairman of the Literacy Committee, was opposed by Musonda, civil servant and secretary to the Committee. A young Bemba challenged a senior Mambwe! The former believed that 'mass mobilization' could be achieved, in this case, because the occasion was a great one; the latter knew that large Mambwe gatherings do not occur spontaneously, if the custom of providing 'free beer for all' is ignored. But that, in Musonda's opinion, was tantamount to bribery, a violation of party ideals, a misplaced strategy for winning votes. Indirectly, the CDA's critique revealed the present inability by the party to mobilize for the right cause. Musonda was critical of what Chikulo once described as 'the tendency of party officials to put personal gain before tasks of mass mobilization' (Chikulo

1979: 209). Musonda's stand also reminded of President Kaunda's regular attacks on alcohol abuse in rural areas.

A second theme, equally important, runs through the case material. The boycott by peasant-students showed poignantly that the Mambwe peasant producers know where their priorities lie. That they were absent had nothing to do with the presumed bad publicity that had followed Kazia's rebuke. The students' failure to attend was due to the bad timing of the celebration, which clashed with an important event in their village, a marriage that had attracted many relatives and friends, including guests from across the Tanzanian border. The wedding was a unique chance for meeting up with a large circle of kin, affines and friends from Tanzania; many of whom were either established or potential trade partners.[7] The prospect of reviewing past transactions, confirming partnerships, speculating about future deals and obtaining general information about who was planning to grow what during the forthcoming season... all these issues, *crucial to survival today*, had turned the wedding ceremony into a social function of far greater significance than the sterile presentation of certificates. The significance of this particular wedding will become clearer in Chapter 7, where kinship and affinity are discussed in relation to cross-border trading.

The final case study brings out further aspects of the contrast between local expectations and practices, on the one hand, and party organization, on the other. This time, however, the branch-level party representatives and their Chief face a really awkward dilemma, a problem which could jeopardize the area's good relations with the free-trading world. Branch-level leaders could not afford to break off good relations, but they still wanted to be seen to be towing the party line. It is with this case that I return to Long's thoughts on the changing relationship between Witnesses and non-Witnesses.

Case Study 10: The Agricultural Show

Organizers of agricultural shows need to put up stalls for the display of produce. They need people to cut poles from the bush, slash grass, and erect the actual structures. The money economy triumphs over the self-help economy here, for no one in charge of organizing such a show in the Mambwe hinterland would consider asking the people to come forth spontaneously.

In reality, therefore, putting up the stalls means employing local people. But money is not only required for recruiting workers; it is also necessary to provide honourable guests with food and drink, as happened in the previous case. Since no committee has the necessary funds at hand, the Party is activated to raise money from the people who live in the Ward. As I was living in Kasunga at that time, I was aware of the unusual interest in this matter, especially when it became known that the nearby royal village of Aron - a Watch Tower community already much in the news during the 1950s (Watson 1958: 54, 97) - had refused to contribute. Today, the royal Siame clan still exerts authority in Aron, as it does in many villages, which implies that the Siame headman is agnatically linked to various chiefs. (Royal status denotes prominence in local politics, but authority may be challenged – see the growing influence of Simuyemba in Chele, Chapter 6, and the case of Chivunzila, Chapter 7.)

The man who had called upon the headman of Aron was one Winel S., vice-chairman of the UNIP Branch comprising Aron, Kasunga and Chivunzila (see Diagram 7). Winel, a most congenial man, also represented his own village Kalinda at the Ward Committee in Mwamba.

Although Seveni Siame, head of Aron, is a UNIP branch secretary, he refused to respond to the appeal for village contributions (5 *ngwee* per family). Siame considered himself to be a village headman first and that he was also a branch secretary of the party was not to alter his decision. Siame's ambivalent stand sparked off a chain reaction in which leadership roles became blurred. When Winel S., as Ward Council representative and vice-chairman of the party branch, approached party secretary Siame for the purpose of raising the funds (which was a Ward Council decision), he was in fact met by Siame the uncooperative headman. Siame's position was reminiscent of what Watson wrote about Aron, some twenty-five years earlier.

Winel reported the incident to Donald S. Although the two men are on an equal footing in the Ward Committee, Donald enjoys higher status, since he is also a *kapitao* for the Northern Co-operative Union. Donald responded by taking the case to those responsible for organizing the show (e.g., the Ward Councillor) and to Chief Mwamba himself. He asked the chief to solve this matter. Chief Mwamba judged that Siame was a rebel headman and that he had to be threatened in the customary way. The Chief told Donald to instruct the villagers of Aron to pay up, even if their headman continued to refuse. And he added, 'Should the villagers also refuse, then I shall expel them from my territory and will depose their headman.' Donald brought the message by word of mouth to headman Siame, who agreed to make his village contribute.

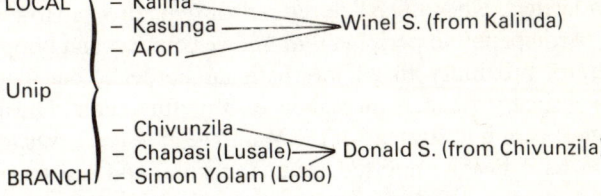

Diagram 7 Ward representation

The sometimes curious intertwining of old and new leadership roles is here exceptionally clear: a low-level party secretary rejects this function to favour his other role as headman of a Watch Tower village. When Party and Council members fail to persuade the headman, it is the authority of the 'traditional' leader which is sought. The 'modern' leader (UNIP branch secretary Siame) who chooses to be a religiously-inspired headman opposed to Party organization (headman Siame) is threatened with sanctions from the 'traditional' authority, lest he acts against the wishes of the 'modern' (Ward Council) organizers of the agricultural show.

Recourse to customary sanction in order to enforce the wishes of the new men in power is a common strategy in developing One-Party states, an extension of indirect rule. However, equally significant is that newly imposed organizational structures may be frowned upon by those who also occupy 'traditional' office. Headman Siame's feelings are those of his villagers, and when these clash with the wishes of the imposed party system, of which he too has become a member, he has no choice other than to reject the 'modern' role. From the villagers' point of view, and that of headman Siame, there are better ways of investing one's meagre financial resources. The village collective in Aron, in other words, view their Watch Tower organization as the more secure road to development. Agricultural shows are associated with UNIP, government departments, the National Marketing Board (NAMBOARD) and the Northern Co-operative Union (NCU); whereas what really counts in the lives of small-scale surplus producers is those networks that do operate when cash crops need collecting. In the Mambwe economy, such operations are more likely to be taken care of – even for non-Watch Tower villages – by independent traders who have close links with the organization.

Maize is still the official cash crop in Mambwe country, but bean cropping is much more lucrative. Bean cropping is even encouraged by local politicians, and especially by Mbala-based politicians who have a stake in or who run their own private transport. Outside the realm of official price controls, bean cropping and trading are better ways of investing money. In Mambwe country, the free-market producer price for beans was double the price paid by state monopoly buyers in Eastern Province. The bean trade dominated all cash-raising efforts. It was part of a non-official but tolerated, large-scale operation in which Copperbelt-based Watch Tower traders had a significant interest.

In order to understand why 'official' development structures fail to generate any grass-roots participation in peripheral Mambwe country (and peripheral, note, often implies proximity to an international border!), one needs to understand how ordinary villagers meet their cash requirements. During my fieldwork, the most common strategy in the Mambwe grasslands was to grow beans (and/or to have beans imported from Tanzania) and sell to visiting Copperbelt-based traders. The long-distance traders who visited most regularly were Watch Tower entrepreneurs who called upon their Watch Tower contacts. The vast and efficient Watch Tower network was the one that counted most when villagers sought to raise instant cash. In contrast, the government-backed buying-up depots for maize never paid cash. And maize, the only crop the depots handled, fetched much lower prices.

It is in the light of the local appreciation of the free-market alternative that Donald's decision to involve Chief Mwamba must be understood. Donald was being very cautious. By taking the Siame case to the 'traditional' Chief Mwamba - who fought his own battles with UNIP! (case study 8) - Donald S. was able to avoid a personal clash with the Watch Tower congregation. Donald could have left the Chief out to try and settle the matter through pressure from the 'officials' (himself, Winel S., the Ward Councillor, other WC members), but that option would have put too much emphasis on the question of Aron's allegiance to UNIP and to the nation-state. Donald chose to settle the dispute outside the Party and outside the 'official' development structures, for it was in his own interest (as the prominent shopkeeper of a large amalgamated village), and therefore in the interest of many other villagers, that he be able to maintain good relations with local Watch Tower groups. The solution was also welcomed by Siame (although he moaned a lot), because he had not lost face by reversing his position. Within the terms of reference chosen by Donald, i.e. within the idiom of traditional politics, headman Siame had merely given in to the old chief, to someone senior in the organization of the royal lineage.

FOOD SECURITY AND SELF-HELP

The apathy and occasional resistance which Mambwe villagers display towards the imposed development structures must be ascribed to two trends. First of all, though current strategies for raising cash (bean cropping; intensive cross-border trade) may be deceptive roads to long-term development, they have nevertheless reactivated the regional flow of cash and are locally perceived to be the best antidotes available against impoverishment. Secondly, the position of the emergent farmer is not the source of much envy. Peasant farmers are aware of the absence of any durable alliances between farmers and bureaucrats. As I observed the situation in Kaka, for example, the hypothetical unitary elitist front between farmers and extension workers was too unstable to be held responsible for the plight of the rural poor. The reason for this instability relates to shortages of consumer goods, farming requisites, loans and subsidies. What Bratton argued for Kasama also applies to the development front in Mambwe country, namely that 'the interests of existing patrons are likely to be jealously guarded', under conditions of scarce or declining resources (Bratton 1980a: 281). The politics of progressive farming in Kaka showed emergent farmers to be in a precarious position.

In the eyes of many peasants, joining the 'emergent' farmers, for instance by trying hard to secure AFC loans, was synonymous with taking unnecessary risks. The pattern of interaction between emergent farmers, field-based civil servants and higher-ranking politicians was too rife with uncertainty and contradiction to appeal to outsiders. Van Donge made a similar observation for Eastern Province, where the possibility of alliance building equally amounted to 'a pattern of interaction in which contradictions and ambiguities were more prominent than the pursuit of common interests' (Van Donge 1982: 89). Hedlund (1984) confirms the precarious, dependent position of 'emergent' farmers who opted for resettlement on a project site in North-Western Zambia.

Observations during the first half of the 1970s led Bratton to pinpoint the emergent farmers as a significant new element in the local social structure. Successful farmers made their presence felt through membership of WDCs (Bratton 1980a: 91). The situation in the crisis period of the late 1970s was different, and many peasants (at least in the context of the grassland economy) viewed the position of the emergent farmer with ambivalence. Emergent Mambwe farmers were looked upon as clearly better off than the average villager, yet their difficulties in the face of low pricing incentives, uncooperative extension workers, and irregular supplies of requisites were thought to obstruct progress. Moreover, since Kaka is in part a red-brick transformation of an existing village, there were many abandoned dwellings that had attracted numerous dependents – like elder parents and divorced sisters with children. Such dependents, farmers complained, were a constant drain on their cash earnings.[8] Peasants were interested in forming advantageous relationships, but they approached local traders, not local administrators.

Returning to the scene of his first research, Long 'discovered that Witnesses and non-Witnesses had worked out a way of accommodating to each other's ideological point of view' (Long 1984: 5). As is clear from my own case material, I too observed such a 'rapprochement' in Mambwe villages, especially in and around areas targeted for intensive development. Cooperation with the Witnesses took the form of free-market bean sales to Witness-controlled buying-up places. For the cash-starved Mambwe the bean sales were a lifeline, the best they could do under the circumstances. The 'rapprochement' did not mean that all tension between Witnesses and non-Witnesses had disappeared, for clearly it had not. What had surfaced was an atmosphere of greater understanding and tolerance towards the Watch Tower ethic.

Set against the background of a nationwide economic depression, this 'rapprochement' supports the idea of a dialectic relationship between religion and economy. As Bond expressed it in the context of social change in rural Zambia, 'major changes in the production relations of society may lead to changes ... in the religious beliefs held by its members' (Bond 1978: 35). In Mambwe country it is the ailing national economy, epitomised by malfunctioning marketing parastatals (NAMBOARD, NCU), which has led to a change of heart, an attitude of greater religious tolerance. By the late 1970s few Mambwe could afford to have bad relationships with Witnesses: hence the chief's intervention, as a traditional leader.

Some of the factors that separated Witnesses from non-Witnesses during the colonial period have also been removed. Witnesses used to challenge the authority of the Mambwe chief by refusing him tribute labour and by trying their own cases (1958: 201). Today, these sources of tension, which Watson discussed specifically for Mwamba and Aron, have by and large disappeared, since chiefs have lost those prerogatives.

Given the endemic need for cash, which affects men and women, a somewhat more enthusiastic response to government facilities could have occurred. Why did this not happen? With reference to Bratton's thesis, I argue that the 'official' development process of the grassland villages is hampered not by local antagonism towards a presumed alliance of successful farmers, politicians and extension workers (for the alliance was stuck, 'frozen' at the embryonic stage), but by the massive local search for a *self-help* escape from impoverishment. UNIP's failure to mobilize the grassland peasantry must be understood in terms of the peasants' preoccupation with meeting the growing demand for food and cash. The more relevant variables in the economic structure of the Mambwe grasslands are the prevailing high price for beans paid on the 'free' market, the declining level in the production of millet, and the scope for 'informal' complementarity regarding food and scarce goods. Such complementarity, which exists in most African regions split by artificial international boundaries, is usually marked by the existence side by side of diverse, even opposed, agrarian policies. The Mambwe area provides an illustration.

On the other hand, as case study 10 shows, Mambwe peasants do not wish to go too far in provoking the party. (Really, the Literacy Day disaster had brought the Mwamba area close to disrepute.) Had Siame stood his ground, the wrath of UNIP would almost certainly have come down, and this could have resulted in NCU blacking out Mwamba, under pressure from UNIP. This would have meant vital cash losses, since the people of Mwamba still invest in maize. They have good reasons for doing so (see Chapter 2). Their basic view on marketing was that they should invest in both systems.[9] The possible ambiguity in Chief Mwamba's behaviour (opposing UNIP in case study 8; taking care not to offend UNIP in case study 10) makes perfect sense when seen in the light of the popular view on marketing. Mwamba's style of leadership is not so much ambiguous as syncretistic, guided by a search for reconciliation. The style is neither modern nor traditional, but a synthesis of both. The political manoeuvre that finally persuaded headman Aron to pay up was successful, because the final move blotted out all possible references to UNIP. In the end, the people of Mwamba safeguarded their trade interests, both with the Co-operative and with the Witnesses.

Cooperation between Witnesses and non-Witnesses was on an extensive scale, for cash benefits were mutual. The reliance on Witnesses was also boosted by their reputation for being scrupulously honest (Poewe 1978: 311).

Other researchers on trading styles in Africa confirm that dominance of private marketing by religious or ethnic groups does not necessarily lead to exploitation or monopoly profits (e.g. Cohen 1969; Lele 1977: 501). But in spite of the 'rapprochement' between Witnesses and non-Witnesses, I was also aware, and increasingly so towards the end of fieldwork, that the average peasant household was losing the capacity to feed itself and struggling to preserve some degree of independence. Two interacting constraints threatened household autonomy: loss of labour power, and loss of fertile land. The labour constraint experienced by poorer households is taken up in the next chapter. An appreciation of the ecological damage inflicted upon Northern Zambia in the course of the twentieth century is given in Chapter 8.

CHAPTER SIX

LAND, LABOUR, AND CASH

The previous chapter established that the 'official' development resources to which local-level leaders had access during the late 1970s were inadequate for boosting subsistence agriculture. Rural incomes stagnated as a result. The reasons for the depressed incomes were manifold. The hybrid maize introduced did not suit local conditions; funds released by the Agricultural Finance Company reached only a small proportion of all maize-growers; and even households that did benefit from AFC credit continued to face constraints. Nor had development policy created new jobs in the rural sector. Certain development schemes were launched in Mbala district in the second half of the decade, but these were not planned to involve the masses (GRZ 1977b: 45-54). Compared with the opportunity structure and the flow of remittances in the 1950s, I could only conclude that cash levels had seriously dropped (Chapter 3).

In this chapter I examine responses to the need for making better use of the local earning capacity. The cash-starved Mambwe have indeed reacted to this need in various ways. In the food production sector, for instance, reactions to the dearth of cash, and to the need for higher production, have taken on a variety of styles. Three such styles can be discerned from the point of view of the Mambwe villager. They differ according to the nature of government assistance, the use made of labour resources, and the availability of land. Gender also influences local opportunities for raising cash, but this will be discussed separately in Chapter 7.

At the time of my research, Zambian village leaders were being urged to think creatively about rural development, since the government pocket manual on village organization held them responsible for working out appropriate strategies for the use of all available resources (see Chapter 5). In everyday language, this creative responsibility largely coincided with finding ways to alleviate the local cash constraint. This was no mean task, since the government-approved strategy for raising money through maize cropping was so poorly implemented in peripheral Zambia.

There is little information in the literature on 'official' local-level responses to the poor performance in state marketing. But one rare account, which deals with responses in Luapula province, suggests that the failure of government strategy may have caused village-level party officials to regulate the fragmentation and distribution of *existing* wealth (Poewe 1979: 82). Poewe observed this reaction in the context of beer brewing and commercial fishing, and labelled it a strategy of 'equal impoverishment'. The Mambwe grassland response to the cash constraint, including the reaction of its local-level party leaders, developed along similar lines. Although this chapter is about specific village reactions to scarce cash, I recall that grassland villagers habitually cash in on the production trends and price differentials that exist either side of the border. As I argued earlier on, especially in Chapter 3, people from either side of the border exploit discrepancies in pricing, they respond to the demand for scarce goods and food, and they import to meet perceived shortages. The age-old principle of economic complementarity between diverse ecological zones (Chapter 2) has been adjusted to the international border situation. This adjustment brings relief through the redistribution of *existing* resources. The broad pattern of taking fish, vegetables, soap, sugar and other commodities into Tanzania in order to 'extract' agricultural produce (millet, beans) for sale on the Zambian free-market was the most widespread single strategy for earning cash in the late 1970s. Without it, many grassland households - including the families of village-level administrators - would have been unable to meet even the most basic of their needs.

UNIP's village and ward leaders did not officially approve of cross-border transactions, although their households too found it necessary to participate in them. Official curtailment of cross-border trade was not attempted in rural areas, at least not at the time of fieldwork, for such action would have been unsympathetic to the needs of the people. Party leaders in rural areas starved of cash faced many dilemmas. Their views and actions must therefore be judged with an understanding of local conditions. 1978 was a real crisis year, in the Mambwe grasslands as in other parts of the country, for the problem of food had reached a critical stage in urban and rural communities (Muntemba 1982:45). Cross-border trade stimulated a more 'equal impoverishment' between two peripheral areas - one Zambian, one Tanzanian - and achieved, in some cases, a similar redistribution between the sexes (Chapter 7).

Not all local leaders, however, responded to the need for cash by agreeing to share out whatever wealth was available. Some leaders were more ambitious. The Village Productivity Committee (VPC) of Chele village, for example, decided not only to democratize *existing* wealth (i.e. by sharing out the technical means of production), but also wished to augment this wealth. The

Chele VPC, with the assistance of the Intensive Development Zone programme, conceived the idea of a model village built on the principles of Zambian Humanism. Chele followed UNIP's guidelines for development close to the letter: its VPC organized large work-parties, claiming to honour the 'traditional' Mambwe ethos of work-sharing, and clearly succeeded in boosting aggregate levels of production. The initiative is my first example of a specific village response to reduced rural incomes. The Chele version of 'modern' agriculture anticipated that cash needs could be overcome through improved levels of production.

For the second illustration I shall go back to Kaka. Being in part a settlement scheme, Kaka is a village where much land had been set aside for commercial farming. The relatively large farms that subsequently emerged in Kaka had attracted a number of 'dependent' relatives (Chapter 5), but there was still considerable demand for seasonal labour. Household heads who had *not* registered as 'emergent' farmers looked to the farms for seasonal work and for raising cash (outside busy periods) on loan terms.

In spite of their idiosyncracies, the two approaches, which could be termed VPC-centred and project-centred, showed up a common trend in relation to the expenditure of labour-time for poorer households. The trend was also present in the third style, which was based on *laissez-faire* politics. In the latter case no administrative intervention was allowed, except for the allocation of AFC credit to a handful of households. This third style has already been described in Chapter 4, when I examined new agrarian relations in Kowa village. In Kowa, AFC credit could only be obtained through joining the VPU (Village Productivity Unit) of a neighbouring village, but there was sufficient cash available for contract work: wage-earners in Kowa contracted the unwaged for a substantial part of all agricultural activities. In this chapter I shall restrict myself to a discussion of the Chele and Kaka responses.

The pattern of interaction between field-based civil servants, farmers and political authoritites, analysed in Chapter 5, was shown to be affected by ambiguities and mistrust. Existing attitudes, I pointed out, were not conducive to the formation of durable alliances, since resource hand-outs were far too limited to stimulate the emergence of more entrenched class interests. The argument is supported by Hedlund's analysis of a comparable settlement in North-Western province, where several farmers became disgruntled about the low level of assistance (Hedlund 1984:245). I wish to take this debate one step further by arguing that the analysis of social differentiation must not be restricted to whether durable alliances are created between government personnel and 'emergent' farmers. As Van Donge has suggested, referring to Long (1968), the allocation of credit is one important issue, but 'a farmer must also obtain land and organise a labor force' (Van Donge 1982: 98). It follows that a full understanding of land and labour allocations will be necessary in order to unravel the question whether or not historical continuity has occurred with regard to social differentiation in Mambwe country. The absence of successful alliances at the top of the social ladder must not be taken to mean that positions lower down are not being perpetuated.

So, it is to land and labour, and to the politics of village life, that I now turn. However, observations on land and labour cannot be fully understood unless one also knows about recent developments in cash needs and sources of income. The latter theme will serve as my introduction to the Chele and Kaka styles in modern agriculture.

THE CASH NEEDS OF MAMBWE VILLAGERS

Under conditions of circulatory outmigration for men, women food producers had secured the right to sell surplus from their kitchen gardens. Such surpluses were small and mainly in maize. Mambwe women used the money thus earned to buy clothes and personal goods (Watson 1958: 110). The scale of the sales was restricted, especially when compared with the later sales to NCU, but the prerogative provided women with a regular and independent source of cash.

By the late 1970s a number of historical changes had weakened the women's hold over the maize trade. These changes had come in the wake of developments in Zambia's political economy. I discern three major changes:

(a) As shown in Chapter 3, urban labour markets had become saturated. Circulatory migration had come to a halt and men had begun to seek out alternative sources of income.
(b) The post-independence policy of village regroupment had put a stop to the periodic movement of villages. Continuous settlement and cultivation had in turn affected the fertility of kitchen-gardens (*ivizule*), so that such gardens lost their significance for raising cash.
(c) The early phase of the campaign for promoting commercial maize had been successful, and the SR-52 hybrid had gained overall popularity, even in peripheral areas.

The impact of these converging factors is not too difficult to guess. Having lost every hope of securing formal, long-term, urban employment (along the Line of Rail and in Mbala), Mambwe men now claimed that state-controlled production of food surplus was the only respectable alternative to wage-labour migration. Would-be migrants in particular insisted that government commit itself to the development of village agriculture. Mambwe men also equated 'state-controlled' with 'male-controlled', and did not feel they needed to justify their taking over the women's monopoly in trading maize. Nowadays, marketable crops are grown not in *ivizule*, but on plots reserved for marketing purposes. These plots, on which some of the family food may also be grown, are cleared by men and allocated to individual women, usually wives.

Mambwe women have well-defined rights over the distribution of *food crops*: women alone have legitimate access to food stored in the household's granaries. Rights over *surplus*, on the other hand, are at best negotiable. With regard to the main traditional staple (millet), custom allows a husband to try and persuade his wife to sell stored grain. But wives have rights of refusal, for instance, on the grounds that the household would suffer if insufficient food were kept. A woman's reluctance to use up food crops for cash purposes makes sense, since she alone is responsible for feeding the household and for entertaining visitors. Any miscalculation in managing the supply would mean that a woman is forced to spend her own cash on purchasing extra food.

It is difficult to ascertain whether environmental constraints diminish or fuel the likelihood of male-female conflict over food allocations, particularly during the period leading up to harvest, when food prices peak. What is causing tension though is that the traditional millet staple has largely been displaced by cassava and maize, and that maize now occupies *the ambiguous position of being both a food and a cash crop*. Which part of the maize crop is for sale and which to be consumed is a matter for local debate and no unambiguous rules do as yet exist.

When they harvested maize, both men and women were explicit that their cash needs could only be met through selling off part of the crop. A woman with children would strive to obtain a large enough share of any 'surplus' sold (millet, maize or beans) by stressing the number of mouths she feeds, the long days she labours in the field, and by pointing out that her mother never needed to beg for the right to sell *ivizule* produce. Husbands usually countered that being cut off from the migrant jobs their fathers used to enjoy, they too now had a great need for cash. Whatever informants said about crop ownership, harvest time brought out that much wheeling and dealing was going on.

In the absence of clear-cut guidelines for the disposal of produce, it is understandable that female-male relations were often tense during harvests. One common solution to the problem of rights over surplus was for the man to claim the proceeds of home-grown food surplus (beans included), while allowing the woman to invest some of the money (i.e. his earnings) in regional commerce. Profits from petty trading were not necessarily large (see Chapter 3), but men claimed that they were not inferior to the profits their own mothers used to make when trading *ivizule* produce. The solution was not popular with the women. Generally speaking, therefore, surplus sales were more a matter for negotiation. There were no hard and fast rules, for example, about how the proceeds from bean cropping were to be shared: some women did receive a quantity of beans as starting-up capital (with or without the obligation to return cash), while others did not. Compromises were often made.

Women producers do not normally achieve full usufructory rights in this patrilineal culture, but many controlled key areas of the regional food supply system. Although men too participated in petty trading, their organizational powers and capacity for making profits were more often than not undercut by women traders who exerted control over partners across the Tanzanian border.

The mechanism that regulated cross-border trading will be illustrated in Chapter 7.

The uncertainties surrounding the control of marketable foodstuffs has enhanced the importance of working for food (*ukupula*). The practice of *ukupula*, which Richards showed to be increasing in neighbouring Bemba land during the early 1960s (Richards 1961), has also become pronounced among the Mambwe. I shall now discuss how labour-time is allocated in accordance with the need to create alternative sources of income.

CHELE: AN EXPERIMENT IN HUMANIST AGRICULTURE

The focus in this section is on the organization of a 'traditional' form of cooperative agriculture which had been streamlined to the tenets of Zambian Humanism. The village of Chele was generally referred to as a place where Zambian Humanism was 'at work'. The relationship between 'traditional' modes of food production and the ideology of Humanism is yet to be given attention in the literature (see Elliott 1983: 163). I present my data on Chele in the light of Elliott's broad hint that Zambian versions of Humanist agriculture may suffer from built-in ambiguities.

Chele, situated near the fertile, waterlogged plains of the Saisi river (Watson 1958: 9), was the home of an elected Member of Parliament (1973-78). This fertile village became an obvious candidate for IDZ patronage when 'rural growth areas' other than Kaka were demarcated (Chapter 5). The MP and other members of the VPC 'reciprocated' IDZ assistance by pledging to re-organize agricultural production in their village, along Humanistic lines. At the time of research Chele's leaders justified their approach to agriculture on the grounds that it sustained a traditional ethos. In contrast to other Mambwe villages, where millet production and communal work-parties had declined, Chele had succeeded in reversing the trends. Most importantly, Chele staged work-parties that brought together exceptionally large numbers of workers.

MAMBWE TRADITIONAL PRODUCTION

Mambwe culture, as described by Watson, did not know any rigid forms of stratification. Watson saw the Mambwe village as a united, economically independent unit, where food was communally produced and consumed (Watson 1959: 42). Essential to cooperation on the land was an institutionalized form of communal beer drinking. Consumption of millet beer (*cipumu*) generated and expressed a high degree of cooperation. Through their village membership, households were united as a corporate working-group and all cooperative work was reciprocated. In Watson's words:

> A man who attends another's work-party obliges the other to work in his own fields in return. Beer is not pay: it is the work which is reciprocated. ... A man cannot get his gardens dug simply by providing beer for others to come and work for him; if he does not work in return, no one will again accept his invitations (Watson 1958: 107-8)

Despite the largely egalitarian overtones of Mambwe cultural ideology as it existed in the fifties, it is essential to make some further points. First, the cooperative groups Watson observed were mainly women's parties. Men pooled their labour only during the initial stage of the agricultural cycle, for instance, when lopping trees in woodland villages. The predominance of female activity did not mean, however, that women controlled land. Nor did they control the product of their labour. It was even questionable whether they controlled their own labour, since some categories of women, widows mainly, were denied return services. While widows often worked for food (*ukupula*), their participation was not reciprocated. The traditional Mambwe mode of agriculture, then, was only partially based on exchange labour. The system had built-in inequalities that made it vulnerable to manipulation.

Secondly, the work-party system required supervision. Watson noted:

> The villagers arrange these work-parties among themselves, but the headman supervises the arrangements in the general interest. Mambwe millet beer takes three or four days to prepare and quickly loses its quality. Thus if two people brew for the same day and one lot must be left over, it is likely to go off. No one wishes to waste grain, and any clash of dates leads to quarrels. The headman must settle such conflicts with some delicacy, if he wishes to retain the confidence of both parties (Watson 1958: 108).

Supervision by the headman, together with the women's lack of control over the production process, suggests that the 1950s system of agriculture was not so egalitarian as Watson presumed.

MAMBWE IDEOLOGY AND THE STRUCTURE OF INTENSIVE DEVELOPMENT

When agriculture becomes organized in the name of Humanism, care must be taken to ensure that the built-in potential for labour exploitation is constantly checked. A continuous assessment of the 'rural development' performance, which I see as crucial to the successful raising of the VPC capacity for production (Chapter 5), should look into ways of minimizing differential access to and control of resources. In this context I accept the argument by Lappé and Beccar-Varela that 'the prime test of policy intervention is whether or not people are achieving food security' (Lappé and Beccar-Varela 1980: 23).

Chele is situated along the Mbala-Kawimbe road in the vicinity of Kowa, where everyday life continues to revolve around members of the 'royal' Siuluta lineage. The Siuluta were also numerically dominant in Chele, but their political dominance had waned. In 1978 it was the Simuyemba, with a minority of Siuluta, who controlled Chele's economic destiny. Their political prominence was reinforced through the well-organized VPC and its programme for agricultural re-organization.

There were two major types of gardens in Chele. Communal/VPC gardens (*viyalo viyakuombela pali pamwi*), cultivated solely to raise marketable crops, and individual (main) gardens, the produce from which was kept for household consumption and occasional petty trading. The third type of garden, *ivizule*, had lost its previous commercial importance. VPC activity was not concerned with kitchen gardens. The distinction Watson made between *ivizule* and main gardens remained valid, but permanent settlement and overcultivation had lowered output, especially in kitchen gardens.

The VPC chairman explained the production process of his village with the following words: 'The idea is to extend the mechanical services that are the privilege of a few among us to those who otherwise have no access to modern farming implements.' Chele's Member of Parliament, a resident farmer I shall refer to as Mr.C., confirmed the VPC approach. Those who owned cattle and ploughs volunteered to plough the land of the less fortunate villagers.

At this point I must note a subtle distinction. Villagers without cattle and ploughs benefitted from the mechanical service *only in relation to gardens of the individual type*! The less fortunate did not have any 'communal fields', and help with *ivizule* was not part of the commercially-oriented VPC programme. Poorer families reciprocated the service of ploughing by working during three specified weekdays, outside the slack season, in the *individual and VPC-type gardens* of those who possessed the mechanical means for intensified production.

The haves and the have-nots were united in what is called the Village Productivity Unit (VPU), the medium for implementing the principles of Zambian Humanism (Kandeke 1977). Between 1976 and 1978 VPU membership in Chele rose from twenty-three to twenty-eight. The increase was nominal though, since inquiry revealed how more than half of all VPU members had still to produce anything at all on a commercial basis. The VPU list also included three old women whose agricultural interests did not go beyond their *ivizule*, and two young men who by 1978 had left the village in search of employment.

The creation of a tradition-oriented VPU for Chele was the work of Mr.C., member of the Simuyemba clan, Member of Parliament and manager of an impressive farm on the edge of the grassland plains. When the VPU idea materialized in 1974, boundaries for the communal gardens had been fixed by the Assistant District Agricultural Officer (ADAO) stationed in Kawimbe. This had occurred on the basis of a 'one man / six acres' government recommendation. Women were excluded, and so were one half of the resident men. The former had no place in 'official' planning; the latter were excluded because of their alleged lack of interest. This situation strengthens the view that when 'VPCs were operating properly, they already had a bias in favour of the already established elites' (Bwalya 1984: 82). After 1974, expansion of the communal gardens went on unchecked. Four years later Simuyemba farmers had acquired substantial tracks of additional land. This explains why people in Chele referred to the communal gardens by the term *viyalo* VPC, and not by the term *viyalo* VPU.

I must now consider how the communal plots had been allocated. With the exception of the plots marked W, X, Y and Z (map 5), all communal land, or well over 65 per cent of all VPU gardens, was controlled by the six male members who constituted the Committee. The plots marked 'W' belonged to S.N., a powerful old man who (although not a VPC member) owned a relatively large herd of cattle and was a widely respected healer (*sinanga*). To include him among the group of people whose economic interests had expanded over the past few years is certainly justifiable. Two other non-VPC men also owned communal plots ('X' and 'Y'). These men were related to S.N. and had an interest in the old man's estate. The remaining non-VPC member, owner of plot 'Z', was the younger brother of a Committee member.

Land grabbing by 'progressive' farmers highlights the problem that land is now in short supply. The seriousness of this grabbing was brought home to me by the two brothers who farm in Namutumi. Their 'village' is now part of regrouped Chele and comes under the auspices of Chele's VPU. The brothers' father was a brother to S.N.; their mother a sister to Mr.C.'s mother. In 1978 I witnessed in Namutumi a real scramble for land, between its two resident households on the one hand, and the VPC on the other.

Map 5 shows how land allocations in Chele developed in the four years following the inception of the IDZ scheme. Developments were influenced by the expansion of the 'Sitanziye' state farm, situated to the west of Chele (map 4), which had an immediate effect on the activities of the progressive VPC. The story is as follows. After an abortive attempt to expand the state farm southwards, the state farm manager, himself a Mambwe, had been forced to look in a different direction. The initial plan for southward expansion had been successfully opposed by Chief Amos Kowa, who had taken the case to the Ministry of Lands and Agriculture in Lusaka, and by the local villagers who had persistently burnt down poles everytime a new boundary was staked out in the direction of Kowa. Local opposition to the expansion of the ranch had a long history (see Chapter 4). Admitting defeat, the state farm manager had encroached upon the vacant land, mainly dambos, that once belonged to the London Missionary Society. This new boundary was not opposed, but it precluded the northward expansion of VPC gardens.

Chele's VPC reacted to the expansion of the state farm by extending its *viyalo* VPC in the direction of Namutumi. The Namutumi households in turn reacted by claiming that the territory between the plains, the state farm frontier and the western boundary of the VPC gardens was theirs. The brothers argued that their father had been the sole cultivator on that land during the past three decades. The land could not therefore be rightfully taken by people from Chele. But Chele today is a regrouped Chele. So, the local court would not intervene to stop VPC people from grabbing Namutumi land. Only the brothers' own swift action could stop the VPC. One of the brothers then ploughed, and in some places even cultivated on, a long thin stretch of land

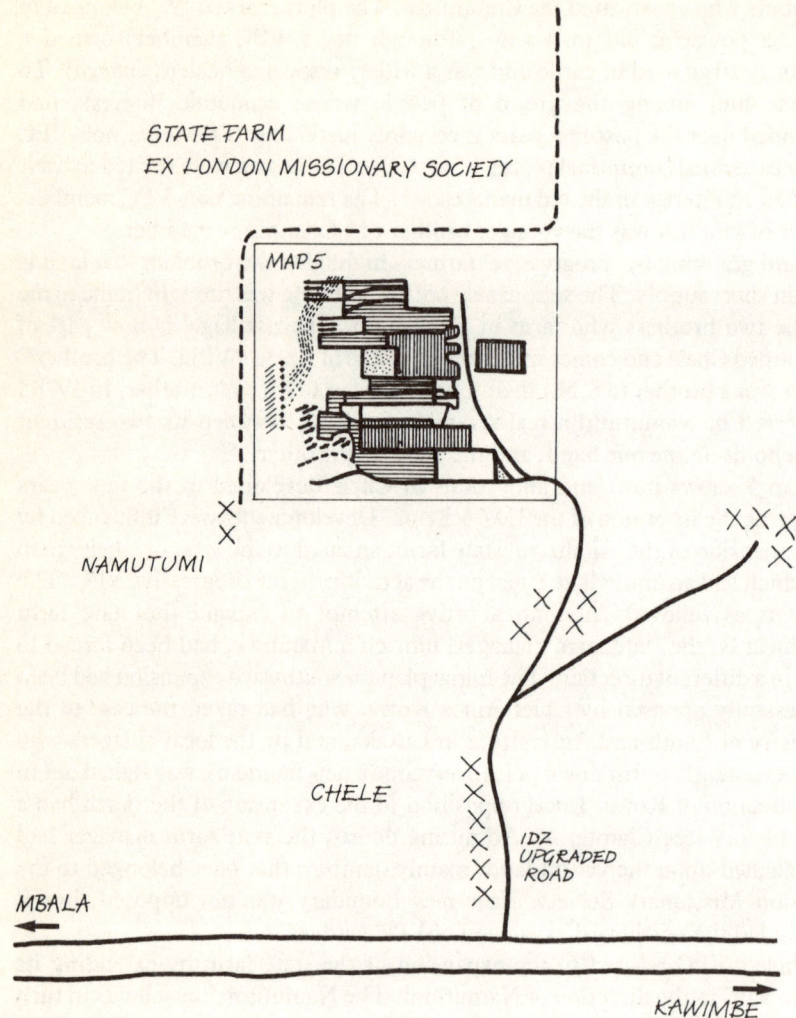

Map 4 Chele regrouped

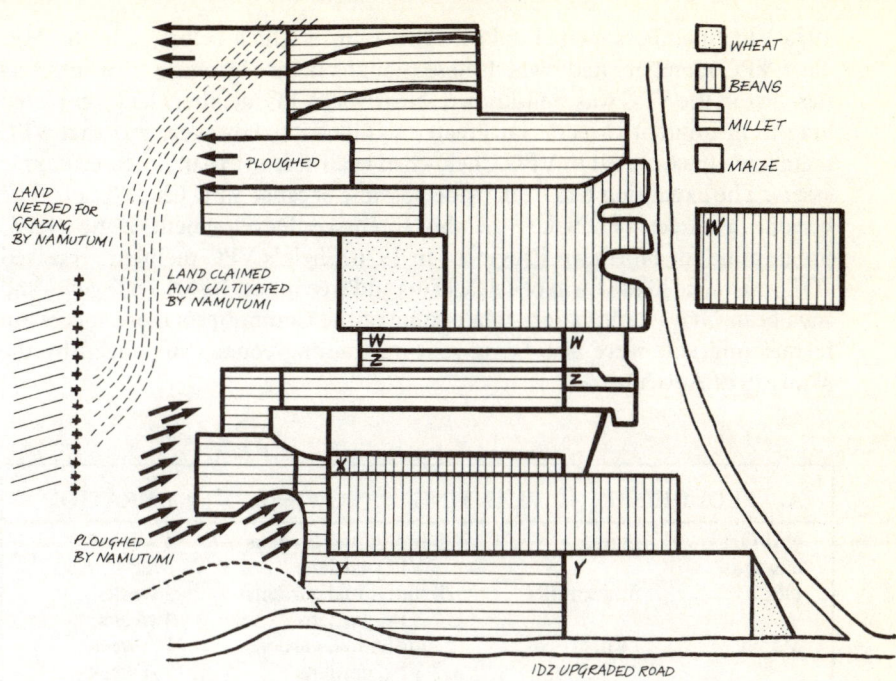

Map 5 Land acquisition in Chele: the VPC gardens

that bordered on VPC territory (map 5). The principle that one 'owns' the land one works is honoured by the local courts. The ploughing ensured that the VPC ended its expansion. Namutumi had won the battle, at least for the duration of one agricultural season.

Namutumi had good reasons for claiming the land. First, the household heads, who claim to live on good terms with their migrant brothers, believe (or say they believe) that the absent kin will return in the not too distant future. Secondly, and this was an urgent matter, Namutumi cattle, like all cattle in Chele, needed adequate grazing land. For year-round grazing, the cattle needed to have access to the plains and to the slopes that skirt Namutumi village. Access to the slopes was essential, since cattle move up to graze when the plains flood between January and March. The westward expansion of VPC land threatened the seasonal movement of Namutumi cattle; hence the quick action taken by the two household heads. The ploughed track, sparsely covered with bean plants, would yield a meagre crop. 'But that does not bother me', explained one of the brothers. 'I am not interested in those beans, of course not. I only wanted to stop the VPC from grabbing more of the family land.'[1]

VPC members emphasized that the ploughs they owned were acquired before IDZ made its mark. 'VPU brought together those with ploughs, so that their unity might serve the have-nots in Chele,' said the VPC secretary. By

1978 VPC members owned ten ploughs, four of which belonged to the MP. That VPC members had owned these ploughs before bringing their interests together in the VPC was well-known. Nearly all VPC members had completed long-term migrant careers. Of greater significance, however, was that VPC members - once united in VPU Chele - had been able to expand their economic assets. The expansion had been made possible because VPU Chele (read VPC) became a direct beneficiary of the Intensive Development Zone (IDZ) programme for Northern Province. In 1976 Chele's VPC members received IDZ assistance in the form of cattle loans and free inputs for wheat (*ngano*) and soya bean (*ntoyo*) cultivation, while some of the Committee's more successful former migrants were also being sent on training courses organized by the Ministry of Agriculture.

A. PLOUGHING	+ PLANTING	/ SOWING	DURATION
mid-Oct onwards	maize	28 individual gardens	4 weeks*
		6 VPC gardens	over 4 weeks
Dec	fingermillet	28 individual gardens	3 weeks
		7 VPC gardens	4 weeks
March	beans	28 individual gardens	1½ weeks
		7 VPC gardens	2½ weeks
Early March	wheat	6 individual gardens	ploughing not on collective basis
		1 VPC garden	ploughed collectively (3x)
*One week equals three working days.			
B. HARVESTING			
June-Sept	fingermillet	*Collective labour*/beer parties/women only	
July-Sept	maize	*Individual labour*/on a family basis	
May-June	beans	*Individual labour*/family basis + wage labour	
End June	wheat	*Individual labour*/family basis + wage labour	

Table 9: Division of labour on VPU land in Chele.

To grasp the full impact of IDZ assistance one needs to understand how agricultural labour was divided in Chele. Land, labour and cash are three major themes in any analysis of systems of food production and supply (Muntemba 1982: 31; Pottier 1985a). The table below presents in schematic form a full agricultural cycle, although it omits the weeding period. Weeding and any other tasks involving the hoe were not regulated by the VPC. This is an important point. My suspicion is that the pattern of weeding closely parallelled the situation described for Kowa (Chapter 4), with poorer villagers being contracted to weed in the gardens owned by 'progressive' farmers. What is certain is that weeding, which is women's work, had increased as a result of the expansion of fields, an expansion made possible through ploughing. I regret the absence of concrete data on weeding, but I observed at the time that paid weeding, a rare occasion for earning cash locally, meant that poorer households often delayed their own weeding, or weeded less thoroughly.

The table above indicates the uneven character of the reciprocity presumed under VPU/VPC regulations. For all major crops it is the *larger VPC fields*, owned by that small group of Committee members and their relatives, *which required the longer period of labour input*. One outstanding fact about the division of labour in Chele, then, is that during the busier weeks of the rainy season some 28 adults deploy their labour on gardens well over 60% of which are owned by a group of ten only.[2] This can be inferred from the 'duration' of activities, as indicated in table 9. Moreover, the ten also own 'individual'-type gardens, and ordinary VPU women, as Mary Namfukwe will make clear below, do not necessarily receive the plough-service. Such women work for food (*ukupula*) in the traditional sense of the word! This is the second major fact about the division of labour in Chele. I may therefore conclude that the 60% estimate is likely to be much larger in reality.

VPU labour was also mobilized during harvesting. In 1978 the latter part of the cycle was marked by the appearance of very large female work-parties. Important here is that harvesting in VPC gardens started *well before* harvesting in the individual gardens of VPU (non-VPC) households. The reward for such work-parties always consisted of a meal and *cipumu*. The time-table, drawn up by the VPC, suited the better-off, resulting in late harvests for the VPU majority. Late harvesting can be disastrous, especially when combined with poor weeding, and Chele could testify to the dangers. I visited several VPU (non-VPC) millet gardens that carried crops destroyed through overexposure to sunshine, or ravaged by birds. Late harvesting, however, was not the only cause of the problem. To add to the misery, the rainy season that year had ended some two weeks prematurely. This had caused so much moisture stress that maize and millet crops on less fertile land could not fully mature.

The combination of bad timing and a shortened rainy season affected, in particular, fields carrying hybrid maize. Hybrids are highly susceptible to improper timing. Late ploughing and planting had occurred in nearly all VPU (non-VPC) fields in 1977-78, and the poor yields were a disaster. Many peasant households ended up with surplus levels (if they were surplus...) that barely sufficed to pay back the credit received at the beginning of the planting season.

In Chele, VPC members had more land, disproportionate access to communal labour, and a much better chance of keeping correct timing. They also limited the mechanical services they were supposedly extending to the have-nots. As one progressive Siuluta who had broken with the VPU put it:

'When my wife brewed beer I invited the VPU/VPC collective to gather on my land and plough it. I was not a Committee member, so they refused. VPC members resented my ambition to achieve proper farming standards. Later, when applying for an AFC loan, the VPC chairman refused to sign the application form. The man, a Siuluta who took the title of headman after it had been held by my own father, argued that Chele was too small for large-scale farming' (details in Pottier 1985b).

NUTRITIONAL COST

When VPU producers spend three working days on predominantly VPC land, their own (individual) gardens suffer neglect because of bad timing. Confronted with the argument, VPC members countered that the have-nots did produce their own millet, a 'capacity' now lost in many other places. They also claimed that poorer households could resort to commercial brewing when intending to purchase supplementary foods.

The VPC counter-argument would be valid were it not that it ignores what poorer households *do* with their millet. Chele was indeed exceptional in its capacity to maintain (and increase) an adequate overall supply of millet, since Mambwe villages were rapidly losing that capacity (I.Schultz 1976: 113). But a further question must be asked. If Chele's big achievement was the maintenance of an adequate millet supply, did this then mean that poorer households still consumed millet in preference to cassava (*kalundwe*) or maize (*cisaka*)?

The answer is 'No'. Apart from occasional consumption at home, the lower-income group used millet for different purposes. First, VPU peasant producers had become caught up in the practice of hoarding. I indicated in Chapter 3 that chronic millet shortages in Mbala township encourage villagers to hoard millet and to sell only when prices in town rise sharply during the latter part of the wet season. Chele's peasant producers responded willingly to such a market. Millet, like beans, was sold rather than consumed. Secondly, millet not set aside for marketing was largely turned into commercial beer. The cash derived from hoarding and brewing was then spent on 'discretionary' items that had become 'necessary' – cloth, soap, sugar, paraffin, matches.[3] Whatever cash remained was spent on starchy root crops, like cassava and sweet potatoes (*visela*).

Was there a nutritional cost? It may be that the balance between protein and calorie intakes in the diet of poor people is better than is commonly thought, as Berg has suggested (Berg 1981). He argues that 'diets often provide enough protein when energy intakes are adequate' (*ibid*: 117; also Miracle 1973). For Chele, however, I would argue that the high cash value of millet and beans had adversely affected the level of protein intake. The two crops were still grown by the poor of this 'model' village, but had largely disappeared from their diet. The village achieved food security only when aggregate production figures were taken into acount. The practice for poorer households was to sell nutritionally superior staples and (after spending some of the cash thus earned) to buy back foodstuffs of a lower nutritional status. Conversion of quality food into nutritionally inferior staples has also been reported for other areas of Africa (e.g., for Malawi, Hirschmann and Vaughan 1983; for Rwanda, Pottier 1986a).

Infrastructural improvements do not necessarily translate into nutritional gain for all, a point also argued by Richards. Upon returning to Bemba country some twenty years after the Great Depression of the thirties, Richards noted how infrastructural conditions had greatly improved, and how 'the gap between town and country did not seem ... to be so great as in 1933' (Richards 1961: xiv). She concluded, however, that certain peasant households had lost the capacity to feed themselves:

A number of women without men to support them were living entirely on the sale of beer with which they purchased food, and drunkenness was more obvious in the villages. Food had begun to be bought and sold even in rural areas, though the practice was prominent only in suburban districts (Richards 1961: xiv).

Although beer brewing is lucrative only when cash and grain surpluses circulate in abundance (Muntemba 1982: 47), the practice of purchasing food with cash earned from brewing seems to have spread throughout Zambia (Hedlund and Lundahl 1984). What is more, the need to purchase food, whether by brewing or selling labour, affects an ever-widening social stratum. Compared with the fifties there are today in Mambwe country many more women who work for food (*ukupula*); and so do many of the poorer male household heads. Throughout Zambia villagers now rely on fewer crops and simplify their diets by sacrificing nutritional balance (Chambers and Singer 1981: 12).

The predicament of the poor raises questions about a possible resistance. Will peasant households react to the straightjacket they are in? Can they react? These questions must now be addressed.

CHALLENGING POVERTY

The effect on the nutritional status of poor families in Chele endorses Moore's argument about the transformation of work-party systems, when he wrote that the poor have few sanctions in cooperating with richer farmers (Moore 1975: 274). It is a similar conclusion which has prompted scholars like Muntemba, writing on women food producers in Zambia, to recommend that 'women must be conscientized to challenge the sexual division of labour which subjects their labour to men' (Muntemba 1982: 48). What then, I ask, stands in the way of this conscientization? What stops women and poor men from challenging the system imposed upon them?

Let me first recall two scenes from fieldwork. The first one is an interview with Mary Namfukwe, an elderly woman. When she took part in a *kusinza* work-party in the communal gardens - on a plot owned by the committee's secretary - Mama Namfukwe once commented: 'It is true that when I brew beer at the onset of the rains you will only find people with hoes on my land. No-one with a plough would turn up. But when those with ploughs organize a party I simply must go - because if you do not work for others, others will not work for you.' 'Others,' Namfukwe added, 'means other women, not men with ploughs.' Thus, when Namfukwe joined the secretary's work-party, she did so *not* because she expected the secretary to reciprocate, but in order to meet the other women, the real Unit, the women who do reciprocate her labour, because 'Namfukwe is always there when work needs doing.' Namfukwe's testimony, which shows how influential men ignore the labour input of poor women, is in sharp contrast to Watson's assertion that attendance at work-parties invariably obliges reciprocity (Watson 1958: 107-108; quoted above).

Work-sharing among women, and the solidarity this creates, of course antedates VPU organization. I therefore suspect that the women's long history of jointly working the land must have been an active element in the consolidation of VPC interests. Women's solidarity, however, was also actively nurtured by a local Christian church organization, run by the VPC secretary and S.N. the influential healer. Church leader S.N. used to be a land shrine priest (*simapepo*), but became a Christian convert sometime before independence. We know from *Tribal Cohesion* that land shrine priests officiated mainly in times of disaster, for example, when drought or locust invasions struck (Watson 1958: 163). Through setting himself up as church leader in his native Chele, S.N. continued to guard over the fertility of its people and their land. After observing the situation in Chele, I hold the intertwining of ties of kinship, marriage and religion responsible for the absence of any spontaneous challenge to its specific brand of humanistic, collectivized agriculture. Challenges will only emerge in the wake of a programme for raising political consciousness.

Committed to a style of fieldwork which honours the idea that interaction with informants must lead to a two-directional flow of information, I sometimes set out to openly discuss my views on the experiment. I believed the system to be an overtaxing of poor people's labour power – but how did they see it? As the harvest period unfolded, I grew more and more eager to hear a VPU or a women's viewpoint.

To me there never seemed to exist a just return for the labour-time the poor expended in the so-called 'communal' gardens. Despite adequate food production for the village as a whole, the distribution of nutrients was far from equitable. Whenever I expressed this opinion on the burden and cost of Humanism Chele-style (and here I pride myself upon Mambwe culture for the importance it attaches to 'speaking one's mind'), I never convinced anyone. My views on what I considered to be justice, Humanistic justice, or on the exploitation of domestic labour, were not taken seriously. At least, this is how it felt. Ignored as they seemed to be, my views were solicited often enough, but I always had to be prepared to have them turned into fodder for a good laugh. Especially around the beer-pot, when drinking in mixed company, male/female or VPU/VPC.

It was not until fieldwork in Chele had entered an advanced stage that I obtained insight into how the burden of labour was locally perceived. I remember the day, the field, and even the time. The discussion came after I had spent several hilarious hours trying to improve my skills at cutting millet. While joking about my damaged fingers, a woman in the work-party pointed out that I would probably remember my ordeal as 'the day I had worked for the women of Chele'. It was good fun. It was also the beginning of a more serious conversation, perhaps the only uninhibited conversation I ever had on the subject of agriculture in Chele. It was then that I realized that personal opinion or prejudice, if handled tactfully, can indeed function as the stepping stone towards a new perception (Gadamer 1976: 216; Cesara 1982: 80). That day the women of the party told me that they did not object to the demands of the Village Productivity Committee (read: the system), because participation allowed them to meet frequently, and without the men.

Context is important here. I learned that work-party cooperation, especially at harvest time, provided women with a regular forum for the exchange of precious information about petty trading opportunities and strategies. Since grassland women derived a large part of their cash incomes from petty trading (Chapters 3 and 7), which sometimes involved perishable foodstuffs, they had a need for opportunities through which information could spread quickly. Work-parties provided just that. Furthermore, the harvesting work-parties, from which men are excluded, were valued since they enabled women to discuss the cash benefits that accrued to petty trading. Such information was not to be disclosed to men. Having lost their prerogative over maize trading from *ivizule*, women guarded all knowledge about their earnings. Cash had become a vital element in the constant negotiation of gender relationships (see Chapter 7; also Pottier 1985a).

One other reason why the women of Chele were unable to challenge the burden they carried may relate to the consequences they faced in the case of divorce. Watson was very clear on this issue. He wrote:

A deserted wife loses her rights to use her husband's fields. When a wage-earner fails to return after an absence of three to five years, and has not sent his wife any clothes or goods, or otherwise communicated with the village, he is assumed to have deserted her. Her rights in his fields then lapse, and she must seek support in a village where she has male kin (1958: 100).

That the consequences of divorce may act as a deterrent against challenging the *status quo* has been suggested by Wright. After researching on why women in Mazabuka refrain from challenging 'male management', Wright wrote about the wives of maize-growers:

On the Magoye settlements, women in 1980 declared that they were not exploited and were they to be, they would divorce their husbands. An appraisal of consciousness among wives must consider the larger environment shaping expectations of women in various sectors of the society. The option of divorce still has all the difficulties pointed out in the 1950s for wives of accumulating peasants, entailing as it does an abandonment of all property associated with the marriage (Wright 1983: 83).

There can be little doubt that similar pressures acted upon women food producers in Mambwe country.

There are also some other practical considerations to be made. First, beer is food, and poorer individuals can economize on their own food reserves, through joining work-parties (see also Hedlund and Lundahl 1984: 64). Reserves are usually running low during the weeding season. Secondly, although continuous maize cultivation may be bad for the soil, nutritionally a poor substitute for millet, and underpaid, its introduction has nevertheless solved a labour problem (see Chapter 2), and remains one of the very few local sources of cash. In spite of the drawbacks related to its introduction, hybrid maize is not a crop that can be easily removed from the area (details in Pottier 1986b).

Increased work-party participation in Chele belied the contractual nature of the arrangements. While the local leaders who masterminded the labour/ service exchanges presented the increased participation in terms of their sustained effort to uphold Mambwe egalitarianism, the evidence gathered indicates that intervention had widened the gap between rich(er) and poor(er) households. This is where Chele differed from Kowa. In Kowa too I noted how social differentiation was clearly visible, in the form of a division between wage-earners and the non-waged, but there was in Kowa no *rigorous* timetable, no evidence of a systematic your-labour-for-a-meal policy. Most of the poorer families in Kowa still grew traditional maize, which is hardier and less vulnerable to timing. Moreover, when rewarded in kind, labourers in Kowa took their produce home.

The Chele version of Humanist development pays lip-service to a 'traditional' ethos that never was. The work-parties described in *Tribal Cohesion* were of an ideal type from which certain groups were excluded. Building upon an idealized notion of the past, Humanist agriculture in Chele perpetuates and amplifies social prejudices and inequalities that characteristically escape the eye of the casual observer. (Or the eye of their President when he conceived the idea of the VPC – see Quick (1979: 99).) The analysis of relations on the land in Chele shows that the more powerful food producers have maintained, indeed stepped up, their interest in growing fingermillet, the traditional staple. The reason for this renewed interest lies with the cash value that millet acquires in times of scarcity and with the VPC need for regular access to 'cheap' labour. The plough-owners have worked out a system which enables them to overcome the problem of labour bottlenecks. In spite of the fact that the labour-power of poorer households is heavily taxed, their co-operation is ensured because of the intermeshing of economic, kinship and moral considerations. Women play a major role in this process. The ties of solidarity they have forged, through centuries of work-sharing, is fed by the moral universe of kinship and religious organization, by the need for close cooperation in trading, and (I speculate) by the rules of divorce. All these factors preclude a challenge to the system.

As a rare case of meticulously implemented policy, the Chele experiment is a perfect example of the 'custom strengthened / custom threatened' syndrome discussed by Parkin in his work on the Giriama (Parkin 1972). The shift from (presumed) reciprocal to non-reciprocal arrangements has been sealed by a shift in the meaning of *cipumu*, the millet beer customarily consumed at the end of a work-party session. The meaning of *cipumu* has shifted from being a symbol of guaranteed reciprocity (Watson 1958: 106) to being a means of straightforward payment – a transition facilitated by the fact that ploughing-as-reciprocity cannot so easily be 'measured'.

The predominance of non-reciprocal arrangements suggests that the current nationwide promotion of millet (Wood 1985) is unlikely to benefit the at-risk group in places like Chele. It is the already better-off who are more likely to have any millet surpluses for sale. This point is also borne out in the data on Kaka, which I now present. Some of the poorer households may still decide to sell, but they are likely to do so at the cost of a switch towards starchy staples. In Chele-type versions of agriculture it is unrealistic to expect that poorer households will be able to take advantage of the new market for 'traditional' staples.

CAMP KAKA

The division of labour in Kaka, by gender and by economic status, resembles the outline I have drawn for Chele. Women strove to preserve the autonomy enjoyed under conditions of circulatory migration; while its demise here too was accompanied by an institutionalized dependency affecting poorer households. The women's prerogative of controlling the sale of *ivizule* surpluses had slipped away, in the same manner that the opportunity structure favoured by IDZ isolated households lacking close links with the programme's initial beneficiaries. This issue will be clarified shortly. There was some overlap between the groups disadvantaged by sex and by economic status, but the groups were not identical.

Who then were the intitial beneficiaries? The number of registered farmers for the whole of Camp Kaka was seventy. Some fourteen lived in Kaka and in the adjacent village headed by David Chikoti. David's village forms a link between Kaka and the village of Ali Chikoti, which is described in Chapter 8. From my survey in Kaka I learnt that there were approximately three non-registered households for every farming unit registered with the IDZ. These non-registered households constituted a convenient labour pool for meeting periodic peaks in the demand for labour on registered farms.

When I first contacted the Agricultural Demonstrator in Kaka, I was given the names of fifteen 'pioneers'. After interviews with thirteen of them I realized that farmers at the centre of Camp Kaka fell into three categories. Registered farmers were male household heads who were either: (a) close kin of the chairman of the Ward Development Committee;[4] or (b) members of Watch Tower; or (c) returning migrants who had completed successful careers: 'townmen' in Bond's terms (Bond 1976). Most farmers registered with IDZ combined two of the attributes, typically a+b or b+c.

All registered farmers grew maize surpluses on plots ranging from 0.4 to 6.0 hectares (see table 10a). But half the surplus producers grew less than 1.0 hectare for commercial ends. In 1978 twenty-four farmers in the camp also grew wheat on a trial basis. They cultivated plots of 0.4 ha and received the necessary inputs free of charge. Kaka Primary School had joined the wheat scheme, and experimented on a 1.4 ha field. Registered farmers also grew beans, most of them on plots of at least one hectare. Fingermillet too was popular as a cash crop. The total hectarage for millet production in Kaka and in David Chikoti equalled that of beans.

The prospect for growing wheat looked bleak at the end of the first experimental year, with only 11 of the 24 farmers declaring they were prepared to carry on. Even the school decided to give up. One common complaint about the wheat project was that threshing, which is done manually, was too hard. Wheat grains are not so easily separated when the traditional technique is applied. Work-parties *were* organized for threshing wheat, but they were not based on reciprocity. Wheat growers also encountered problems with selling their crop. I found that at least eighteen 50kg bags, or the output of approximately eight farms, had still not been collected by NCU when the rains started in late October. Late collection meant the produce had to be stored, which increased the risk of post-harvest losses and delayed payment even further. Small wonder then that about half of the farmers lost heart after the very first attempt. Those who decided to continue, the Kaka Agricultural Assistant said, would be joined by some twenty-five new farmers. These farmers lived farther away from the centre of Kaka. Presumably, they still had to learn the full facts about growing wheat. Overall enthusiasm was dampened, however, when it was rumoured, with reason, that the fertilizer requirements for 1978-79 would never reach Kaka in time.[5]

Despite inadequate supplies, poor assistance and a strain on the potential alliance with IDZ/NCU personnel, Kaka farmers knew that their immediate future was still secure. The political and administrative backing they enjoyed *within* the village, through patronage, ensured that the original project settlers would continue to be 'first choices' of the WDC, whenever resourceful villagers were recruited for new trials. Although experiments may fail to satisfy, the fourteen households that had settled near the centre of Kaka knew they would continue to be 'innovators' for quite some time to come. At the time of my stay in Kaka, ten trial fields for sunflower, a novelty in the area, were planned for 1979. The restricted number implied that only resettled people qualified, and that political patronage and achieved social status by far outweighed the importance of merit. The strategy of favouring initial settlers, for which IDZ reserved the dubious label "Intensive Extension Approach", also applied to the sheep scheme. Only farmers who had benefitted from earlier assistance and free hand-outs had been allowed to subscribe to it.

One further characteristic of the farmers as a group was that many earned additional incomes from off-farm activities. The secretary of the Kaka VPC, for instance, ran a *Chibuku* bar; one other farmer was a builder-driver employed at the clinic; while a third worked as a tailor. The scheme's most successful farmer owned a Land Rover – not a negligible source of income when public and official transport services break down, as they tend to do in every rainy season. He was a member of Watch Tower and had begun business as a shopkeeper looking after his father's property. The father had been a long-term miner in Luanshya.

Emergent farmers made use of the credit facilities offered by AFC, but allocations were not very large. Farmers did not usually secure loans other than those of the short-term, 'seasonal' type. Restrictions imposed at ministerial level were locally blamed for the non-availability of medium-term credit. The restriction reflected Line-of-Rail bias and a lack of national commitment to infrastructural development for outlying regions. There was (and still is) an urgent need, for instance, for spreading the production of farming implements and building materials. Only when prospects for regional investment are created, in the light industries especially, can projects like Kaka become viable.[6]

I shall now consider how the project has influenced the division of labour. In contrast to Chele, Kaka did not pay lip-service to the ideal of the 'traditional' work-party. Large work-parties did occur, and they too mobilized the poorer, non-registered households, but no attempt was ever made to disguise the fact that such arrangements were based on pay, not on reciprocity. The farmers' reliance upon wage labour is documented, in table 10b, for the year 1977-78.[7] The reliance, substantial by local standards, implied a certain entrenchment. I was not, however, in a position to forecast the rate at which contractual ties could be expected to increase. What the interviews with peasant cultivators did bring out was that 'having a patron' was vital for securing an all-year-round flow of cash. Typically, a man would tell me:

We clothe ourselves with beans. It is no good to show your stomach. But when the children start a new year at school, I need to find more cash. Money, always money. Money for shoes, money for uniforms, money for party membership. I then go to Mr. S. [a well-known Kaka farmer] who advances me what I need. When the rains come in October, I go and make ridges for him.

Not everyone in Kaka was prepared to accept as virtuous or inevitable the predicament that cash must be earned through selling labour. The women of

REGISTERED FARMERS: KAKA VILLAGE	MAIZE	WHEAT	BEANS	FINGER-MILLET	GROUND-NUTS
01	57 bgs (1 ha)	-	16 bgs (5 ha)	? (2 ha)	4.5 ts (0.5 ha)
02	360 bgs (6 ha)	8 bgs (0.3 ha)	11 bgs (4 ha)	25 bgs (3 ha)	8 bgs (2.5 ha)
03	1 int. + 60 bgs (2 ha)	7 bgs (0.4 ha)	4 bgs (1.2 ha)	15 bgs (1 ha)	? (0.2 ha)
04	56 bgs (1 ha)	-	1bg+3ts (0.4 ha)	8 bgs (0.6 ha)	-
05	30 bgs (0.4 ha)	-	10 ts (1.2 ha)	? (1.8 ha)	? (0.2 ha)
06	35 bgs (0.6 ha)	-	5bgs +3ts (2 ha)	30 bgs (3 ha)	-
07	33 bgs (0.6 ha)	-	7 ts (0.8 ha)	35 bgs (3 ha)	-
DAVID CHIKOTI					
08	2 int. + 39 bgs (2.5 ha)	-	11 bgs	1 int. (5 ha)	-
09	140 bgs (2.5 ha)	-	3 bgs (0.8 ha)	-	-
10	226 bgs (4 ha)	? (0.4 ha)	7bgs +2ts (2 ha)	9 bgs (0.2 ha)	-
11	118 bgs (2 ha)	5 bgs+1t (0.4 ha)	8 bgs (2 ha)	25 bgs (1.6 ha)	1 t (shelled) (0.2 ha)

Table 10(a): Harvests in Kaka Camp (1978)/Production

Note: bg(s) = bag(s); 1 int. = 1 *intanta* (granary) or 55-60 bgs approx; t = tin (1 bg = 6 ts).

See also footnote 7.

REGISTERED FARMERS: KAKA VILLAGE	HOUSEHOLD COMPOSITION	PLOUGHING & PLANTING	WEEDING	HARVESTING	THRESHING	SHELLING
01	2w + 11ch	-	18 ♀-d (salt or 50ng/d)	24 ♀-d	-	-
02	1w + ?ch	information not available				
03	1w + 9ch	-	18 ♀-d (50ng/d)	22 ♀-d (50ng/d)	-	-
04	1w + 1ch 1 div. da + 1ch	28 ♀-d	?	40 ♀-d	w-p	-
05	1w + 8ch	hired plough (2 days)	4 ♀-d	-	w-p	-
06	2w + 2ch 1 div.da + 1ch	-	-	-	-	-
07	2w + 8ch	-	9 ♀-d (50ng/d)	24 ♀-d	w-p	4 ♀-d

DAVID CHIKOTI

08	2w + 13ch	60 ♀-d (1t millet for 5 days work)	60 ♀-d	?	? (salt)	? (salt)
09	1w + 4ch 1Mo + 4ch 1S + 3ch	hired plough (K4/acre)	-	-	-	-
10	2w + 6ch	hired plough occasionally	45 ♀-d (50ng/d)	50 ♀-d (50ng/d)	w-p	-
11	1w + 5ch	17 ♀-d (salt) 2 w-p (ploughs only)	24 ♀-d (salt)	35 ♀-d	?	?

Table 10(b): Hired Labour and rewards in Kaka Camp (1978)

Note: w = wife; ch = child; Mo = mother; S = sister; div. = divorced; ♀-d = women-days; da = daughter of household head;
w-p = work-party; ng/d = ngwee per day's work; K4 = 4 Kwacha.
See also footnote 7.

the literacy class, for instance, were bitterly disappointed when their Women's Club failed to obtain seeds for its vegetable project. The women, who came from registered and peasant households, were unanimous that no amount of cash earned in other people's fields could compensate for the collapse of their scheme. Vegetable growing is important to women in rural Zambia, since it is a crop they can control (Muntemba 1982: 47). Unfortunately, it is also a wet season activity, which demands much attention at a time when women are already burdened with tending the staple crops.

Members of peasant households agreed that selling their labour on local farms was the major and often only means by which they could obtain cash outside the bean season. Commercial brewing too was one way of earning cash, but only farmers' wives had continuous access to surpluses of millet and maize. Women from non-registered households knew that labour for wages delayed work on the family plots and that such delays could result in neglect. But they usually remarked: 'What else can we do?' There was really no answer.

When asked in grassland villages outside Camp Kaka, that same question usually solicited a more positive reply: 'There is the market' - a suggestion that speculative petty trading was a commonly adopted strategy for raising cash and, ultimately, for ensuring survival. Kaka, however, remained outside the regional network for active petty trading. Its poorer households therefore tended to borrow small amounts of cash from their patron employers, to spend at the 'marketing shed'. Whether intended or not, the shed had the effect of keeping the labour force within the Camp. Peasant household members did not need to leave Kaka in order to satisfy their needs for cash and for basic goods. Nor were they expected to. The situation was akin to that reported by Tallantire for some of Uganda's cotton-producing districts, where

The increased pace of life no longer [allowed] women to spend ... periods away from the home for the collection of leaves and fruits over considerable distances (Tallantire 1975: 244; quoted in Porter 1979: 72).

With regard to Kaka, I substitute 'Tanzanian produce and regional foodstuffs' for 'leaves and fruits'.

Local politicians, project personnel and emergent farmers occasionally experienced strains on their relationships (Chapter 5), yet they were united in advocating a national profile for their project. They wanted a Kaka independent of other Mambwe villages, a Kaka which enabled the returning migrant to extend the urban way of life. Kaka accepted a high price for its achievements and ambitions. It accepted high-level external dependency upon a most erratic national supply system and tolerated a high incidence of internal dependency.

Kaka had become a self-contained unit which restricted the mobility of its agricultural labour force. I suggest that several variables were responsible for this development. First, the credit arrangements in Kaka controlled the peasants' labour. The arrangements heightened the dependency of peasant households and prevented the value of labour from rising too fast.[8] Secondly, there was an overall increase in the pressure on labour-time, because of acreage expansions and the introduction of hybrid maize. The increase in labour-time expenditure affected both rich(er) and poor(er) sections of the project community. In this respect, the workload of women from registered and peasant households alike was close to reaching very high levels indeed. The intensification of agriculture not only imposed physical hardship and production risks (related to inputs, timing,...), it also supplanted women in trading activities.[9] Production in Kaka did not need to be 'topped up' with produce from villages around the settlement. Instead, the scheme favoured direct trade with Zambia's industrialized Line of Rail.

In the final analysis it was the combination of the credit factor with the demands made on productive labour-time which restricted the mobility of Kaka's poorer producer-sellers. After a long tradition of Mambwe involvement in labour migration, peasant households found it acceptable, and indeed necessary, to enter into informal-but-binding contracts with registered patron farmers. Peasant cultivators thought of such contracts increasingly as the one realistic means by which their cash demands could be met.

TRENDS AND MICRO-LEVEL VARIATIONS

It is important to emphasize the interplay of sex and poverty in the economic disparities I have described. The data presented in this chapter point to the need for a perspective which links the variables of sex and poverty. They reinforce what Staudt has argued in her work on women's participation in rural development, namely, that 'we can no more deal with poverty while ignoring sex disparities than we can deal with sex disparities while ignoring poverty' (Staudt 1979: 2). Poverty goes beyond gender, and the practice of working for food (*ukupula*) and/or for a landclearing service is spreading to households that command only limited resources – land, labour, and cash.

Better-off farmers, whether they lived in Chele, Kaka or Kowa, occasionally rewarded their workers in kind, paying with salt for example, which was highly valued by the labourers. But this is where the similarities ended. Chele farmers preferred to reward labour with a good meal and with *cipumu*; in Kaka they paid cash; in Kowa they paid cash or gave produce. These differences reflected the degrees to which labour sales had become institutionalized. In Kowa 'paid' labour was usually recruited from within the immediate neighbourhood; in Kaka groups of families attached themselves to a specific farming household, through borrowing; in Chele one half of the village was tied to the other half.

The institutionalization of labour arrangements - strongest in Chele, weakest in Kowa - has implications for the timing of agricultural activities: the more advanced the institutionalization, like in Chele, the more precarious the position of the client/peasant families. Precariousness, moreover, augments with the introduction of hybrids. In Kowa, unwaged households grew traditional maize (unlike the poor in Chele who benefitted from 'development'). They were better able to cope with delays in their own fields. Still, taken together, the three cases illustrate that 'increasingly, the independent decision-making of the peasant farmer has been undermined' (Long 1984: 2). Existing nuances result primarily from the interplay between highly specific local-level factors and views on development ('traditional' Kowa; 'humanistic' Chele; 'project' Kaka) and the forces of external determination, especially the growing need for cash. This illustrates, as Long has himself repeatedly argued, that it is 'theoretically unsatisfactory to base one's analysis on the notion of external determination alone' (*ibid:2*). Such a perspective, for which *Tribal Cohesion* had been an intellectual landmark, in that it highlighted the importance of local variables, remains very useful.

It is sometimes said that food production in rural Zambia has become individualized. The claim is mostly correct. But commercial farmers may also, as in the Chele experience, embark upon *a process of retraditionalization*. Individuation and retraditionalization are not incompatible concepts. The agrarian scene can be just as ambiguous as the realm of local-level politics. In the previous chapter I showed how ward leaders ('modern' and 'traditional') oscillated between two authoritative structures, sometimes using one set of ideas to validate the other. Likewise, emergent farmers did not necessarily live by the money economy alone, but used, through rediscovery and remoulding, values and life-styles that at one stage seemed on the brink of oblivion. I sometimes wonder whether Chele agriculture might not be an extension or even a rediscovery of Watson's observation that 'the chief had rights over the labour of his people, who had to cultivate his fields and those of his wives, each man working for two days a year' (Watson 1958: 159). Chele's Member of Parliament had adopted something of the lifestyle of a chief.

The food-for-work strategy, already in existence in the fifties, had expanded to include more people and different modes of reward. Depending on the availability of scarce commodities and on the stage reached in the agricultural cycle, labour was rewarded with cash, food and drink, or payment in kind. Cash needs had become acute, everywhere, but Chele farmers kept their cash payments down. Interestingly, Chele was not just re-instituting the 1950s food-for-work strategy, its village leaders had also re-introduced the landclearing service as a reward for labour. There are no references in *Tribal Cohesion* to landclearing-for-work practices, but the strategy existed in other parts of Africa (Henn 1984: 15). Kaka, on the other hand, was mainly cash-oriented, while more flexible labour arrangements for paid work prevailed in Kowa. Where true reciprocal arrangements had survived, like in Kowa, they already involved smaller numbers (no longer the entire village) and were made between equals. Plough-owners joined other plough-owners; hoe-owners did likewise.

Emergent farmers in Chele viewed the work-party system as economically more advantageous than payment in cash. Calculations made in this respect, for corn-growing villages in Chipata District, have revealed that cash payments are indeed more costly than when food and beer is provided (Hedlund and Lundahl 1983: 71). Commercially inclined farmers in Chele had 'discovered' how *cipumu* could also be used as cash, i.e. as payment which did not require reciprocity. To borrow an idiom from Barth, they had broken through between spheres (Barth 1967). In the process of breaking through, they rediscovered the value of millet, the value of communal labour, the importance of women's solidarity. The looks of 'traditional' work-sharing are no guarantee for justice – a conclusion development planners must bear in mind (Pottier 1985a: 41-42).

Throughout the discussion there has been ample evidence of social differentiation, of differential control over land, labour, implements and inputs. The question now is whether the uneven distribution of resources and benefits was becoming entrenched, more stratified. My inclination here is to point out that the commercial sector had remained embryonic in the twenty-five years between Watson's fieldwork and my own – too embryonic and too unsteady to foster entrenched interests or stratification. However, there is a further point to be made. I have also shown how land scarcity had already resulted in the occasional scramble for land, and how prominent locals were trying to lay their hands on choice plots. Landlessness itself was as yet unknown and female-headed households still had access to some land (mainly through male relatives), but the situation was certainly ripe for the emergence of the first incidences of landlessness. When this occurs the tendency to acquire food through *ukupula* is likely to reach the point where it will take a much greater effort to break the cycle of poverty.

CHAPTER SEVEN

KINSHIP AND THE BORDER ECONOMY

The trade avenues that are typical of the Mambwe economy are small-scale, diversified, influenced by seasonal availability, and the privilege of no-one in particular. The scope of this trading, which is mainly in foodstuffs, is intimately bound up with changes in the pattern of circulatory migration for men and with changes in the exploitation of the land resource (Chapters 2 and 3). My interpretation of this trade, which I now present, is based on first-hand observation in the regrouped village of Chivunzila, an administrative unit made up of sections that enjoyed autonomy in the 1950s. Dominant sections in the make-up of this village derive from the older villages of Kosam and Simukulwa, both of which were described in *Tribal Cohesion*.

When working in Chivunzila I became impressed with the importance attached to riverside (*mianda*) cultivation. It is in riverside gardens that the villagers of Chivunzila grow vegetables, such as tomatoes, rape and cabbage (mostly male crops), in addition to beans and maize (crops often, but not necessarily, controlled by women). The interest in riverside gardening is in contrast to the fifties, when *mianda* gardens were rare. Watson wrote about *mianda*:

The grassland Mambwe sometimes cultivate riverside gardens (*mianda*) on the sides of dambos, near the perennial streams. There are few suitable sites for these, and they [do] not appear to be a significant element in the Mambwe economy (1958: 29).

In a footnote he added, 'I saw only two of these gardens among the grassland Mambwe' (*ibid*: 29).

The very intensive exploitation of riverside gardens today may be explained from a variety of angles, but all point to the fact that *mianda* gardening, and bean cropping in general, has become an important strategy for raising cash. Put simply, men need to exploit *mianda* to make up for the loss of income due to the decline of migrant opportunities; women need to exploit *mianda* to make up for the loss of income due to declining soil fertility in the kitchen gardens (*ivizule*) on which they used to produce their cash crop. By the late 1970s the demise of 'classical' migration and the ensuing 'return to the land' had led to new approaches to cultivation, a heightened significance of petty trading, and some remarkable structural changes in the composition of villages.

In this chapter I shall continue the focus on the changing structure of the Mambwe village and will consider the trade in foodstuffs, with its implications for gender. The chapter falls into two parts. First I shall discuss developments in relation to labour migration and residence for men, paying attention to the position of young men. Next I shall develop the notion of a border economy. This will involve discussion of women's secondary marriages, their residential preferences, and their involvement in the cash economy.

OF MALE LABOUR MIGRATION, CASH CROPS, RESIDENCE AND TRADE

Chivunzila comprises both Kosam and Simukulwa 'village' and lies on the main road to Mwamba, less than half a mile from Kasunga. In addition to Kosam and Simukulwa village, Chivunzila includes Mbunga, a small settlement not discussed in *Tribal Cohesion*. Simukulwa 'village' 1978 was very different in outlook from Simukulwa as it existed in 1952, since the important Simpemba section had moved away from the site. The Simpemba lineage, however, was part of the amalgamated village, even though the partnership with Simukulwa had lapsed. The core of Simukulwa 'village' 1978 consisted of Donald Simukulwa (George's son) with one of his own married sons, together with Odilon Sikambula (pseudonym) and one married Sikambula son. The Simukulwa-Sikambula partnership was an influential force in the amalgamated village and beyond, as will be seen in the case study at the end of the chapter. Unlike his father, Donald Simukulwa did not exert domestic authority over a fully-fledged agnatic group, but he had influence over the economic life of the village. His 'official' role was that of an administrator, for Donald was steering the village through its first experience with the cash crop economy and the development institutions (see Chapter 5).

At the time of fieldwork this experience was turning traumatic, as hybrid maize cropping proved an alternative inferior to the migrant option. In this respect, the ILO commission who reported on the Zambian rural economy in 1977 argued that the cash constraint had existed in rural Zambia ever since its 'first sorties into cash agriculture' (ILO 1977: 77). According to ILO figures, deterioration in the rural-urban terms of trade was of the order of 20 per cent for the period 1964-74 (*ibid*: 77). With the national economic downturn of the mid-1970s the situation in rural Zambia deteriorated quickly. By 1979 a rural producer had to market three times as much produce as in 1965 in order to buy the same urban goods (Chambers and Singer 1981:9). These adverse terms of trade did not quench the need for cash, but rather accentuated its compelling nature and pervasiveness.

The worsening terms of trade for hybrid maize set the position of the Simukulwa administrator into perspective. From the official point of view, Donald Simukulwa fulfilled the triple role of Village Productivity Committee (VPC) secretary, Ward Committee (WC) member and NCU depot *kapitao*. He had an authoritative say in the allocation of seeds and fertilizers within the ward, and his functions conferred considerable status. But now the times were changing. Not only did Zambia's agricultural extension services pay badly, they also failed to deliver inputs on time, and never paid promptly for the commercial maize that peasants grew. Criticism of NCU mounted throughout 1978. The overall dissatisfaction with 'official' development efforts, however, affected Donald only slightly, for he also held un-official functions. Donald's role was important in coordinating opportunities for informal trade, which were based on regional exchanges.

Simukulwa was indeed only occasionally approached in his official capacity of institutional broker. The reason, quite simply, was that few villagers in Chivunzila bothered to contact town-based institutions for satisfying their agricultural needs. They still produced hybrid maize for the Cooperative Union, sometimes up to twenty-five or thirty 90kg-bags per household, but maize was no longer the main source of income. When fertilizer for maize was available from the NCU depot, interested villagers would come forward to buy with cash, but only very rarely would they approach Simukulwa with requests for credit on the terms proposed by the Agriculture Finance Corporation. The dwindling interest in formal agrarian institutions and development committees related to the villagers' disillusionment with what these superimposed bodies had had to offer thus far (Chapter 5). Their one-time enthusiastic response to the government call for nationwide food security had been stifled by late collections and very late payments. As a result, many villagers were already investing in beans rather than maize. Indifference to NCU and WDC surfaced during my fieldwork, when a formal NCU request for the building of a storage shed in Chivunzila was turned down. The villagers insisted that NCU had no right to mobilize free labour for the purpose of building the shed.

The basis of Simukulwa's prominence needs to be sought not in his connections with the Department of Agriculture or with the extension services, although these may have been significant before the collapse of Zambia's Co-operative Movement in 1972, but in family history. Building upon the reputation and business assets of his father, Donald Simukulwa had become important for his role as middleman in the bean trade. Donald followed in the footsteps of his father in the sense that he too belonged to that 'class of men who obtain wealth and influence through money' (1958: 82), but his economic assets were much less impressive than were those of his father. His 'grocery' contained only a small range of essentials: blankets, soap, paraffin, matches, and school necessities. These could be bought with cash or alternatively with beans.

Although he still enjoyed relative influence and some material wealth, Simukulwa had not found the opportunity to further the economic interests of the estate he had inherited. In the same way that Chivunzila's younger people were denied the chance to work as migrants or entrepreneurs, so Simukulwa was only allowed to be a village-level middleman. His own standard of living was just minimally above that of other villagers. Watson's observation that successful trader-farmers face severe competition in a limited market (1958: 209) remained valid. Trader-farmers encountered difficulties when trying to expand their businesses, since there was a great shortage of 'indigenous capital' (Baylies 1980: 193). However, it would be erroneous to assume that Donald remained unresponsive to existing opportunities, for his economic interests had benefitted from the already mentioned partnership with Sikambula, a man influential within the local Watch Tower community. Later on I shall discuss the nature and scope of this partnership in relation to the border economy.

One other prominent villager was the headman of this administratively regrouped unit, John Chivunzila. His position was not unopposed. Though it is common for village headmen to preside over VPCs, the presidency is not automatically respected by all the villagers – especially not in situations, like Chivunzila, where a number of older villages have merged. Opposition to the appointment of Chivunzila as village and VPC head was regularly voiced by two former headmen and also by the Simukulwa-Sikambula alliance. Being relatively successful farmer-traders, the Simukulwa-Sikambula group exerted more *de facto* control over the villagers than did the nominated head.

The monetization of village agriculture - which has put a price on maize, beans and millet - has modified the pattern of village leadership. In addition, it has caused local exchanges to become more speculative, less aimed at satisfying immediate consumption needs. But the strategies adopted for generating cash through exchanges are complex. Since the level of maize surpluses produced in the area remained low (organizational constraints, acidic soils), cash could not so easily be generated through the 'normal' NCU channels. If a villager wanted 'quick cash', which was what most households needed, then she/he invested in beans and maximised on bean sales in the free market. The Mambwe area is suited for bean production, government tolerated the free market (for the distant urban centres have to be fed!), and the trade was lucrative since long-distance traders paid well and on the spot. What was more, the demand for beans was such that the high price paid to the producer had stimulated a flow of 'surplus' from across the Tanzanian border.

The mechanism regulating the cross-border flow of foodstuffs worked on the basis of ties of kinship and affinity. A century ago, the European powers had halved Mambwe country, but that arbitrary split had never led to any real separation. The border was a stimulant for close contact, not a line that separated. Modern cross-border exchanges are regulated by cultural principles and by the social networks they have generated. To understand the mechanism

142 KINSHIP AND THE BORDER ECONOMY

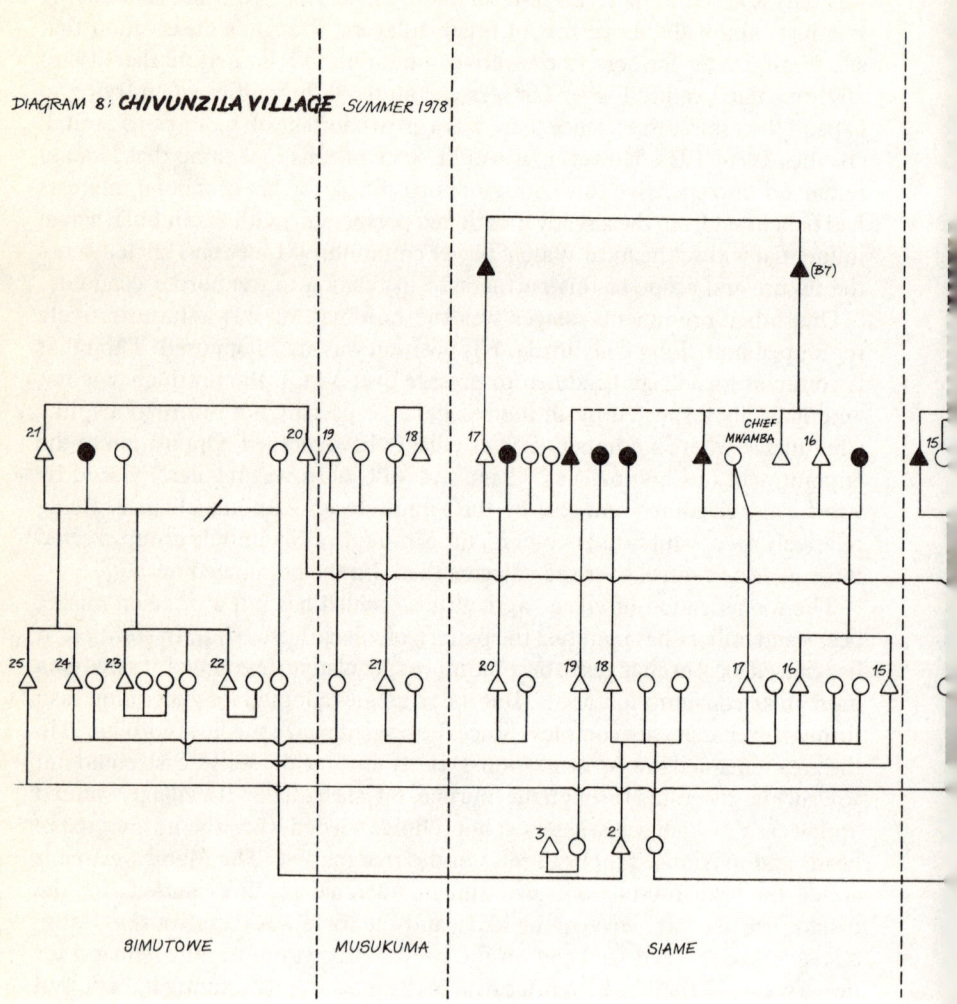

Diagram 8 Chivunzila village, summer 1978

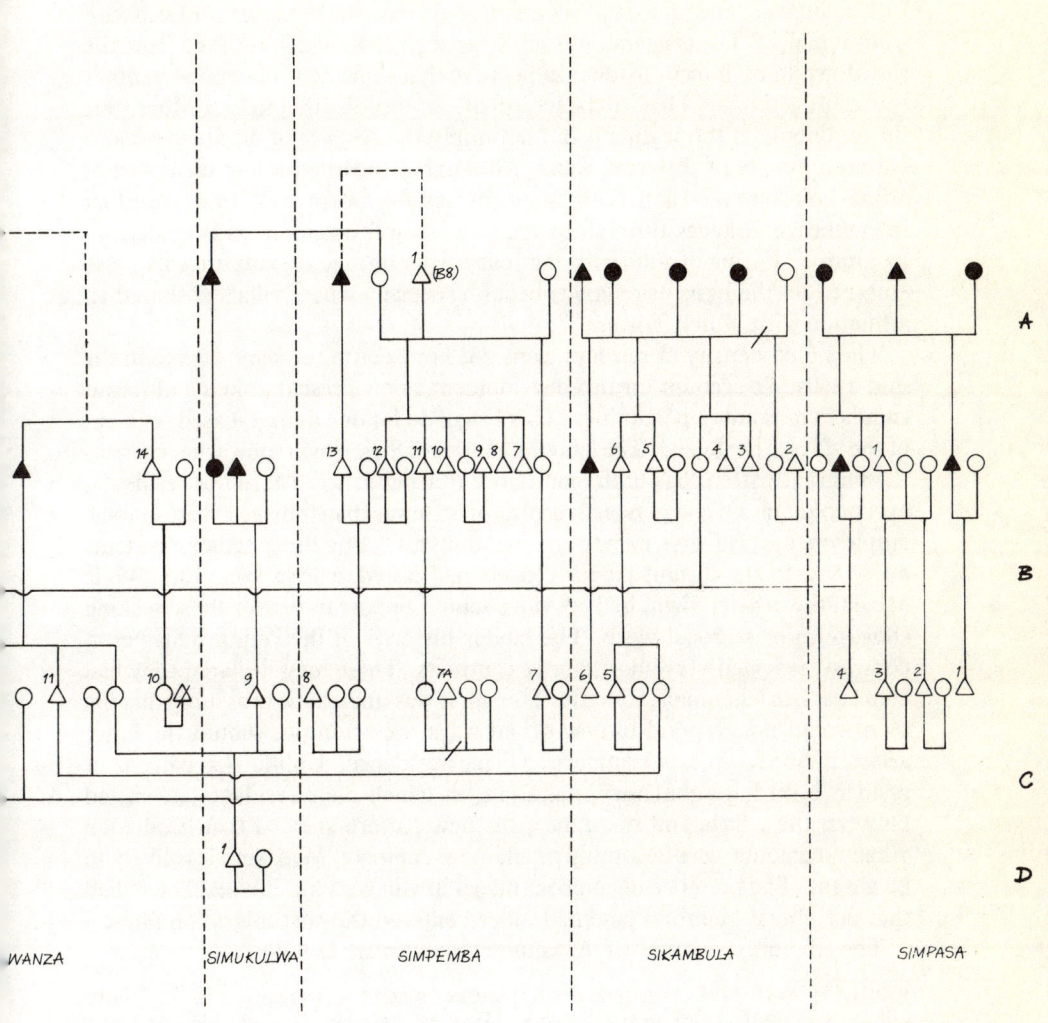

it is useful first to take a look at Chivunzila's social groupings and at the linkages that have evolved within the village, and beyond.

Chivunzila counted some five residential clusters based on lineage affiliation. These were the Siame segment (with 9 adult males), the Simpemba (with 8), the Simwanza (with 6), the Sikambula (with 6) and the Simutowe (also with 6 adult males). The existence of such large segments, which resulted from the slowdown in migrancy, made it imperative that clansmen cooperated in other economic activities. This will be seen in the case studies that follow. Moreover, the autonomy of the segments did not imply the absence of durable relations between people of different clans. Although I recorded a low incidence of affinal links into the Siame 'core' segment (see also Chapter 4), it was clear that inter-lineage linkages through marriage were still common, as is evident in diagram 8. Forms of solidarity that cut across lineage organization had also emerged on the basis of religious belief, especially where villagers shared an affiliation with Watch Tower.

The noted density of resident clans did not exist to the same degree in the mid-1950s. To account for this development I now present a sketch of recent trends in migrant opportunities. This I shall do for one lineage-based segment of the village: the Siame. The labour histories of Siame men show what changes the migrant pattern has undergone since independence. All senior residents, except one (Jack), had personal records of no fewer than fourteen years in wage employment. (All first names are pseudonyms.) For these senior residents every trip to the distant labour centres had lasted at least two years, while Mbala, the district town, had provided labour opportunities for those seeking short-term or seasonal work. The labour histories of the younger Siame, in contrast, revealed very short labour contracts. These men declared they had come back to Chivunzila to settle. Though it was unrealistic to assume that the men would not respond to new urban wage opportunities should the latter arise, they saw no alternative to village residence. Unlike the pattern of residence during circulatory migration, in which male residents alternated between the village and the mines, the new pattern showed that residential village segments were becoming much more compact. Men were less likely to be absent. The presence of compact nuclei in villages like Chivunzila testified that peripheral Mambwe land had indeed entered the post-migration phase.[1]

The labour experiences of the younger Siame were as follows:

Jim [C15] (born 1953) became a general worker when the Tanzania-Zambia Uhuru railway was built. The line runs close to Mambwe country. This was his first job, a contract for one year. He then worked on the construction of a dam near Mulefu village, after which he was recruited for a local cattle innoculation campaign. Both jobs were in the vicinity of his home; on the dam he worked for three months, in the campaign for four. Jim left early in 1977 and headed for Lusaka. That same year he was back. On his first long-distance trip Jim had only secured a three-month contract as a manual labourer in construction.

Godfrey [C20] (born 1957) left for Lusaka in 1975. He held three consecutive jobs in the capital: as a general worker for a private company (nearly a whole year), as a factory worker in a cooking oil processing plant and, finally, in construction (seven months). Upon leaving the capital he took up employment as a bricklayer in Serenje, to come home towards the end of 1976. He returned to Lusaka no later than the following year. After a four-month job in the construction of a water-pipe scheme, Godfrey failed to clinch a new contract and decided to rejoin Chivunzila.

Gregory [D2] (born 1952) took his first job at a bakery in Kabwe, where he worked for eighteen months. Ndola came next. After a six-month contract as a builder there, Gregory travelled south to become a factory worker at the Kafue textiles for two years. He found subsequent work at the Mukonchi Farming Training Centre. At Mukonchi Gregory received practical training in growing vegetables. He held two contracts as a labourer/trainee farmer, each one lasting six months. Now 26 years of age Gregory had 'settled on the land' and grew vegetables in his experimental, well-irrigated *mianda* gardens.

'Experimental', in the case of Gregory, has several connotations. First, obtaining vegetable seeds was no easy task. The NAMBOARD depot in Mbala had failed to obtain seeds for public distribution at the outset of the 1977-78 rainy season.[2] Secondly, there was no obvious market in the Zambian grassland area. Village markets were non-existent, while the district town lacked the storage facilities needed to attract marketable vegetables from beyond a radius of, say, five miles. In spite of these constraints, the vegetables Gregory grew did serve a cash purpose and had a specific destination, for he had set out to create his own market. It was a market in which vegetable production had become part of a wider interest in buying up Tanzanian millet and beans. Gregory's vegetables were usually taken across the border, where his contact was the mother of his classificatory uncles, Jim and Jack.

Vegetable growing in the Mambwe grasslands is an activity which requires skill and initiative, for no villager can possibly succeed if he relies solely upon the existing parastatal services. Chivunzila villagers who in 1978 grew a variety of vegetables (usually men) had all obtained their seeds through personal contact with friends and relatives living in the larger towns. Although such men appeared successful, they bitterly complained about the narrow range they were 'encouraged' to grow: onions, rape, tomatoes, and cabbage - there was little else. It was also unfortunate that growing vegetables contributed so little to the local diet. The effort was mainly a strategic device to boost the syphoning of Tanzanian beans; a means to ensure long-term participation in the cash economy.

The villagers' interest in beans made sense because of their life-long involvement with wage labour migration and the ongoing need for inflation-proof cash. The latter was needed for purchasing basic commodities such as clothes, salt (also used for rewarding labourers), school uniforms, bicycle spares, seeds (when available), church and party dues, beer, etc. In 1977 Copperbelt- and Lusaka-based entrepreneurs toured the Mambwe area and paid K8 per four-gallon tin of beans; in 1978 they offered K10. One further attraction of intensified bean cropping (or trading) was that beans could buy what money could not. As became clear during the acute sugar shortage of

1978, it was the villagers with beans in their pockets, so to speak, who managed to obtain refined sugar when at long last supplies began to trickle in. The first consignments of sugar that reached the grasslands were almost entirely channelled through to Tanzanian border villages, but once their needs were satisfied, the exchange of sugar for beans became a major activity within Zambian villages.

The situation in the Mambwe grassland area - a redoubtable importer of beans - parallelled scenes observed in other parts of rural Zambia where scarce goods (e.g. soap) were used to acquire beans cheaply (Dumont and Mottin 1983: 142). The history of inflation, for which Dumont and Mottin provide some telling examples (*ibid*: 57), and the buying power of scarce commodities and beans were well understood by the grassland Mambwe. The trade in beans had reshaped the local perspective on production and exchange.

Not so well understood by local producers, however, was the existence of a direct link between the smoothly-run collection of beans (which was not a Watch Tower monopoly) and the fast deteriorating NCU service, which I documented in Chapter 5. Equally difficult to grasp was the notion that so-called super profits from bean sales occurred in a setting of infrastructural underdevelopment. The near-unavailability of so many basic consumer goods[3] and the absence of any form of light industrial development in the area need hardly be repeated. But the impact was unique. At some 650 miles from Lusaka the sudden influx of cash, because of the free market in beans, contrasted sharply with the poor supply of consumer items and resulted in the mobilization of the young and the more enterprising. With money in their hands but very little to spend it on locally, the potential migrant force ended its seemingly 'idle' existence. Young people now travelled to distant towns (men in particular) or visited regional food production centres (women and men), from where they acquired goods and produce that were badly needed in the home district. To recall a general point: from underpaid migrant workers (Watson 1958) the rural Mambwe workforce had turned itself into an underpaid distribution unit for basic and scarce goods (Pottier 1983a).

I can now return to the scene in Chivunzila. The area over which the producer-sellers of Chivunzila operated included the Mwamba area itself, Mbala, Mpulungu (*kapenta* trading centre), the market at Kasama (where fish from Lake Moero could be bought) and a number of Tanzanian border villages. Mbala, the nearest market, was of double interest. First of all, the town had retail shops where basic goods could be bought for further retailing in villages. Secondly, Masaiti Compound, the town's squatter settlement, had a large, informal market for millet, fish and other produce, which flourished during the scarce season. Rural petty traders hoarded millet at home and sold to Masaiti beer-brewers when this vital ingredient became scarce towards the end of the rainy season. It was well-known that producer-sellers in Chivunzila and other border villages imported millet from Tanzania on an extensive scale

– 'because it is cheaper there'. Part of this millet was then consumed, while some was stockpiled and sold when the price for millet began to rise.[4] It is impossible to provide figures for this trade, but it met two kinds of demand: a) from the informal sector in Masaiti, and b) from poorer rural households that failed to produce sufficient millet.

The young Siame, whose labour histories I have described, also specialized in trading fish, an activity which requires close cooperation. The dry season is ideal for trips to lakeside villages near Mpulungu, since *kapenta* is then normally abundant and in demand in the hinterland, where large supplies of fingermillet are imported around that same time. Most of the fish, however, is taken straight across the border. The word 'abundant' needs to be used cautiously though, since the local fishing industry was not achieving its 'production' targets and since local millet yields were down. To take the example of fish production, Zambian fishing activities on Lake Tanganyika peaked in 1969-70, but achieved weak results thereafter (GRZ 1977b: 13). By 1978 lakeside sales were marked by the dual structure which I discussed in the context of Masaiti marketeering. Fish sold at the SOPELAC depot was bought up by Zambian long-distance traders, while local petty traders invested in cheap Tanzanian imports.[5]

The decline in local millet production was of little concern to the Siame, since the mother of Jim and Jack, who was divorced from their father, had 'gone home' to a nearby Tanzanian village. The brothers visited their mother regularly during the dry season and always took a few baskets of dried fish along. Across the border the fish was exchanged either for beans or for millet. Since these exchanges took time, the brothers usually returned to Chivunzila, leaving the collection of Tanzanian produce to Jack's wives. (The rules governing access to profits from cross-border trade are important for understanding the evolution of gender relations, and will be explained in the following section.) Before returning to Zambia, the brothers usually made sure that they obtained a few Tanzanian hoe blades. This sometimes meant using profits from previous transactions. Tanzanian hoe blades were thought to be better than those sold by NAMBOARD. They would be sold back in Chivunzila, at a price.

OF SECONDARY MARRIAGES, WOMEN'S RESIDENCE, CASH CROPS AND TRADE

As an administratively regrouped village Chivunzila is unlikely to move its site in the near future. Individual households may move to new sites within Chivunzila, but new villages – breakaway villages like those described in *Tribal Cohesion*, e.g. Simukulwa – have become a thing of the past. Zambia's rural administrators would stop such moves. Consequently, all available space within Chivunzila is likely to become fully occupied within a decade or so, and the concentration of houses close to the main road is certain to become very dense indeed. The demise of the migratory system and the tendency to build new houses near the road to Mwamba (a trend which started in the mid-fifties) have resulted in a significant increase in land-person ratios. The increase, in turn, has led to the adoption of new methods of cultivation.

I noted four major changes in the method of cultivation: fallow periods had shortened; cultivation time had increased; riverside gardens (economically insignificant in Watson's days) had become very important, and finally, cassava and maize had to some extent displaced the more labour-intensive millet.

Substitution of cassava, as Miracle has calculated, enables the innovating community 'to reach the upper range of capacity in terms of population density' (Miracle 1973: 6). Miracle's calculations may be correct, but the increase in capacity refers to caloric yields. This means that extra efforts are needed to maintain or achieve nutritional balance. One solution here is to complement the diet through increased consumption of fish or meat. However, meat consumption among the Mambwe is very low and fish, although available, serves a different purpose. Fish is not so much consumed as traded. The full response to decreasing land availability in Chivunzila has been a combination of switching to cassava and hybrid maize. But the shift has done little to reduce the pressure on land. For instance, since hybrid maize became both a family crop and a cash crop, its introduction led to the extension of gardens rather than the saving of arable space. I have already offered an explanation for this: cash flows, in the form of migrant remittances or government hand-outs, had ceased by the late sixties, which made the intensification of local agriculture and trade in produce seem like a reasonable strategy for bringing in more cash. The pressure on land will remain high, despite the poor performance by NCU, since continuous cultivation is now necessary, and because ploughing has become popular with many households.

The exploitation of riverside (*mianda*) gardens was also geared towards 'the market'. But unlike commercial maize farming, which was tightly controlled by men, *mianda* cropping (when beans were involved) was much more of a negotiated activity. This stemmed from the fact that women as well as men needed to find an alternative, reliable source of cash. If Mambwe men had lost their foothold in the urban/industrial labour market, so Mambwe women had lost their (1950s) source of income. Negotiations were prompted by the fact that both women and men had already found their first alternative sources of cash to be unreliable. Maize cropping for men, as already established, had proved a disappointing alternative, since the Northern part of Zambia is too acid, too heavily leached, and has too long a rainy season to be suitable for maize cultivation (Marter and Honeybone 1976:50,77), and since the rural-urban terms of trade had steadily deteriorated. When, during the early 1970s, Mambwe men switched to maize, Mambwe women lost control over their source of cash, which, during the colonial period especially (the heyday of circulatory migration) had rested with the cultivation and occasional sales of kitchen-garden maize. The loss was also caused by the exhaustion of the soil in and around kitchen gardens. The alternative for women was (and still is) greater participation in trading foodstuffs. The Mambwe women's alternative had proved equally unsatisfactory. Full-time commitment to trade, sometimes coupled with more beer brewing, not only lengthened working hours, but was hazardous too. Hazards related to the risk of arrest in contraband commerce, and to the risk that produce might get spoilt because of poor regional infrastructure.

Consequently, when in the mid-1970s bean cropping became commercialized, both women and men declared their interest, with both sides showing determination to get a share of that promising activity. In spite of the fact that their men controlled the land by custom, Mambwe women proclaimed their acquired right to an independent source of cash. This was a right which, the women said, they themselves and their mothers had enjoyed for decades. The riverside garden was to become the Mambwe woman's new source of cash. About the disposal of riverside produce it was generally agreed, by both men and women, that arrangements concerning the sale of beans usually came about through hard bargaining. Because of such wheeling and dealing, a number of women in Chivunzila were also growing maize in *mianda* gardens to make up, so they said, for poor or non-existent maize yields in *ivizule*. It seemed to me that no hard and fast rules existed about who owned *mianda* produce and that arrangements about the disposal of crops resulted as much from the recognition of embedded cultural variables, such as formal land ownership or the senior status of a headwife, as from the right to earn cash, a right acquired by both sexes in recent history.

But *mianda* gardening was not purely a question of 'Who would own the crop?' The issue was often: 'Which crop would be grown?' Apart from beans and (some) maize, *mianda* plots produced crops such as cabbage, rape and tomatoes. The logic behind the diversification was as follows: if only beans (often a woman's crop in *mianda*) were grown, the husband might press for a share of the earnings, especially should he be dissatisfied with (or have to wait for!) the money earned from maize cropping; if only vegetables (often a man's crop) were grown, the men were likely to want to sell in Tanzania - in which case their wives were likely to press for a share, since Tanzanian trade partners are usually 'traced' through Chivunzila-based women. What factors led to crop selection in *mianda* was difficult to determine, but that both sexes usually had a stake in its produce, by acquired right or because of the cultural mechanism involved in cross-border activity, stood out as a central issue.

The facts about kinship and marriage are all-important for understanding the mechanism that regulated cross-border trading. From detailed genealogical inquiries I inferred several basic facts about Chivunzila. These were: a) that *few* men had fathers who originated from Tanzania or brothers who lived there; b) that *some* men (e.g. the Siame traders) had mothers who lived in Tanzanian border villages; and c) that *many* men had Chivunzila-based mothers, wives or sisters-in-law who were born on the other side of the border. Invariably, such women had relatives and close friends living in Tanzania. Especially important was that numerous Chivunzila women - the categories 'mother' and 'co-wife' - had daughters from previous marriages who lived across the border. The mother-daughter link, apparently severed by international politics, was the one most frequently activated for the cross-border trading in foodstuffs. In short, it was a genealogical advantage which gave Chivunzila women both the right and the means to claim a share of any profits their men made in exchanges across the border.

I have two points to make in respect of women's residence. The first point is straightforward: when a marriage breaks up it is still both norm and common practice that the wife returns to her natal village, usually her father's, while her children remain with the ex-husband. Estrangement and divorce are frequent, and the number of women who at one or more times in their lives have had to 'return home' is high. This means that several Tanzanian women previously married to Zambian nationals have by now returned to Tanzania (e.g. the mother of Jim and Jack), while *vice versa* many Zambian women once married in Tanzania have likewise returned to Zambia. Of course I have no systematic record of the former category of women (except in the case of some individuals), but I did know several Zambian Mambwe women who had 'returned home' after their Tanzanian marriages had ended. This leads to my second point – and here we do have a new and significant trend. Not only have many women 'come back home' to Chivunzila after their marriages broke up, the majority have subsequently stayed on in the village, even after re-marrying (see diagram 9).

It is still expected that a divorcee, an 'estranged' wife,[6] or a widow will leave the village when she remarries. The expectation is not always brought out in actual behaviour, as became clear during the settlement of a dispute over land, in which a divorcee was involved. Chisasa Nayame, the woman in question, had returned to her father's village. She 'belonged' to Kosam's. Soon after she arrived she bought (but I am not sure about the actual financial arrangements) the house and gardens of one F.Simbeya. His father having just died, Simbeya had decided to leave Chivunzila to join his mother in Kaka. After acquiring the property, Nayame was approached by one E.Sikazwe, son of the deputy headman. Sikazwe asked Nayame for permission to cultivate the land she had bought. Nayame refused. An angered Sikazwe then took the case to the Ward Councillor, and an inspection tour followed. The outcome of the inspection, which I attended, was that the councillor and the four local witnesses who accompanied him sided with Nayame. Sikazwe was ordered to stop cultivating Nayame's land. The decision surprised me. However, while returning from the fields, the witnesses reassured Sikazwe that when Nayame would marry again, which they thought likely within a year or so, she would leave the village and he, Sikazwe, would be allowed to cultivate her gardens.

At first I took it for granted that Nayame would indeed leave the village in due course. The assumption was challenged when I learned about the trade interests of that large number of women for whom Chivunzila was home. A thorough checking of genealogies then revealed that no fewer than twenty-two married, resident women were 'of Chivunzila', and that sixteen of them (or about 25 per cent of the total female population) had lived with their previous husbands in other villages or in town, before returning as divorcees. Also of interest was the realization that thirteen of those sixteen had subsequently remarried and stayed on in the home village. Hence, I presented an incomplete picture when earlier on I suggested the existence of compact clan segments. Taking account of the evidence in Diagram 9, I must now add that all the major clans also have an average of about three adult women residing in the village. In addition to the women who returned to stay (often re-marrying local men to become co-wives), there were six young women and five men - all from Chivunzila - who had established monogamous households. In sum, twenty-two adult women who lived in Chivunzila – which is one third of all married women – were in fact 'of the village'.

The contrast between anticipated and existing behaviour is a powerful challenge to the old pattern of patrilocal residence after marriage. And the new pattern is likely to continue. On re-marriage, women usually have good reasons for not leaving their home of origin. Firstly, as already discussed, re-marriage (with or without a divorce certificate) gives women little security. Secondly, the extension of acreages under ox-plough cultivation implies a heavier burden on labour-time, female labour-time in particular. Given that work-party arrangements based on reciprocity have broken down throughout the grasslands (Chapter 6), and that an individual's time budget cannot expand *ad infinitum*, it is now increasingly common for women to cooperate on the land with other women drawn from the immediate extended family. This contrasts with the village base which determined work-party formations in the fifties. The retaining of a residential core of adult women linked by close family ties could be one way of enhancing the likelihood that the extra demands on labour-time can be accommodated. In Kowa, a large cluster of agnatically related women had formed around Kaputula; here in Chivunzila, similar clusters (although smaller) existed within every lineage segment.

One further explanation must also be considered. Since the lucrative trade in beans towards the Copperbelt and Lusaka encourages the extraction of Tanzanian surplus, many women who returned to Chivunzila upon their being widowed or divorced, found themselves extremely well placed to act as go-betweens in the cross-border trade. Living in Chivunzila has in many cases proved the near-perfect answer to a woman's need for independent cash.

152 KINSHIP AND THE BORDER ECONOMY

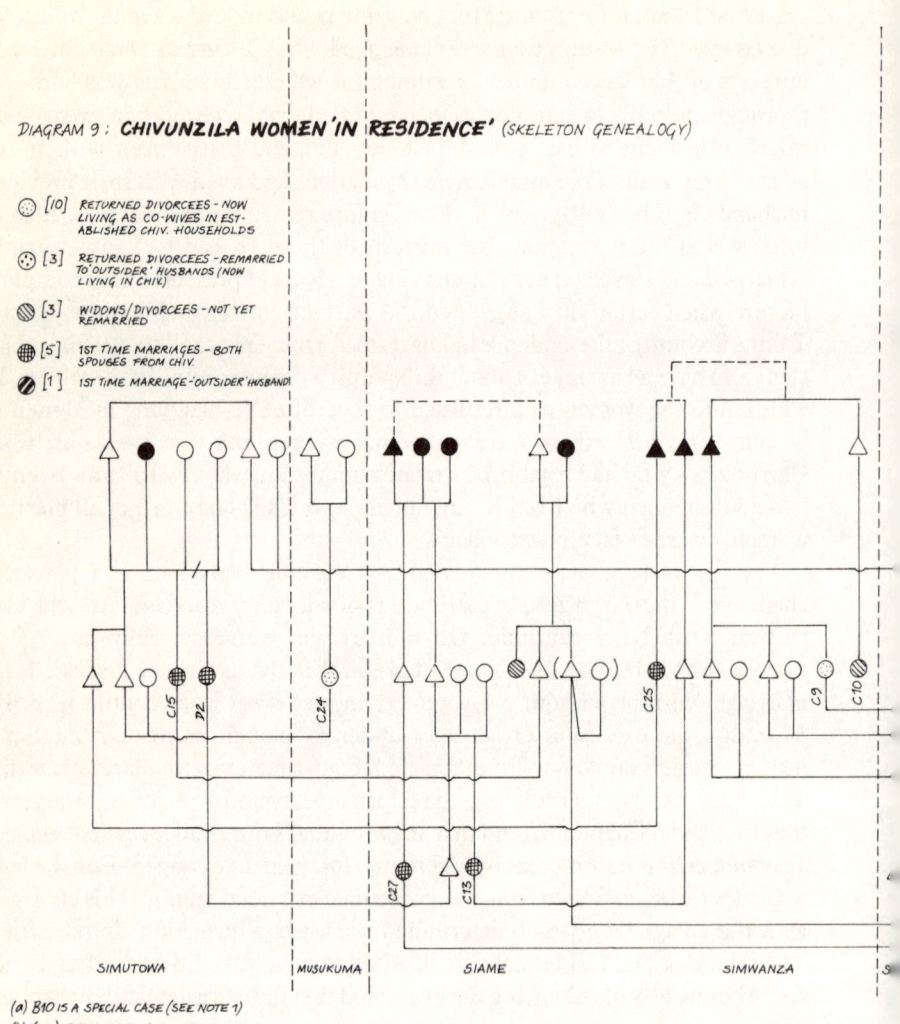

Diagram 9 Chivunzila women 'in residence' (skeleton genealogy)

MIGRANTS NO MORE

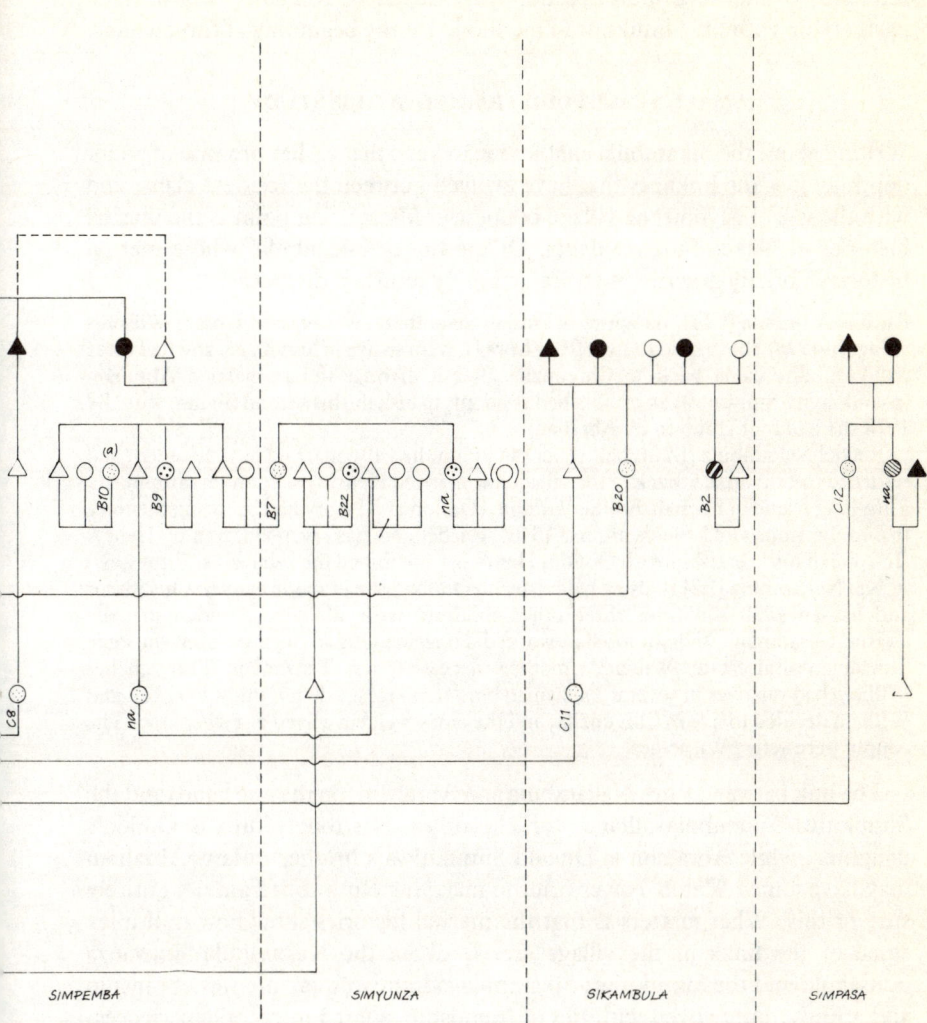

I now propose to illustrate what I mean by 'extremely well placed', with reference to the Sikambula (pseudonym) cluster of residents, whose trade partnership with the Simukulwa I mentioned at the beginning of this chapter.

SMALL-SCALE FOOD TRADING: A CASE STUDY

Writing about the Sikambula enables me to keep that earlier promise of an in-depth look at the linkages that have evolved between the resident clans, and with the world beyond the village boundary. My starting point is the marital histories of Nakambula residents. Of the three Nakambula, whose marital histories I briefly describe, two are definitely returned divorcees.

Ruth Nakambula [C11], daughter of Odilon Sikambula, was born in Kosam Wilson's village in 1924. She married a man from Lobo's, went to live in his village, and had three children. She came back to Chivunzila after a divorce and re-married Abraham (pseudonym) Simwanza, an established resident, to become his second (living) wife. By 1978 she had four children by Abraham.

Rachel Nakambula [B20], half-sister of Odilon, had also married out, divorced, and returned to Chivunzila. Back in the village she married Henry (pseudonym) Simutowe, a life-long friend of her half-brother Odilon. (Odilon and Henry had been together on a trip to the Lupa Gold Fields around 1940.) Rachel now has seven children by Henry. (In spite of his friendship with Odilon, Henry has not joined the Jehovah's Witnesses.)

Kai Nakambula [B2] is also a half-sister to Odilon. She is about ten years his junior and has an adult son (plus three other children) with William (pseudonym), the assistant headman. William too had worked alongside Odilon during a stint on some Tanzanian sisal estate. William's mother, deceased, was Tanzanian. Through her William had relatives in several Tanzanian border villages. I do not know why Kai and William decided to live in Chivunzila, and they may well have lived elsewhere too. The couple were active Witnesses.

The link between Ruth Nakambula and Abraham (on the one hand) and the Simukulwa-Sikambula alliance (on the other) is strong. Ruth is Odilon's daughter, while Abraham is Donald Simukulwa's brother-in-law. Abraham may have joined Watch Tower prior to marrying Ruth, but I am not entirely sure of this. What matters is that the marital histories show how multiplex some of the links in the village are. Between the Nakambula-Simwanza household and the Simukulwa-Sikambula 'administration' are ties of kinship and affinity, interwoven with ties of friendship, shared migrant experiences, and religion. The ties that link the three Nakambula women are equally intricate, and may explain, in part at least, why it is that these three women had chosen to stay on in Chivunzila. They called on each other for help with agricultural work, child care and domestic chores, and seemed genuinely to enjoy life in the village. However, to understand their positions more fully, I now need to look at their interactions and activities beyond the village boundary.

As a cooperating unit in the trade of foodstuffs, the three Nakambula were often joined by the two headwives with whom Rachel and Ruth shared husbands. It deserves to be mentioned that one of those senior wives, Jessie Namukozwe (pseudonym), headwife in Henry's household, was a central figure in the women's struggles to secure independent incomes. Jessie was a keen gardener, with excellent trade connections. The allocation of land within Henry's household was as follows. Husband Henry had his own bean garden (a steady source of income), each wife had one millet and one cassava garden, while Jessie (as headwife) also had her own *mianda* garden. Jessie's *mianda* plot was mainly used for growing beans, but she also grew a little maize and some Irish potatoes. The produce from this garden was entirely Jessie's. As a rule she took her beans and potatoes to Donald Simukulwa's grocery, where she exchanged or sold for cash. Donald's grocery - and here I link up with the first part of this chapter - was a major buying-up point east of Mwamba. Since Donald's son George was married to one of her daughters, Jessie knew that she would be given a fair price. The close link with Donald made Jessie popular with other women who were involved in the bean trade. Jessie, moreover, had a daughter who lived in Tanzania.

Jessie's daughter was one reason why Gregory Siame (mentioned above) was so enthusiastic about producing vegetables for exchange across the border. Although Gregory, as I have indicated, could call upon the mother of his classificatory uncles, this cross-border tie was not the only one at his disposal. He was just as likely (and may indeed have preferred) to call upon Jessie's daughter, because the daughter was also his sister-in-law. When Jessie's daughter acted as a contact, and especially when Gregory had taken dried fish across the border, it was his wife and her mother Jessie who took it upon themselves to collect the Tanzanian beans, or the millet, at a later date. In practice though, because of Jessie's age, it was more common (or such was the arrangement at the time of my fieldwork) for co-wife Rachel Nakambula to join Gregory's spouse.

In 1978 Jessie's daughter also acted as contact for Rachel's niece, Ruth. This did not mean that Ruth always used Jessie's daughter. Indeed, like Gregory, few people in Chivunzila had just one contact. As an alternative to headwife Jessie's daughter, Rachel could call upon a contact via half-sister Kai's mother-in-law. Although Kai's husband's mother had died, husband William had half-sisters from one of his mother's later marriages – and they too were living across the border.

There is also a seasonal aspect that needs mentioning. Beans are harvested twice a year, and the November crop (which was not collected at the producer's doorstep) usually belonged to the woman who tended it. However, the Mwamba-Mbala bus service became very irregular by November, due to the first heavy rains, so transport had to be found. In addition, it was necessary to have contacts in Mbala, with whom one could stay overnight.

At the time of the November bean sales, the proverbial tables turned for co-wives Jessie and Rachel. Although Rachel would once again act as Jessie's agent, this time she would choose a contact from within her own family network, i.e. a half-sister who lived in Mbala. This did not mean that Rachel would visit Mbala - after all, she had seven children to care for. Someone else would be sent. The more likely person to take responsibility for transporting Jessie's beans was Rachel's half-sister, Kai, who was a real sister to the Mbala contact. Transport was by bus, unless there were too many bags to be taken. In the latter event, Kai approached Odilon Sikambula, her half-brother, to arrange for transport through Watch Tower. The road had deteriorated by that time of year, but fellow church members who owned transport could always be found ready to lend a hand.

CROSS-BORDER COMMERCE: AN ASSESSMENT

Any quick assessment of the ethnography of cross-border commerce would probably suggest that men controlled the trade, for indeed it was men, not women, who could be seen taking goods towards the Tanzanian border. Such men often used bicycles as their means of transport.

The apparent control by men was much in evidence during a peak period in cross-border activity (August 1978), when sugar had just become available again in Zambia, after an absence of about six months. Many men from Chivunzila had managed to buy up small quantities of sugar after visiting Mbala, where they had stayed with friends or relatives. During the first few weeks that sugar trickled in, the bulk of the supplies was taken across the border, together with dried fish or soap and matches, non-perishables that were also in demand. Exchanges took place at the house of the trader's contacts. With the exception (perhaps) of fresh vegetables, Zambian goods taken across the border were sold at fixed points, not traded from door to door. Chivunzila men could usually call upon several Tanzanian contacts, since the availability of surplus goods tended to fluctuate. No trader wanted to overburden a contact, as this might flood the market.

The necessary interval between taking the goods to Tanzania and returning with merchandise (beans, millet, sometimes hoes) required trust and discretion. These prerequisites to successful trading often dictated a choice of trade partners from among close relatives and affines. The basic strategy for choosing cross-border trade partners was to call upon (Tanzanian) households who had female kin living in Chivunzila. On returning from Tanzania, and depending on the season or availability of scarce goods, the male traders were likely to resume their search for more sugar, more soap, more fish... thereby leaving 'their women' in charge of the collection of Tanzanian products. This was not so much a chore imposed on the women as the latter's prerogative – their way of ensuring that other female kin and they themselves obtained a share of the profits.

I cannot comment on whether women ever received a fair share. But that it was women who collected, once the exchange completed, was some indication that profits from cross-border trade were indeed 'negotiable'. However, the women returned with produce, not cash, and it took another transaction (e.g. selling the beans to Simukulwa) before any cash became available! At that point men could reassert control.

Few Chivunzila traders ventured deep into Tanzania in order to exchange, although some might travel to Mbeya on a shopping trip. Whenever I met Tanzanian contacts on Zambian soil or talked to Chivunzila people en route to (or returning from) Tanzania, the signs were that their journeys never took them much beyond villages near the border. Therefore, what I have described as a border economy was indeed very small-scale and perhaps applicable only to villages in the vicinity of the Zambia-Tanzania dividing line. On the other hand, the narrow confines to which the term applied do not preclude the existence of a whole string of such micro-economies.

Whatever the scope of the border economy, I stress that cross-border trading takes place in a 'family' setting and that its aim is to raise the rural incomes of local people. Cross-border transactions are little else but mutual favours between relatives and affines who happen to belong to different states. One advantage of this 'spontaneous' setting is that the risk factor can be reduced: produce taken across the border is seldom exchanged by the producer-seller. The exchange itself is left to a relative or affinal contact, mostly traced via women who reside in Chivunzila. It is this tracing which explains why Chivunzila women have some control over the profits that accrue to the border economy.

Peripheral Mambwe land of the late seventies experienced supply constraints of goods and cash. Tanzanian produce was cheap against the background of inflation-hit Zambia, and the Zambian petty traders offered relatively attractive 'prices' in the form of goods not otherwise obtainable in Tanzania.[7] The organization of the cross-border trade had clearly developed into an extended-family affair, in which all parties stood to gain, because of the differential pricing systems involved. From this point of view cross-border trade was indeed some kind of redistribution of existing wealth (see Chapter 6).

But lest the mild success of cross-border trading be interpreted as approval on my part or even justification of the system, I hasten to add that I cannot wholly sympathise with the *laissez-faire* attitude which underlies the food leakages. Seen from the perspective of an impoverished rural economy, the profit-making (or redistribution of wealth) is little more than a nervous attempt to mask the absence of a serious national commitment to the cause of rural development in outlying areas. There are profits to be made from trading across the border, but such profits rarely last. The real pay-off lies elsewhere. As the administrators who tolerate this trade fully realize, it is the Zambian Line of Rail towns which ultimately benefit most from the food leakages, since the cross-border trade satisfies their high demand for beans.

CHAPTER EIGHT

NEW DEVELOPMENTS IN SHIFTING AGRICULTURE

In preceding chapters I have repeatedly argued that population increase and pressure on the land have led to a process of soil depletion. The question which therefore arises is whether shifting (or swidden) agriculture can be improved as shifting agriculture or whether it is doomed to be phased out by other, more intensive forms of land use?

When Grandstaff posed that same question in an article published in 1978, he affirmed that swiddening could be a potential modern adaptation, provided certain conditions were met. Concentrating on two important variables of adaptation - higher yields and improved system viability - Grandstaff suggested that increased productivity be monitored for possible negative effects on viability, especially those resulting from unwise cropping (Grandstaff 1978: 553).

Theoretically speaking, several measures can be taken to stimulate both productivity and viability. No such measures are needed when fallow periods are long enough to ensure regeneration of secondary forest growth (in forest swiddening) or bush vegetation (in savanna swiddening); yet, the maintenance of adequate fallow periods is an increasing problem in many parts of the world today. An overall shortening of fallow periods, with a corresponding increase in the period of cultivation, is frequently observed. Such shortening results from natural population growth and/or from the imposition of settlement policies that heighten person-land ratios. With regard to the measures to be taken, Grandstaff argues that 'real efforts should be made to limit population ... [or alternatively] to provide outmigration if population cannot be internally limited' (Grandstaff 1978: 555). At present, in the case of Mambwe villages, neither outmigration nor other forms of reducing population pressure appear to act as safety valves. Mambwe cultivators have opted for improved productivity via increased exploitation of the resources at hand and, in some cases, increased reliance on technological assistance from outside.

Grandstaff also warns, and this is a focal point for my discussion, that 'income-generating activities must ... be appropriate to the nature and timing of the subsistence labour activities so that the system viability is not lost through conflict between the two' (Grandstaff 1978: 562). Loss of system viability, as other researchers have pointed out before him, may be expected when returns from cash crops are particularly attractive (Dasmann *et al* 1973:63; Janzen 1973:1216; cited by Grandstaff). The production system of the Mambwe poses a dilemma in this respect. The system is not one in which cash cropping is 'particularly attractive', since the terms of trade for maize cropping do not act as a great incentive; yet, maize cropping did solve a labour problem, and there is a second crop - beans - which is well suited to the area and highly attractive as a cash crop.

In this chapter I shall respond to Grandstaff's call for a micro-level monitoring of the effects of cash cropping (and outside assistance) on system viability. For this I have chosen a village which until three decades ago met its full food requirements through extensive swiddening. Until the late 1950s, the village - called Chikoti - practised a swidden system based on secondary forest fallow. Chikoti had 'emerged' from the forest by the time of my field study, but continued to rely on woodland ash-planting (*citemene*) for the production of fingermillet (*malezi*).

In order to assess the direction of change for the production system of the woodland Mambwe, it is necessary to discuss the analytic tools at my disposal. The tools are those provided by the time-space perspective which Carlstein proposed in his evaluation of why and how swidden communities change (Carlstein 1982). Carlstein's time-space structural approach to change revolves around the close relationship between the land cropping cycle, the residence cycle and the size of the local territory (Carlstein 1982: 158). Space-time budgets accommodate a variety of space-time consuming activities. These include variables such as land area (with productivity reduction over time), time expenditure (with likely increases when gardens become territorially spaced out), and the crops themselves. Grandstaff has urged analysts to adopt such a 'budget' framework whenever they assess the viability of micro-level habitats. An illustration of how crop selection may influence space-time budgets can be found, for example, in the switch from cereal to root crop cultivation. While millet or rice are comparatively more labour-intensive (than, say, cassava), these cereal crops are also less space-time intensive, in the sense that they have much shorter cropping cycles. Millet and rice reduce space-time inputs because they have a quality which releases both land area and cultivation time (*ibid*: 70). However, since cereal crops are also labour-intensive, it would be misleading to talk about an absolute release of cultivation time.

I shall concentrate on how space-time shortages have developed in Chikoti and on how the substitution of a root crop (in this case, cassava for millet) is best understood as a solution to such shortages. The popularity cassava enjoys in much of Africa today has its rationale in the fact that it feeds 'more people ... per acre with less effort', in comparison with millet (Ludwig 1968:105; quoted by Carlstein 1982:225).

The development of space-time shortages is usually linked to changes in the pattern of settlement. And shortages emerge as populations grow. This growth can be natural, imposed through settlement policy, or the result of reduced opportunity for outmigration. Chikoti, the village for which I shall present a space-time profile, has had to cope with the impact of two major policy decisions. First, after Chikoti refused to move to an adjacent territory selected for development (i.e. the Kaka resettlement, Chapters 5 and 6), its location became fixed because of the national ban on moving village sites for purposes other than infrastructural development. Secondly, because of the closure of the urban/industrial labour market (Chapter 3), Chikoti, like other Mambwe villages, has for some time now experienced perceptible population swell. It is with the long-term implications of this double restriction on spatial mobility that I am concerned. The implications for village-level agriculture come under the heading of space-time shortages.

Population growth, whatever its origins, has long been recognized as a major force in the transition towards intensified agriculture. Boserup, who has expounded on the adoption of more intensive forms of ecotechnology, defined intensification quite simply as the shortening of fallows and, in her own words, 'the gradual change towards patterns of land use which make it possible to crop a given area more frequently than before' (Boserup 1965: 43). Carlstein criticizes the approach for dealing mainly with regional levels of change, while smoothing over the 'many structural features at the local or household level' (Carlstein 1982:189). As an alternative, he suggests that the analyst be concerned with 'processes of intensification [that] are operative at different structural levels' (*ibid*: 189) – processes that can be conceptualized as changes in the space-time budget of the habitat under study. In Carlstein's framework, such a budget is made up of spatial demarcations and activities which, like all activities, consume space-time. The latter, he clarifies, 'is merely a short hand for expressing that the component individuals, artifacts and organisms occupy space-time' (*ibid*: 150). In concrete terms, the analyst is asked not to restrict his or her discussion to a focus on population growth at the regional level, but to pay equal attention to the distribution of land and labour-time among (and within) households.

Returning now to Grandstaff's approach to the development of swidden systems, it does indeed seem reasonable to conceptualize the transition from extensive (forest fallow) to medium intensity cultivation (bush fallow or grass fallow) as a multi-level adaptation to the quest for 'a denser packing of parcels with acceptable day-prism range' (Carlstein 1982: 201). The actual form the adaptation takes may well consist of a variety of systems of cultivation, but it will reflect the community's capacity to mobilize human time resources (*ibid*: 162) and expose its principles for the protection of soil physical properties (Richards 1983:5). The reference to local principles is a reminder that the allocation of space-time resources is more than a mechanical reaction to demographic pressure. It is a reaction which is also a cultural event. I shall develop the cultural aspect, especially in relation to the division of labour by gender. Gender relations will be discussed in the light of Richards's argument that 'minimization of fluctuations in labor supply requirements across the agricultural year is an organizational issue of considerable importance' (Richards 1983:31).

Having accepted the broad contours of a structural framework for understanding the transformation of the Mambwe woodland system, I now consider the ultimate analytic problem of how the long-term viability of such systems can be assessed. I shall treat adaptation to space-time shortages as 'viable' if responses reverse the process of (space-time) resource depletion; i.e. if a balance is struck between the maintenance of soil fertility and productivity on the one hand and labour-time input on the other. If, on the contrary, the measures taken to maintain soil fertility and crop productivity result in an overtaxing of labour time, or if time allocations are such that they lead to neglect in matters related to fertility or productivity, then I shall reserve the label 'not viable'.

MAMBWE FOREST CULTIVATION, 1952

In order to discuss changes in the woodland system, it is useful to first recall some of the attributes outlined in *Tribal Cohesion*. In 1952 the Mambwe occupied both a grassland zone and a stretch of forest. In the open grasslands - with their sandy soils and outcrops of dolerite - the Mambwe practised 'a fallow system of cultivation, marked by a distributive method of green manuring and crop rotation' (1958: 21); in the forest, where the soil was equally leached, a variation of the ash-planting (*citemene*) system existed (1958: 21-22). The woodland system was of a more advanced type than the method used by the Bemba (see Richards 1939), since it was based on 'the practice of spreading mounds in the main [i.e. millet] gardens during the latter part of the cultivation sequence' (Trapnell; cited in Watson 1958:24). Trapnell also informed that the Bemba, according to their own oral tradition, had adapted their large-circle *citemene* system from the more progressive method of the Mambwe (1958: 24).[1]

Traditional Mambwe agriculture was characterised by natural fertilization (through clearance of woodland or green manuring, depending on the ecological niche), burning, short-term cultivation and relatively long fallow periods. The two systems (woodland and grassland) were efficient in terms of the demands they made on people's labour-time. But although they produced reasonable returns per person-hour, both systems were potentially vulnerable to population pressure (1958: 16).

Regarding the main features of social organization, I would like to mention the following – bearing in mind, of course, that Watson is writing in the present but about a time now long past:

First, with reference to the division of tasks, Watson reports that

Among the grassland Mambwe both sexes have an equal share in the work of hoeing the fields,... [Men] and women are ... interchangeable units in this fundamental activity. In the woodlands, the men specialize in the task of lopping the trees, but share all the subsequent cultivation with the women, [except for weeding, which is a] specialized task confined to women (1958:33).

It is true that ash-planting, as Watson says, takes care of weeding (1958:26). However, it is also well-known that labour requirements for weeding rise considerably in 2nd and 3rd year gardens.

Secondly, regarding access to land, I note that

Women's rights to the use of land differ from those of the men. There are no 'estates of holding' for women; they work land whose rights are held by men. A man must make a garden for each of his wives, and if he does not, his wife may leave him and claim a divorce (1958: 99).

If we can talk at all here about women's rights in land, it is in the sense that a husband needed to provide every wife with a garden of her own. Once the 'wife is provided with her own garden by her husband,... she is expected to provide food and beer for her husband and family' (1958: 109). But the story does not end here.

Thirdly, with regard to access to produce, it is married women who controlled the disposal of commercial crops. They, and they alone, decided how to manage the food stores and how to dispose of surpluses. The latter were grown in the kitchen gardens. Thus Watson writes:

Women sell the surplus crops (mainly maize) from these gardens and use the money to buy clothes and personal goods. As a result, these gardens are personally tended and jealously guarded (1958: 110).

These surplus crops should not be thought of as bumper harvests, for the Mambwe village of the fifties aspired not to surplus production but to self-sufficiency and economic independence at village level (1958: 34).

Fourthly, it was one of the main findings of Watson's research that the women's right to male labour, needed during the initial stage of cultivation, was safeguarded by institution. A safeguard was required since the Mambwe were 'no longer simple subsistence cultivators,' but actively involved in wage labour migration (1958: 21). The safeguard against possible labour shortages was the communal approach to agricultural labour. Thus Watson argues:

The work-party ensures that no woman left at home needs fear that she will be bereft of labour to cultivate her fields. When a young man goes off to work, he knows that his wife and family will not have to beg (1958: 110).

Cooperative labour based on reciprocity was grounded, according to Watson, in a cultural ideology intrinsic to the patrilineal system. The system existed in its own right, irrespective of conditions in the wider environment at that time. The productive system of the Mambwe, so Watson maintained, conditioned them to work regularly and to cooperate in production (1958: 35). Viewed in retrospect, the above is not a position which I share in its totality. During fieldwork in the now-almost-grassland village of Chikoti (woodland in 1952), I arrived at a different conclusion. My interest in the mechanism underlying work-party cooperation had been triggered by the fact that Chikoti's people emphatically denied that cooperative work was still the norm. The diminished importance of cooperative labour became clear when I reconstructed the composition of female harvesting teams for millet. The information pointed to recruitment on a kinship basis, which cut across the village boundary, with the occasional addition of paid female labourers, who received salt rather than money as their reward. The mode of recruitment was consistent with behaviour in the grasslands (see Chapter 4).

The demise of the work-party system was intriguing, since headman Ali Chikoti's village seemed remarkably cohesive in its response to opportunities in the wider economy. One collective response, already mentioned, was that Chikoti had refused to join the nearby development project in Kaka, arguing that the residential move would widen the distance to millet gardens in the forest. The village had also registered as a 'group practice' (which was absolutely unique!) for the purpose of acquiring hybrid maize seed and chemical fertilisers on credit.

I emphasize that the cohesive aspects of Chikoti pertained to its response to external forces, i.e. the government-backed scheme for intensified agriculture in Kaka. There was no corresponding cohesion in the internal structure of the village. Unlike the typical Mambwe village of the 1950s, Chikoti already had a high number of resident clans (11 for 25 households) and no core residential group. Its genealogy manifested several affinal linkages within the village, but the end-result was a structure of the 'chain of affinity' type which has spread throughout the grasslands. From the point of view of residence, the village had embarked upon a process of "dissolution" (Murray 1980:144). The continuing absence of men of (potential) political prominence underscored that process. At the same time, I found evidence of what Murray has called the conservationist trend towards maintaining the traditional ethos, as indicated by the collective approach towards the incentives offered by agricultural extension. Chikoti village had become an appropriate illustration of Murray's argument that 'processes of "dissolution" and "conservation" are simultaneously at work in rural communities of the [Southern African] periphery' (Murray 1980:144).[2]

Before I can clarify the mechanism for work-party cooperation in the fifties, it is useful to add to the general picture of Chikoti's physical appearance. The people of Chikoti continued to practise ash-cultivation, even though the forest was already a good one and a half hours' walk away from the village.[3] In the 1950s Chikoti had been surrounded by woodland; but population pressure over the past three decades had resulted in the virtual depletion of surrounding forest. Two factors directly responsible for this development were the constant cutting of young vegetation and the precocious re-use of fallow plots. The village site had remained the same for well over 20 years, which is an excessively long period for any system based on woodland swiddening. Zambia's farming populations no longer move 'en bloc'. This is partly because the Government encourages concentration of villages with a view to boosting rural infrastructure, and partly because *citemene* is officially banned (GRZ 1977:28; Hedlund and Lundahl 1983: 25, 29). The ban - which works best in the vicinity of political centres - came about after the system was identified as the main cause of forest deterioration (Dumont 1979: 26).

Despite Chikoti's cohesion vis-à-vis the outside world, a condition which I initially believed to be conducive to work-party activity, I was soon forced to drop the idea that cooperation based on reciprocity was alive and well. How could I account for this development, especially since the village seemed united in some contexts and showed very few signs of internal differentiation, between households, with regard to wealth and access to means of production?

Whenever I voiced surprise over the collapse of the work-party system, I received the same simple reply: 'there is no millet for *cipumu*'. *Cipumu*, or millet beer, I was told, required a level of production which was no longer achieved. The work-party system, that hallmark of cohesion, had disappeared as a consequence of the drop in millet production. Although shifting systems can be described as producing no significant surplus (e.g. Goody 1982: 208), it is fair to suggest that producing a specific kind of surplus for internal distribution (which is usually converted into beer) must be common practice. After all, it has been shown that swiddening produces high yields, particularly in forest areas (Harris 1972:247; Watson 1958:27), and especially when there is some institutionalized mechanism to call it forth.

When I probed the work-party system in Chikoti as it had existed a few decades earlier, I found the underpinnings of that system to have been threefold. It is here that my interpretation differs from Watson's. I inferred from discussions that work-parties had thrived in the days of circulatory migration, not because everybody lived by custom, but because at the time nearly every male adult was either a middle-aged retired migrant worker who could guarantee reciprocity or a younger temporary resident who had the cash to pay for the millet that was needed for *cipumu*. In the early 1950s, access either to cash or to millet did not exist as a problem. Both were relatively abundant. Moreover, and this is the third important attribute, the 'guarantee to reciprocate' also applied to the absent migrant since his children and wife (or wives) usually remained in the village during his absence.

Nearly three decades later the 'homogeneous' village of Chikoti was made up of a substantial number of young families, who as families would leave for the towns as soon as realistic job opportunities arose. Although such opportunities were scant, young village men were unlikely not to want to duplicate the migrant successes of their parents' generation, and young women/wives were not prepared to stay behind should their husbands 'chance upon' urban employment. A second point on which the new system differed was that young families did not have easy access to money or surplus millet. These social developments explain why cooperation on the land had become eroded, notwithstanding the existence of other - even recent - manifestations of cohesion and solidarity towards the outside world.

As shifting cultivators the Mambwe of 1952 displayed a remarkable degree of togetherness. Like other peoples who practised swiddening, the Mambwe too displayed sustained cooperation between individuals and between households in terms of the volume of food that was produced and consumed (cf. Bayliss-Smith on Maring agriculture, 1982:29; also Goody 1982:208). Large tracts of land were always in fallow, and plots seldom exceeded a hectare. But the work-party system practised in the fifties was not simply an expression of some abstract cultural ideology. As my explanation for the virtual disappearance of the work-party system indicates, the collective approach which Watson observed existed already as an adaptation; it existed as a response to the opportunities for migrant labour. I argue that three factors, prevailing in the 1950s but gone by the late 1970s, accounted for the existence of large work-parties at the time of Watson's fieldwork: firstly, residential permanence was a guarantee for labour reciprocity - a 'rule' which applied to all women and to retired migrants; secondly, a sufficiently high level of surplus millet was produced (without which no *cipumu* could be brewed); and thirdly, there was access to cash, in the form of remittances brought back by younger temporary residents.

To conclude on work-party organization in the fifties, I suggest that the system was more than an example of that pre-industrial mode of production which was 'well adapted for fulfilling traditional needs' (Bayliss-Smith 1982: 26). It was also as a system finely tuned to the 'new cultural aspirations' of the era (*ibid*: 26). But tuning was at a cost, especially when labour input along gender lines is considered, since the burden of the 'traditional' Mambwe work-party system fell disproportionately on some categories of women (widows in particular) who worked for food (*ukupula*) and were denied return services (see Chapter 6). At the time this overtaxing of female labour power did not constitute a threat to the village habitat – defined earlier on as a time-space construct. As Watson's observations suggest, all the basic requirements of a stable system of agriculture were met: fallow periods were sufficiently long, returns per person-hour relatively high, and crop assemblages and sequences well adjusted to ensure soil fertility through full regeneration of the forest.

Twenty-five years on, resource budgeting had reached the point at which several modifications to the system had resulted in an overexploitation both of the land resource and of labour time – two resources now also in short supply in grassland villages (Chapter 1).

FOREST CULTIVATION IN TRANSITION: CHIKOTI 1978

By 1978 millet production in Chikoti had declined seriously. This was due to the recession of the forest line, in response to which a new cropping sequence had been introduced (details below), and to the adoption of cassava as a substitute for millet.[4] Two further changes must be added: young women had ceased to be a permanent workforce in the village, while the flow of cash had reached an all-time 'low' for Chikoti's young men, whose aspirations for a migrant career remained unfulfilled. Under such conditions the work-party system could not continue.

There can be little doubt that the forest Mambwe of 1952 practised a type of agriculture which was well adjusted, both to the natural world and to the changing socio-economic environment. Forest cultivation showed 'a quite elastic capacity' (Ellen 1982:40), not only with regard to land-use, but also regarding the allocation of labour-use. Today the scene is different. Population pressure on the land has drastically increased (through reduced migration, village regroupment, settlement along major roads); the forest has vanished from the immediate vicinity of Chikoti; fallow periods have been shortened, while cultivation periods are longer; a first move towards fixed-field cultivation, supervised by agricultural extension workers, has taken place; chemical inputs and hybrid varieties of maize are purchased; and a centre for the promotion of large-scale agriculture has emerged nearby (Kaka). Forest cultivation continues for millet, but at the expense of making time allocations more precarious.

Before I look at allocations of labour-time in Chikoti, I should say a few words about the influence of Kaka. Seen from Chikoti, the Kaka centre for intensified agriculture has become the focal point for earning cash. Kaka is where the poor sell their labour or their (so-called) surplus crops. Although the people of Chikoti had refused to join Kaka when the scheme was launched in the mid-seventies, they nevertheless set aside some of their labour-time for seasonal work on Kaka's farms.

But why did Chikoti refuse to be resettled? Was this refusal a sign of resilience, grounded in fear of drastic change, fear of the presence of an extractive economy perhaps, or did it reflect faith in the old ways? The short and probably the more realistic answer is that re-housing would almost certainly have ended the practice of woodland cultivation. Such a condition - as the following paragraphs illustrate - was difficult to accept. A further reason, equally forceful, was fear of sorcery, i.e. fear that powerful sorcerers (like that rival headman who did join Kaka) would ruin Chikoti's efforts to produce more food.

What state were the gardens in by 1978? To answer this question I shall concentrate on the millet gardens, which (without exception) were still laid out in the forest. Although the distance to the forest was not something Chikoti's people were happy about, they felt it was worth putting up with the long walks.

The main reason for this appeared to be their understanding of how labour requirements in the forest compared with those in grassland gardens. In short, the villagers of Chikoti maintained that ash-planting took care of the problem of weeding and that it reduced the burden of cultivation in general. As they told Watson, so they told me: that 'after the intense activity of tree-cutting and preparing the bed for seed, little work [was] needed in woodland gardens' (1958:26). Also, only millet beer (*cipumu*) tastes like 'real' beer; maize beer (*katata*) is deemed inferior.

The strong preference for the woodland method is well documented in the epic story of Meli (Mary), the young Mambwe girl who came back home at the turn of the century, having spent several years in slave captivity (Wright 1975:812ff; 1984). When Meli's brother, a forest cultivator, joined the returned sister at the Kawimbe mission station (situated in the grasslands) to represent the family, he was, the story has it, 'unable to adjust to the grassland ... method, with its mounding, deep hoeing, and more continuous attention' (*ibid*: 815). Wright is not convinced that the brother's premature departure was entirely due to his inability to adapt to the agricultural method, yet even so, the difference in cultivation techniques was being used by Meli as a suitable idiom for expressing her brother's dissatisfaction (*ibid*: 815). The almost-ex-woodland Mambwe of Chikoti had not changed their point of view by the late seventies, and they seemed reluctant to ever want to do so.

Nevertheless, the phrase 'mounding, deep hoeing, and more continuous attention' points precisely to some of the more profound changes that the system of food production in Chikoti has undergone. The continued interest in ash-planting does not mean that the pattern of cultivation has remained the same. When the current cultivation sequence for main fields (late 1970s) is contrasted with the woodland practice described in *Tribal Cohesion* (early 1950s), one realizes that adaptation, for better or for worse, is indeed very central to understanding swiddening systems under pressure. The contrast is significant from a technical point of view, but equally in view of the claim that swidden systems constantly test the validity of their horticultural rules (Johnson 1980:63; Reining 1970:140-42).[5]

In the fifties the cultivation sequence on a single forest field was as follows. It was customary to grow fingermillet, sometimes intercropped with cassava, in Year 1; groundnuts in Year 2; beans (two harvests) in Year 3; fingermillet again (or cassava) in Year 4. A Mambwe household living in the woodlands would lay out a new *citemene* field every year, just like the Bemba did, so that all the crops in the cycle would be at their disposal simultaneously (see J.Schultz 1976:56). But unlike the Bemba, the forest Mambwe resorted to the practice of making mounds and spreading them from the third year onwards.

The modified system differs in a variety of ways:

a) fingermillet is grown for three consecutive years, and a new citemene garden is not laid out until after the third harvest (which is indicative of the reduced amount of land available for millet cultivation);

b) millet in Year 2 is nowadays sown on mounds;
c) a period of about 16 months now lapses between cutting the new millet garden and harvesting the first millet crop;
d) cultivation of groundnuts and sorghum (the latter is mentioned in *Tribal Cohesion*) has ceased, but beans (now a cash crop) are harvested twice in Year 4;
e) most households now have at least one cassava field crop ready for harvesting, usually in a garden between the forest zone and the village site;
f) green manuring (not ash-planting) is practised in gardens set aside for cassava.

While the above shifts relate to forest (main garden) cultivation only, I also note for the local habitat as a whole, a clear transition away from forest cultivation towards more intensive forms of cropping. For instance, the fixed-field 'collective' plot on which hybrid maize is grown, in the immediate vicinity of the village centre, is managed on a short fallow basis. In 1978 the land cropping cycle for the fixed-field plot was expected to be about four years (according to field-based extension personnel) but the villagers themselves were in no doubt that after the initial 4-year period the plot could still be annually cropped with the help of chemical fertilizers. Also, in between the fixed-field plot and the forest was a broad stretch on which bush vegetation had begun to reappear. This middle zone contained a large number of cassava gardens at different stages of maturation.

The various adaptations must now be assessed with reference to the long-term viability of the village habitat. The broad picture is as follows. Population increase and the higher demand for land have led to a considerable depletion of the forest resource and an increase in the time it takes to walk to the main gardens. Chikoti has begun to experience some real space-time shortages. Its solution to these shortages has been to cut down on growing millet, to more or less abandon cultivation of groundnuts and sorghum, and to substitute cassava. Being less labour-time intensive during cultivation, less demanding in terms of soil quality, and relatively high yielding (but a calorie provider), the introduction of cassava would seem to have offered some advantages for redressing the imbalance developed within the space-time budget.

But new problems have arisen, especially in relation to soil fertility and crop productivity. Adopting cassava and dropping groundnuts/sorghum does make sense, since perennial crops do less harm to the process by which natural growth recovers (Grandstaff 1978:557). Yet regrowth, as Grandstaff has stressed, is also stimulated through ensuring that 'in a second consecutive year,... the second series of crops be of different species than the first' (*ibid*: 557). On this score, the adaptation in Chikoti has been less successful. It is true that the number of new millet gardens cut every year has been reduced (a space-time saver), but the forest gardens now carry millet crops in their first, second and third year of cultivation. The immediate implications of this development are the increased demand on women's labour, since weeding in second and third year millet gardens is very time-consuming, and the reduced importance attached to crop rotation. Less rotation of crops further implies that extra demands are being made on the soil. These extra demands are met through mounding in the second year of cultivation - which, of course, increases labour-time for men and women. Consequently, the time gained by reducing the overall number of millet gardens is lost as a result of increases through the practice of mounding and the higher need for weeding. Mounding in the second year becomes necessary since there is no forest vegetation left to be mulched.

Other space-savers, in the sense that the new operations contribute to maintaining soil fertility, are the intensification of bean cropping in Year 4 and the use of cowdung (*citindi*). The latter has led to some socio-cultural adjustments, since cattle were not kept in the forest zone during the 1950s (details follow). With regard to beans, the increased importance of this crop would appear not to have been detrimental, since the bean plant fixes nitrogen. On the other hand, Carlstein warns that crop rotation schemes with nitrogen fixing plants require expert advice (Carlstein 1982:227) and such advice has to my knowledge not yet been made available by extension agents. When visiting Chikoti, extension agents restrict themselves to the fixed-field plot nearer the village centre, on which commercial maize – the nation's food – is monocropped. As in other parts of Africa, there is here too an urgent need for re-assessing and re-instating the practice of intercropping (see e.g. Pottier 1986c, Richards 1986, Steiner 1984).

A further effort to maintain fertility, and hence crop productivity, is that 16 months now lapse between cutting a new millet garden and harvesting its first crop. The change is of some interest, for villagers explained that the lengthening of the cycle was a response to declining soil fertility and to the now common practice of having shorter fallow periods. The new approach is to make mounds (say, in February 1987); ash-fertilize from June onwards through to September 1987; open up mounds, make flat fields (*impepe*) and sow millet in December or January, in order to harvest in June 1988. Unlike in the fifties, the practice of spreading mounds in main gardens now permeates the whole of the cultivation sequence (with the exception of second-year millet). So, once again, adaptation - in the sense that less land is used for cultivating millet - does not mean that much labour-time is being saved.

Before I assess these adaptations in terms of their labour requirements along gender lines, I should take the opportunity to put the use of cowdung into perspective. As an adaptation to declining supplies of wood for ash-fertilization, the use of cowdung from cattle kraals has begun to prove popular, although it was not yet very general at the time of fieldwork. Cattle manure was only used for fertilizing mounds in cassava fields. Its use, however, had already had significant social consequences. When Chikoti was surrounded by woodland, the villagers did not look after their own cattle. It was common then for 'a Mambwe living in the forest, where there is little pasturage, [to] own cattle herded in a village on the [grassland] plains' (Watson 1958:31). This meant that the 'herding arrangements effectively concealed the actual number in which a man [might] have rights' (*ibid*: 32). By the early 1970s the pattern had changed for Chikoti. With so much of the woodland gone, herding could now be done by the villagers themselves. A kraal was erected, and the people of Chikoti made arrangements for the transfer of their own cattle. These cattle manoeuvres resulted in complicated financial negotiations (e.g. over compensation to be paid to kinsmen who had acquired rights over offspring by virtue of the herding service) and occasionally led to quarrels over unsettled debts or outstanding bridewealth transactions. Local Mambwe courts now frequently deal with such quarrels.[6]

Drastic change in the natural environment has prompted the villagers of Chikoti to abandon a system of herding which only a few decades ago looked fairly entrenched. The use of cowdung, locally perceived as a remedy against the decline in soil fertility, has become a valid reason for 'calling back' the cattle. I suspect, however, that the need for cowdung is by no means the only motivation behind these cattle manoeuvres. The decision to retrieve cattle also points to the increasing popularity of ploughing in fixed-field gardens, an innovation which carries the seal of government approval. The cattle manoeuvres could well be a first real step towards marked social differentiation.

Adjustment to changing conditions also means that tenurial claims are no longer lost after gardens become abandoned. This is new to Mambwe culture and must be accounted for in terms of population pressure, the government's attempt to fix village settlements, and the possibility that long-term migrants may still return.

To argue that swidden agriculture displays considerable adaptability, as is clear from some of the changes discussed, does not mean that every adjustment is in the best interest of everyone. The changes in time-budgeting should make this clear. The increased distance at which the millet gardens are now situated has been noted, and cattle care, I add, will be time-consuming. The number of hours spent in the gardens has also gone up: hoeing and mounding demand extra labour input from both women and men, while the time needed for weeding (still almost exclusively a woman's task) is on the increase too. More weeding is required to eliminate competition from non-cultigens, especially in second- and third-year millet gardens. Although it is a general characteristic of medium-intensity cultivation systems that they require more careful weeding than long-fallow systems do (Carlstein 1982:189), the extra demand falls disproportionately on Mambwe women.

Before reaching conclusions, it is useful to be precise about where exactly labour-input has been reduced and where it has increased. I note reductions because of the smaller number of fields on which millet is grown, and because groundnuts and sorghum have virtually disappeared as field crops. At the same time there are increases because of a) the extra walking time, b) the greater emphasis on mounding, c) substantial weeding in millet fields that produce for the second or third year running, and d) cattle care. Given the absence of figures about the increase, in terms of hours spent, it might be safe to argue that increases do not necessarily outweigh reductions, and that we are therefore still dealing with a well-adapted, viable system. However 'safe' the position, such a view underrates the total impact of the transformation. There are three comments to be made:

First, the quality of the diet has suffered: while calorie intake is almost certainly adequate, protein levels have dropped. Beans, I repeat, are sold and not much consumed outside harvest times.

Secondly, even should the demands on labour have increased only minimally (which I doubt), it is very clear that labour resources are no longer spread evenly throughout the village. The collapse of the work-party system implies that not every family can secure regular access to sufficient labour-power.

Thirdly, and returning to Grandstaff's warning, I need to consider ways of generating income and assess whether they are 'appropriate to the nature and timing of ... labour activities, so that the system viability is not lost through conflict between the two' (quoted earlier on). System viability in Chikoti looks much less guaranteed when income-generating activities are taken into account. I shall now elaborate this point.

Kaka offers casual, seasonal employment to many women and men in Chikoti. Most men and women who go out to work on Kaka farms are struggling to reverse a reduction in cash flows (migrant remittances having dried up; declining importance of kitchen gardens). The important point is that such casual labourers cannot really afford not to work for wages. For instance, Chikoti women who need cash have little choice but to sell their labour in Kaka. A greater involvement in petty trading (common in the grassland area) is not a lucrative enterprise in the Kaka/Chikoti area, since it is too far removed from the markets of Mbala, Mpulungu and from the Tanzanian border. Working in Kaka, for wages, increases women's time expenditure considerably.

I am not implying that only women go out to work in Kaka, since the trend is for both women and men to work on the farms, in greater numbers and for longer periods of time. What I am arguing is that the need to raise cash through casual wage work is much greater for women than it is for men, since the nationwide promotion of hybrid maize has been accompanied by the 'belief', spread and wholeheartedly supported by men, that 'state-controlled surplus maize' equals 'male-controlled surplus'.[7] On the other hand, and this too is important, a man's income from maize cropping is often delayed through bureaucracy and is almost never sufficient to cover all his cash needs. So, men too are increasingly dependent on selling their labour. One aspect of the problem of ensuring system viability for Chikoti is that this whole village risks being turned into a cheap reserve labour force recruited for Project Kaka. Critics might point out, of course, that there isn't anything unusual here, because the Mambwe are reputed to be a reserve labour force that manages all right. This would be too glib a comment, since the 'reserve' situation in the fifties did not preclude the Mambwe village from being self-sufficient in terms of its food production capacity.

By way of a conclusion, I now return to the main question set at the beginning of this chapter: does the Mambwe evidence show shifting cultivation to be well or poorly adapted to the cultural and political aspirations of the independent state? The test here is the local response to the government call for nationwide food security. I am afraid that the evidence, on balance, reveals a precarious response for woodland villagers. Without wishing to underestimate the problems which even successful farmers in Kaka face (for the Mambwe area remains highly peripheral to the national economy), it is becoming very clear that the gradual disappearance of the forest is forcing 'traditional' cultivators to look in new directions that hold very little promise. Some of the adaptations discussed above point to resilience as well as to a remarkable degree of 'elasticity' - both in the cultural and in the physical sense; yet time for reaching a long-term viable adaptation is surely running out.

I should like to pursue this point about the exhaustion of time by highlighting the importance of timing with regard to the adaptations discussed in this chapter. In particular, I should like to argue that the problem of timetabling in food-crop production is going to become more and more crucial in the future development and transformation of agrarian societies, and of central importance to our understanding of the processes involved.

Calling in the cattle, after so many decades of hidden wealth (or better perhaps, security) has suddenly brought into the open that from now on some in Chikoti may be 'more equal' than others. Of course, it will take time before the differences in cattle ownership will be translated - via the system of intensified agriculture - into more permanent differences of status and wealth. The villagers need not and do not worry about this. What is more worrying to them is the prospect of having to sell their labour for petty cash and food, while at the same time seeing the family fields in need of attention that cannot be given. The most telling illustration perhaps, which I have yet to mention, is the practice of early digging in fields that carry family-food crops. While this practice releases household labour for paid employment elsewhere, it also increases the amount of weeding that will need to be done later in the season. Once again, the consequences fall heavily on women. So long as rural wage labour (i.e. the quest for national food security) does not interfere with the food security which the Mambwe village once enjoyed (Watson 1958: 34), so long the people of Mambwe country will be able to retain some of their autonomy. And they have for a long time now expressed their keen sense of independence: in fending off Bemba raids[8]; in opposing the colonial administration; and even in terms of gender ideology there is evidence from the fifties that some form of respect for mutual financial autonomy existed.

Today the future looks bleak, as hybrid cultivation, which requires rigorous timing, is spreading in spite of the erratic distribution of inputs. Since many poor families cannot afford not to work for wages, it is increasingly common for them to have to bring forward or delay important tasks that need doing in the main gardens or on the fixed-field plots. As far as the latter are concerned, ill-timed farming, as is well known, can seriously reduce output, for hybrid varieties are highly susceptible to bad timing. I believe that developments related to timing are likely to accelerate the rate at which shifting cultivators in transition become dependent, for cash and ultimately for food, on those who have successfully broken away from small-scale farming.[9]

The outcome of this process cannot, however, be predicted with any great certainty. At present it is the poorer women and men of Chikoti village who go to work in Kaka, but will this continue? Should Kaka become self-sufficient in terms of its labour requirements (as has already happened, e.g. on Mazabuka farms – Wright 1983), then the poorer women and the poorer households of Chikoti will have to obtain their cash either from trading (which is unlikely) or from selling labour within Chikoti itself (more likely, if, for example, extensive ox-ploughing catches on). In either case, such families will find it difficult to remain self-sufficient and will find it very difficult to observe rational time-tabling. In the fifties some women worked for food; by the late seventies a whole stratum of poorer households was struggling to maintain self-sufficiency.

Thirty years ago Watson noted a genuine, local awareness of the importance of timing with regard to millet cultivation (Watson 1958:26). Today it is very doubtful whether Mambwe cultivators from forest-depleted areas will be able to go on demonstrating their awareness for much longer.

CHAPTER NINE
SETTLEMENT AND SURVIVAL: CONCLUSIONS

The Mambwe economy is coming to terms with a deteriorating physical resource base and with an ailing national distribution sector. Its capacity for overcoming these constraints must now be considered. I propose to do this by going back to a question posed in the introductory chapter: can the deployment of local organizational resources become an effective strategy for long-term survival?

In spite of the emerging antagonisms which Cliffe (1978) discerned in Watson's data, my own observations tell me that such antagonisms are still emerging, that differential treatment has not yet led to class consciousness or class conflict, and that potential conflict situations fail to ignite because there are loopholes left to be explored by those who are disadvantaged by sex or social status. Thus, although it is reasonable to view intensified petty trading on the Northern Plateau as an expression of growing rural impoverishment, it is equally reasonable to regard it as proof that the poor can organize themselves with efficiency and (sometimes) with substantial benefits. Context is paramount in dealing with this issue; there are no 'universal' truths. In some instances where poor peasants sell their labour, as in Chele (Chapter 6) and Chikoti (Chapter 8), there simply is no alternative. In other cases, for example in Chivunzila (Chapter 7), and quite often in relation to so-called 'gender antagonisms', I have found evidence that strategies do exist through which the disadvantaged can 'fight back'; not always with success, but not inevitably ending in defeat.

I have described one such a strategy in the context of cross-border trade. The intricate ins and outs of the networks involved in cross-border transactions reveal how such activities may help redress situations of overt inequality and exploitation. This perspective was impressed upon me when I solicited an exchange of views on the nature of labour exploitation within the setting of model village Chele. I must stress, of course, that ways of coping with inequality and hardship are highly localized and that some of the exploited groups or individuals are better placed than others in the pursuit of their just rewards. Kaka, for instance, in contrast with Chele, exhibited a social dichotomy in which the taxation of female labour power was less pronounced; but its dependent peasant households could not make use of the trade loopholes that presented themselves to men and women in border villages.

Village conditions vary a great deal in Mambwe land. We should therefore guard against generalizations or the use of blanket terms. The need to drop the term 'tribal cohesion', for instance, has already been the subject of much debate, some of which referred directly to Watson's monograph. Cliffe (1978) and Murray (1980) have both argued, in the words of Murray, that 'it is unrealistic to impute to a given population such uniformity of response as is implied in the notion of "tribal cohesion"' (Murray 1980: 141). Both comment on Watson's Mambwe study and remark that the term 'tribal cohesion' masks a complex variety of social processes. Yet there is a level of analysis where wider processes and local circumstances intersect. Murray illustrates this in his comments on conservation and change within the structure of 'the family'. In his work on changing family structures in Lesotho and Botswana, he identified two processes of 'family' constitution: one a replication of alignments in terms of the prevailing agnatic idiom; the other a process of dissolution through the rapid turnover in household membership (Murray 1980: 147). Dissolution was rooted in the economy of migrant labour. Identification of these social processes led Murray to suggest that they transcend ethnic and cultural boundaries, even though their impact varied between particular communities.

Part of my argument in this book has developed in the same vein. In spite of intervening local factors, I too have concluded that exploitation of labour, along lines of household differentiation or gender or both, has become a recurrent feature of the entire Mambwe economy. Most participant observers would hold this to be an objective fact, and I would endorse their view. Moreover, the category of 'poor villagers' has expanded, for it is clear that the number of people who now need to sell their labour in order to meet their most basic needs has grown. I repeat that such differentiation has not yet culminated in class conflict or class consciousness, but the line of demarcation that separates the resource-poor is much firmer now than it was in the 1950s.

THE TRANSFORMED LABOUR RESERVE: IS GENERALIZATION POSSIBLE?

Life in Mambwe villages today can be suitably understood within the framework of a political economy of migrant labour. The long history of Mambwe involvement in wage migration is the ultimate wider reference for understanding the more important aspects of village life. Current patterns of residence, gender relations and the division of labour have all been influenced by the migrant economy. Migration from Mambwe land has now come to a halt, but it has been replaced by an equally hazardous and potentially short-lived development, which is the regional involvement in commercial cropping and trade. The transition towards an extractive economy confirms the analytical advantage of viewing migrant labour as but one particular manifestation of the spread of capitalist relations of production.

Against this broad canvass the observer is aware that the impact of macro-level forces is mitigated by local circumstances. The data collected during my restudy of the Mambwe economy convey the diversity of social configurations. If they can help it, local actors are never passive onlookers. Today, as in the fifties, life in Mambwe villages can only be grasped in terms of how Mambwe cultural ideology interacts with dimensions of national planning and core-periphery politics. I may have rejected the broad 'tribal' framework, fashionable in the 1950s, but Watson's insistence that local production processes and cultures interact with 'the money economy' still proves valuable. Looking back, the interactions have led to some uniform changes, particularly in respect of settlement policy, village membership, and land management. At the same time, the Mambwe economy also testifies to the existence of multiple local responses. Local responses to externally imposed constraints can be found for the region as a whole and at the level of individual villages. I shall deal with village-specific responses first.

Long-term immersion in the field enables the anthropologist to challenge the assumption of uniformity of response – an assumption often made by radical theorists of dependency or in centralist perspectives on policy implementation (Long 1977). In the preceding chapters I hope to have done justice to this view. The villages where I researched were all unique in some respects. Kowa, for example, the one village where men still had a foot in the local wage-labour market, had developed into a production unit in which the waged contracted the un-waged during peak labour periods in agriculture. In most other villages the distinction between waged and un-waged was replaced by the opposition between emergent farmers and peasant producers. However, I noted further internal differences. Emergent farmers in Kaka contracted labourers from within and from outside the village, whereas contract labour in Kowa and Chele was recruited from within. Furthermore, peasants and emergent farmers in Kaka had developed diadic ties of dependency similar to those in Chele and Kowa, but theirs did not have the kinship overtones found in the two other villages. Another difference related to trading. Kaka's peasants worked in a strongly encapsulated economy and could not participate in local food trading on a scale matching the involvement of border villages like Chele and Chivunzila. Kowa and Chele, in turn, differed from one another in that labour relations in Chele had become more institutionalized, and because many resource-poor households in Chele were encouraged to grow hybrid maize.

Among the broader developments, it is the impact of the cash economy on land and labour which has been most uniform throughout the area. Land has become a relatively scarce resource, and is now being 'mined' to the point where a process of irreversible soil degradation may have set in. The demands made on labour power are also being stretched. In the fifties the overburdening of poor people's labour power was mainly along gender lines. This process has now developed in such a way that the extra demands cut across gender and affect households headed by both men and women. Even when I allow for the existence of location-specific loopholes that enable households to organize themselves, to create space for themselves (Long 1984), I must still face up to the possibility that Godfrey Wilson's reservations about the soundness of the migrant system were not too exaggerated after all (Wilson 1941/2). Wilson held that outmigration from villages was invariably devastating for the rural economy. His approach may have been unsophisticated, in that it was deterministic in the extreme, yet some aspects of the gloomy forecast are now visible throughout Zambia – even in a so-called 'patrilineal' rural economy.

Ways of coping with declining cash flows and pressure on land and labour do not necessarily result from village-level idiosyncracies. One coping mechanism in particular has asserted itself on a regional basis. This regional response relates to the structural changes I have recorded in respect of the residential make-up of Mambwe villages. To account for the changes we need to concentrate again on how local conditions interact with developments within the country as a whole. Flexible arrangements existed already in the fifties; today the Mambwe village exhibits an even greater structural flexibility. The longitudinal analyses of Kowa (Chapter 4) and Chivunzila (Chapter 7), for instance, indicate how core groups that Watson presumed 'perpetual' can be displaced, how links with the core group have become less dominant, and how clusters of agnatically related women can now be found in many village situations. The latter change is significant and deserves to be explained.

The insecurity which follows divorce for a Mambwe woman has now forced many women - especially women who returned from the urban centres - to go and live in villages where they have male kin. In the 1960s, when 'spontaneous' population movement became permitted, many Mambwe women left for the towns. It was then feasible to think of the towns as places where one could settle permanently. The prospect was short-lived. From the early 1970s onwards life in the towns became increasingly difficult (Chapter 3). One result was that many Mambwe women returned home when their marriages terminated. Returning women, as I have shown for Chivunzila, did not all return from urban centres. Many came back from Mambwe or Lungu villages, sometimes situated across the border, where they had lived with their husbands' kin. The high incidence of return migration for women contrasts with the record of return migration for men (Chapter 4). By the late 1970s the attachment of such women to villages where they had male kin had begun to make its mark. Clusters of agnatically related women had appeared. The capacity of the Mambwe village to incorporate returning women is one of the more notable features of its structure today. However, these women find themselves in a paradoxical situation: while they are welcomed as additions to the labour force, their presence is also frowned upon because it increases the pressure on the land even further.

But a more optimistic view on the emergence of clusters of agnatically related women is also possible. Given the need for agricultural labour and the fact that small-scale food trading has become an important way of carrying on in the cash economy, it is feasible to see the new pattern of residence as a positive response towards the constraints affecting the Mambwe economy. The view, attractive in my opinion, has consequences for the debate on the organizational capacity of lineage-based societies. Anthropologists today may be disinclined to continue Watson's argument about the superior organizational capacity of patrilineal cultures, yet the debate itself has been reopened in discussion of Africa's current food crisis.

MATRILINY VERSUS PATRILINY: THE DEBATE CONTINUES

It would be erroneous to think that the debate on the merits and disadvantages of matrilineal and patrilineal cultures came to an end with the publication of Van Velsen's Tonga material (esp. Van Velsen 1960), with Douglas's paper 'Is the matriliny doomed?' (Douglas 1969) or with Needham's warning that paradigms of descent systems are conventional but unrealistic (Needham 1975: 351). The names of Van Velsen and Watson are twinned in the literature on the rural impact of outmigration, but discussion of the link between survival strategies and lineage mode is by no means confined to migration studies. Related fields of inquiry, such as the study of food production and consumption, are also concerned with the meaning of lineage organization.

Survival in Mambwe country today is very much a question of whether and how poorer households control their food supply, and of whether access to regular cash can be ensured. The answers, as I have indicated several times, are not encouraging. For instance, acute shortages of cash and of basic food commodities (sugar, salt, cooking oil) have already forced many poor households into dependent positions. A poor household's food supply is no longer invariably or entirely grown on the family farm: part of the supply may be derived from trading, just as it may be derived from selling labour. The *local* capacity for food sufficiency, so effective in the fifties, has become seriously impaired. Seasonal hunger, virtually unknown at the time of Watson's observations, now affects a large proportion of poorer households. Even in Chele, where the aggregate food production record is sufficient to feed the entire village throughout the year, I have found that many of the poorer - yet productive (!) - households go hungry in the months preceding the millet harvest (Chapter 6). The problem is compounded by the newly emerged ambiguities that affect the status of certain food crops. These ambiguities are epitomised in the practice of selling high-value foodstuffs (millet, beans) and substituting low-value foods, such as cassava or sweet potatoes.

It is in relation to poor women's control over household food supplies that the patriliny-matriliny debate has been revived. Although the matriliny-patriliny dichotomy was once thought to be basically flawed (Guyer 1981: 88), there seems to be sufficient evidence now to suggest that matrilineal organization may have certain advantages for women. Case material is available to confirm this view. For example, access to produce, as conceived by the matrilineal Cewa of Malawi is fairly straightforward: '*Dimba* [riverside] gardens are women's gardens, and the proceeds of sales of *dimba* produce usually accrue to them' (Hirschmann and Vaughan 1983: 94). Cewa women also have a great deal of control over the disposal of non-*dimba* foods (*ibid*: 93). Another example is from West Africa, where Senufo women take advantage of their matrilineal kinship system to ensure life-long rights in land and the freedom to earn their own incomes from commercial crops raised on personal fields (Guyer 1984). Senufo men, in contrast, grow staple crops and take responsibility for meeting the day-to-day subsistence needs. Poewe too, writing about the Zambian Luapula, argues that women reap considerable advantages from matriliny, for example, in their ability to control land. She adds that 'matrilineal inheritance provides security and holds out to the poor the hope that they may at any time improve their material well-being' (Poewe 1978: 304).

If Audrey Richards failed to present an optimistic picture for the (matrilineal) Bemba economy, it was probably because she worked among the Bemba in the days of the Great Depression. Watson, on the other hand, studied Mambwe organization at a time when the Zambian and the world economy boomed, and he was struck by the positive response of the Mambwe. As a result, Watson equated rural hardship (the Bemba case) with residential instability for men (prescribed by matrilineality). On the basis of my own fieldwork, I find this thesis ill-founded. The contrast on which Watson dwelled, I contend, had more to do with wider economic forces than with local cultural ideology and social organization. When survival is at stake, networks 'organized round a core of women' (Watson 1958: 227) can prove very effective indeed. One of the surprises fieldwork had in store for me was precisely the efficacious organization of border village Chivunzila, where several 'cores' of agnatically related women had emerged. The cores, or clusters as I have called them, ensured a comparatively adequate supply of food and cash in the face of falling production levels. Although the incidence of virilocal residence for women and uxorilocal residence for men (young men) is still developing in Mambwe villages, the emergence of groups of agnatically-related female residents means that Mambwe villages are now beginning to resemble situations where matrilocal residence prevails. Of course, Mambwe women do not control land, but their presence has greatly enhanced the potential for organizing the deployment of labour and trading skills. Moreover, as the data on cross-border transactions show, the women-centred clusters involved in this trade are able to exert control over the cash flows that accrue to the trade.

Brabin (1984) suggests that the practice of matrilocal (uxorilocal) residence facilitates a more equitable distribution of available food supplies, 'by giving women more control over food resources' (Brabin 1984: 33). This is especially so where uxorilocal residence combines with low-level polygyny. Although she qualifies her approach, Brabin would seem to endorse the view shared by Hirschmann, Vaughan, Poewe, Douglas, and Guyer, notably, that women in matrilineal societies enjoy a comparatively higher degree of security of tenure and have (comparatively) more say in controlling the overall supply of food. Douglas made the point long before it attracted its present interest: 'It is for ... low-yield agricultural economies that certain advantages are written into the constitution of a matrilineal descent system' (Douglas 1969: 130).

However, Mambwe history suggests that there have been swings from brideservice to bridewealth (during colonialism) and back to brideservice, at least in some instances I recorded. This revival of brideservice, which is by and large related to scarcities of good quality land and/or labour, might be read as an adjustment in the exertion of patriarchal power. Such swings expose the weakness, indeed futility, of continuing the debate on Africa's food crisis in terms of the matriliny-patriliny dichotomy. Brideservice and uxorilocal residence, as the Mambwe evidence shows, are not exclusive to matrilineal organization; their re-occurrence in Mambwe villages during the late 1970s, therefore, force me to go back to a well-known reservation about anthropological paradigms of descent. In particular, Needham's argument that taxonomic concepts, such as 'matriliny' and 'patriliny', are insufficiently discriminative must once again be brought to attention (Needham 1975: 351). Quasi-technical terms like 'matrilineal' and 'patrilineal' denote polythetic classes of social facts (*ibid*: 365) and do not demand the presence of any specific feature. The observed swings in 'acceptable' patterns of residence for rural Mambwe corroborate Needham's point about the shortcomings of working with such a dichotomy. I cannot comment, on the basis of my fieldwork, on the usefulness of the concept 'matrilineality', but 'patrilineality' has most certainly a limited role to play in the local design of survival strategies.

SETTLEMENT FOR SURVIVAL?

In spite of the limited function that patrilineality has for action beyond the sphere of inheritance, recent debate on the organization of food systems suggests that structural features at the level of lineage organization, where they concern cultures conventionally labelled as matrilineal, are still useful for understanding survival. The practice of uxorilocal residence in Mambwe villages must not, therefore, be thought of as merely a 'passive' response to changing circumstances (divorce; shortages of land or labour or bridewealth-cash), it may also be the beginning of an 'active' strategy that might enable Mambwe villagers to go on exploring the money economy. Given the great need for enhanced cooperation, in trade as well as in agriculture, it appears logical to expect that the increasing incidence of agnatically related women will boost the survival chances of the (patrilineal!) Mambwe village. Women-centred agnatic clusters, as I have shown in the Sikambula case study (Chapter 7), are assets that enable clan segments or villages to make the most of trading. Such clusters, I have also argued, are a positive answer to the breakdown of 'traditional' work-party cooperation. From those two points of view, the changing face of the Mambwe village must be conducive to survival.

This is the theory. Whether the adaptation will work in the long-run still needs to be seen, for some disturbing evidence about conditions on the Tanzanian side of the border has now become available. From the evidence, presented below, I deduce that survival today is likely to depend not so much on the organizational responses to trading as on whether protective measures can still be taken to ensure that the process of soil depletion is reversed. Since 'horizontal' organizational resources (across the border with 'foreign' nationals; within Zambia with people of a different religious ideology) are activated in a setting of severe soil depletion and fast falling production levels, cross-border traders may soon find themselves in a frustrating *cul-de-sac*. The uncertainties surrounding the natural resource base make it improper that I would defend the Mambwe self-help system as it existed in the grasslands during the late 1970s. The ecological situation poses far too serious a threat to the prospect of long-term survival. I do accept the villagers' viewpoint that intensified food trading and cooperation with long-distance entrepreneurs (Watch Tower and/or other private traders) is the best short-term strategy under the circumstances (marked by the absence of migrant remittances and widespread parastatal inefficiency), but I think the overstretching of the natural resource base too great a price to pay.

The Mambwe self-help programme for economic survival, which I observed during crisis years, may indeed be at the end of its lifespan. The end is foreshadowed in recent developments on the Tanzanian side of the border, which I must now consider.

FUTURE OF THE MAMBWE ECONOMY

The economy of South Rukwa has also been researched from the Tanzanian end, independently of my own work. In fact it was not until 1983 that the research undertaken by Wright on the agrarian history of South Rukwa, and by Bury on the human ecology of Fipa villages, came to my attention. What we observed independently reinforces the notion of a long history of periodic food flows towards deficit areas. Our respective investigations also establish that women play a central role whenever organizational networks are activated. On the theme of coping with food shortages, Wright wrote in her 'Sketch for a Paper on the History of the Border Zone':

> Over centuries, there were movements of people from deficit to surplus areas and a need for the receiving community to support the destitute. Marriage connections were important among the bases on which to seek hospitality and render service. In reviewing marriage custom in the region, it becomes plain that it served to maximize claims along maternal and paternal lines and that both the husband and wife retained their rights to invoke relationships in their respective families for the sake of their own and their husband/wife's well-being. So women conveyed and could exercise a number of choices (Wright 1985: 2).

The emphasis on historical continuity is important, but must not divert attention away from equally important processes of dramatic change. I have already mentioned some such processes in the context of Mambwe food production: soil erosion, declining yields for (protein-rich) millet, substitution of nutritionally inferior staples, and a large-scale syphoning of (protein-rich) beans towards towns along the Zambian Line of Rail. These processes are bound to have an adverse affect on the future evolution of household-level coping strategies. The organizational structures that evened out food supplies in the past, and still did so in the late 1970s, will cease to operate if current threats to the natural resource base continue unchecked.

Likely to have an immediate effect on the economy of South Rukwa is the very significant, recent shift in Tanzania's agricultural policy. I have occasionally suggested that the 1978 millet flows into Zambia could dry up at some point in the near future, perhaps as a result of tighter border controls (e.g. Pottier 1983a). At other times I have felt uneasy about such negative predictions, because, as many Mambwe elders told me, such imports have been going on for as long as they could remember. The point I now wish to make is that a long history does not guarantee that food imports will continue.

In their own view of the situation, the Mambwe villagers I worked amongst believed that their import strategy had a secure base. They took the seemingly unlimited supply of Tanzanian millet for granted. As an outsider, however, I often wondered about the contradiction between the large scale of those millet imports and the knowledge that Tanzanian agriculture was going through a bad patch. Fieldwork by Bury has since brought to light that the millet imports I witnessed in 1978 were indeed artificially sustained. Bury provides the key to a better understanding of the millet flows into Zambia, by informing that the

> 1974/75 ... [Tanzanian] price hikes ... resulted in a proportionally higher price for fingermillet, at 2 [shillings] (per kilogram), favoring fingermillet production (1983: 272)

By 1980 the price hikes had created 'a vibrant fingermillet black market' for which Rukwa had become a major provider (1983: 272, 273). It was from that vibrant economy that the Zambian Mambwe satisfied many of their dietary needs in the crisis period of the late 1970s. By 1981/82, however, there was reason to doubt whether the Tanzanian side of the Plateau - where people were having to cope with increasing population pressure, *eleusine indica* weeds, and increasing periods of drought - could go on being a provider of millet for much longer. In 1981/82 the pricing incentive to grow millet fell away. As Bury writes:

The 1981/82 producer prices announced a fifty cent drop in the price of fingermillet ... a grain that had always enjoyed a higher demand and a higher price than maize. (1983: 271)

Figures to illustrate the effect on production are not available, but Bury states categorically that the new pricing policy was strongly felt in Tanzania's major millet-producing regions. The once vibrant black market in fingermillet was seriously affected, and the risk of a substantial reduction in the availability of millet for export within Tanzania and towards Zambia became much more of a possibility. How much the Zambian Mambwe have been affected by the reduction remains guesswork, but it is most unlikely that the 1977/1978 levels of importation could have been maintained.

In view of the already low levels of millet production in many Zambian Mambwe villages (Chapter 2), and the unsuitability of hybrid maize, many producers must now be concerned about production trends across the border. The 'traditional' millet imports on which (grassland) villagers periodically rely must be slumping (or more expensive), and there are no signs that the trend will reverse to 'normal' over the next decade or so. If nothing is done in Zambian Mambwe villages to enhance food sufficiency and stimulate production in a manner which reverses the process of environmental degradation, then, we will very soon have to admit, perhaps for the whole of South Rukwa, that there isn't much left to be exchanged! Urgently needed is a programme for re-instating intercropping systems, in an attempt to restore soil fertility and intensify production under conditions of decreasing land availability. Current practices in the grasslands (Chapter 6) and the woodlands (Chapter 8) have become too simplified for an effective maintenance of the structure of the soil. Research on the intensification of millet-based cropping systems is already well under way in other parts of Africa (Steiner 1984). Similar programmes are needed for re-instating and improving such practices in the Mambwe economy.

Scott, looking back to life before the drought, has written about the Sahel: 'Over time, [the people of this region] lost entitlement to food, especially through an inability to produce it and to purchase it' (Scott 1984: 16). The Zambian Mambwe are running a similar risk. By the late 1970s they too were rapidly losing the ability to produce, but they were still doing everything possible to acquire additional food. For some this meant selling their labour; for others it meant exploiting riverside gardens; for others still it meant trading and making full use of organizational resources. Developments within the structure and organization of the Mambwe village facilitated the transition. The emphasis at the time of fieldwork was on organization-through-trading rather than production *per se*. The 1990s will be a time when the ability to import and purchase essential foods will be put to serious testing.

Under conditions of falling productivity and decreased opportunities for importation, peasant households may soon find that they have lost the ability 'to fight back' in the manner to which they have become accustomed. The no-win position, the 'catch 22', is all too clear. Introducing hybrid maize solves a labour problem but harms the soil; maize cropping does not pay well, yet the harsh environment demands that households diversify food production; bean cropping yields precious cash, but does not replace the proteins lost by the displacement of millet and the selling of beans; many villages have become structurally better equipped to play a more active role in food trading, yet the food flows themselves are now at risk. Decision-making and ecological processes have developed in such a way that observers cannot justify sitting back to marvel at the ingenuity of horizontal relationships or interface manipulation. Social networks remain a viable and crucial resource, but the exhausted soil needs attention now.

The Mambwe data are also relevant for the debate on food production priorities. Commentators on the food crisis in Africa sometimes assume that poorer families give priority to food crops when cash and food crops compete for labour (e.g. Marter and Honeybone 1976: 67; McLoughlin 1970: 8). I have no faith in such categoric statements. Whether or not family crops take precedence over cash crops is more likely to depend on the availability or absence of alternative sources for generating income and on whether such sources can be spread through the agricultural calendar.

A NOTE ON PRIORITIES FOR FUTURE RESEARCH

There is a notable increase in the number of references to the ambiguous status of staples. Ambiguity, in this case, means that certain staples are now considered to be both a food crop and a cash crop. Wright's discussion of the ambiguous status of maize (Wright 1983) applies to Zambia as a whole, but other food items too have become affected by status ambiguity. The maintenance of adequate supplies of millet, I learned in Chele, is valued by the poor – not as a food crop but as a partly commercialized crop. For North-Western Province, Hedlund (1984: 229) adds further 'ambiguous' food items to the list: game and honey (men's produce), mushrooms and berries (women's produce). All of these are either eaten or sold. In Mambwe country too, some periodic foods (mushrooms, caterpillars, fish) must now be considered ambiguous.

What has yet to emerge in the literature on Zambia, and must be given priority in future research, is an assessment of the scale on which the noted 'ambiguities' apply. The central issue for research can be stated in the form of a question: Is the ambiguous status of food items an advantage which allows a choice between consumption and sale, as Hedlund suggests (1984: 229) or is it a development which will have disastrous consequences for the health of the rural poor, as I have argued for Chele? It may be premature to want to answer the question, not least because of the great need for cash, which makes evaluations difficult. But the question must be asked. Stromgaard, for instance, recently presented for the Bemba a long list of nutritious food items, implying that a balanced diet was achieved (Stromgaard 1985: 52-57). He did not, however, consider the status of these foodstuffs. All future research on labour and diet must address the full implications that arise from the ambiguous status of foodstuffs essential to the diet.

A related concern is the effect bad timing has upon the maturation of hybrid crops. Research in rural Zambia has already exposed the increased labour demands that come with hybrid cropping, especially in the context of settlement projects (e.g. Cowie 1979: 65-66; Hedlund and Lundahl 1983: 87), yet future researchers will need to pay more attention to the intimate link between timing and yields, and especially in the case of peasant households that produce hybrids.

APPENDIXES

APPENDIX 1   Genealogical Modification to the Kowa Lineage

Watson's genealogy of Kowa village contains an interesting inaccuracy. Below is a copy of the relevant section.

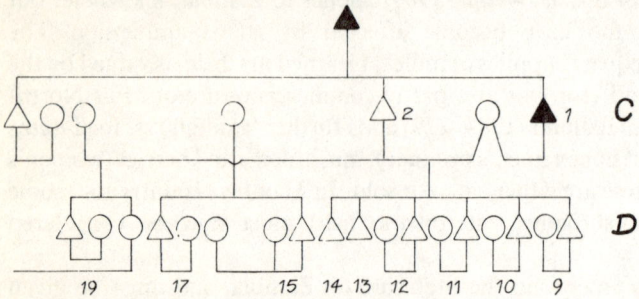

Diagram 10: Succession in Kowa (from *Tribal Cohesion*).

My criticism concerns Amos Kowa (D9). Chief Amos Kowa, who headed the village during my own fieldwork, is not a real brother to D10-D14. The six men have the same mother – Chenda Sumbukeni (C1), daughter of Nsokolo – but Amos's father was the pre-predecessor to Chief Kasimba (C2), acting chief during Watson's fieldwork. Kasimba died in 1962.

Sumbukeni was not only inherited by Kasimba, but also by his predecessor, Chief Chimutwe (C1). This gives us the following picture:

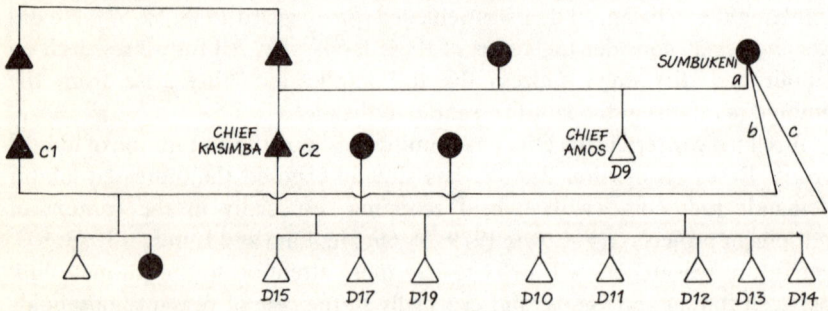

Diagram 11: Succession in Kowa (my evidence).

The end result is that Kasimba Kowa, chief in the 1950s, inherited a spouse who had once been his father's second wife. At first I found the picture too spectacular to be true, even though one man (Sitbet David, D10) had given me the evidence exactly as presented in diagram 11.

I spent considerable time cross-checking the genealogical position of Chief Amos, mainly through interviews with Kosam (D15), Jason (D17) and Lamek (D19). None of these three men, two of whom are a lot older than Amos (!), included the present chief amongst their brothers or half-brothers.

Nor is Chief Amos a son of Chief David (C1), Kasimba's predecessor. Chief David's children, Julius and Silika, are omitted from Watson's genealogy – presumably because they spent their childhood in Chele village. Kosam (D15), Jason (D17) and Lamek (D19) all agreed that Chief David had only those two children with Sumbukeni.

APPENDIX 2 Further evidence concerning out-migration

The following information shows the residential position of all brothers and sons (over 18) of adult men who lived in villages for which I constructed genealogies. The figures relate to residence outside Mbala district.

Mambwe Villages	Residential position of brothers and sons (over 18) residing outside Mbala District	
I. Kowa area	in Lusaka	: 43 (incl. 4 students)
	on Copperbelt	: 31 (incl. 4 students)
	other towns	: 37 (incl. 13 students)
II. Kasunga	in Lusaka	: 12 (incl. 1 student)
	on Copperbelt	: 17 (incl. 1 student)
	other towns	: 10 (no students)
Chivunzila	in Lusaka	: 15 (no students)
	on Copperbelt	: 5 (no students)
	other towns	: 5 (no students)
III. Chikoti	in Lusaka	: 1 (no students)
	on Copperbelt	: 3 (no students)
	other towns	: 7 (incl. 4 farm workers)
Kaka	in Lusaka	: 5 (no students)
	on Copperbelt	: 10 (no students)
	other towns	: 11 (incl. 3 students)
IV. Masaiti/Mbala	in Lusaka	: 15 (incl. 1 student)
	on Copperbelt	: 19 (no students)
	other towns	: 17 (incl. 5 students)
TOTALS	in Lusaka	: 91
	on Copperbelt	: 85
	other towns	: 89 (*)

Note (*): this figure includes 13 people who live in Tanzanian towns.

I also gathered information on job selection for absent men. Of interest here are the high number of migrants employed as either carpenters or bricklayers (21 out of 71 known cases, in Lusaka), the general variety in work orientation, the low number in 'business' and the disengagement from mining, which contrasts with the concentration of Mambwe in Mufulira in the 1920s (Watson 1958: 196).

Lusaka (91)	students	: 6	clerks	: 10	unemployed	: 4
	carpenters	: 7	security	: 8	unknown	: 20
	bricklayers	: 14	factory w.	: 14		
	drivers	: 7	businessmen	: 1		
Copperbelt (85)	students	: 5	clerks	: 8	unemployed	: 3
	carpenters	: 3	security	: 6	unknown	: 11
	bricklayers	: 7	factory w.	: 8		
	drivers	: 7	businessmen	: 2		
	mining	: 16	marketeers	: 6		
	farmers	: 1	cooks	: 1		
	electrician	: 1				
Other Zambian Town (excl. Mbala) (76)	students	: 21	clerks	: 13	unemployed	: 1
	carpenters	: 1	security	: 8	unknown	: 3
	bricklayers	: 2	factory w.	: 10		
	drivers	: 1	businessmen	: 4		
	farmers	: 8	barmen	: 3		
	electrician	: 1				
Tanzania (13)	game ranger	: 1	sisal w.	: 1	unknown	: 9
	clerk	: 1	retired miner	: 1		

Table 11: Migrant destination and job selection outside Mbala district (total sample: 265 male migrant workers).

NOTES

CHAPTER TWO

1   Zambia's agricultural administration distinguishes between subsistence farmers, who produce almost no surplus; emergent farmers, who sell about half or more of their main harvests (maize especially); and large-scale commercial farmers, whose production is specifically geared to the market (see Bates 1976: 275ff; Hedlund 1984: 239).

2   In the light of Alder's views it is tempting to suggest that Watson went rather lightly over the probability of a quick-and-drastic transformation of the Aisa Mambwe food strategy.

3   It is curious that Alder's reference to considerable outmigration for women is confirmed by Watson's own data. Watson collected statistical evidence from eight villages and showed that three-quarters of the women whose husbands were absent had actually joined them (1958: 44). The difference in perspective between Watson and Alder is that Watson saw outmigration for women as conducive to the maintenance of village agriculture (since it reduced the risk of a 2:1 female:male ratio), whereas Alder saw the loss of female labour as precipitating the decline of the traditional production system.

4   Evapotranspiration is the total water loss by evaporation from soil and by transpiration from plants from a surface covered with vegetation (Bury 1983: 57)

5   Records were not kept for the entire period: the 1960s are a major gap (Bury 1983: 53).

CHAPTER THREE

1   A similar point has been made by White (1959: 42), in the context of trade in rural areas.

2   The correspondence between female economic independence and presumed immorality, also noted by Watson (1958: 44), implies that Hansen's observation is applicable to married Mambwe women living in town. See also note 4.

3   The increasing dependence of urban women upon the wider environment, or upon men, has also been described for Lusaka's elite women (Schuster 1976: 6).

4   Disputes over earnings are frequent. These quarrels often result in urban unions breaking up and sometimes force women to return home. Past records at the Mwamba local court (for 1973-78), which I consulted, confirmed the link between income, quarrels and separation.

5   The estimate assumes a mean of 4.3 inhabitants per household. I derived the 4.3 index from my sample, which covers 150 households and just over 650 people.

6   In 1978 the district health authorities decided to seal off Mpulungu harbour because of an outbreak of cholera. This was a difficult time for contraband traders who operated via the lake. The action was followed by a massive "Clean Up" campaign against unwanted foreigners. Both these campaigns affected small-scale *kapenta* traders rather badly.

7   Chinese imports are not only part of a strategy to repay the national loan required for building the Tanzania-Zambia railway link (Tazara), they also help curb price inflation. On the negative side, the reliance on Chinese imports does little to stimulate Zambia's own manufacturing sector.

8   Although groundnuts were not grown in Mambwe country on a commercial basis, and had been displaced in some areas (Chapter 8), I nevertheless noted that 'progressive farmers' in Kaka did show some interest.

CHAPTER FOUR

1   The omission of other Siuluta-Simpungwe links in *Tribal Cohesion* may have resulted from the fact that Mambwe men only reluctantly admit to having wives in other villages. Such women often live in concubinage, a practice of which Mambwe men say they disapprove. At the time of my fieldwork both Nkolo Kowa (D11/[B5]) and Gentile Siuluta (E25/[C15]) had wives living in nearby villages, but neither was keen to mention the fact.

2   Church of God activities (on the land) are discussed in the final section of this chapter.

3   The reference to Kowa, in the case of Sichimba, should really be to Sinyangwe's village. The marriage of Mwanaboy Kaulwe and Kaputula's daughter took place after both men had left their respective villages in the Fwambo chieftaincy. The marriage was one of many that linked Kowa, where Kaputula lived, with Sinyangwe's village.

4   Headman Adam Sikaombe of Kasunga village had one son and one daughter living in the village. The daughter, who returned to Kasunga after

her divorce on the Copperbelt, had remarried and lived with her new husband not far from Adam's place. Adam's daughter and new son-in-law provided most of the labour the headman needed. Adam himself had found the couple some land to work on. He did not live on good terms with his own son (see footnote 7).

5   Watson's discussion of 'residential stability' was within a comparative framework. The Mambwe may have been more residentially stable than the Bemba (1958:227), or the Kaonde (Watson 1954: 23-28), but the relevant data in *Tribal Cohesion*, plus hindsight, compel me to take the view that the Mambwe village was not residentially stable in any absolute sense.

6   Although the Sichimba left Fwambo for Lunzua (1920s), they consider themselves to be Lungu. Lunzua falls under the jurisdiction of Chief Fwambo, but borders on the area over which the Lungu senior chief Tafuna reigns.

7   I did not collect any additional information on Kaputula's *muchape* treatment, but gathered data on the visit of a *muchape* witch-finder (called *Muchape*) during my stay in Kasunga.

When it was known that Muchape had arrived in Mwamba, some villagers from Kasunga, including the assistant head and headman Sikaombwe's own son, invited 'the doctor' to visit their village. They complained of poor crops.

Muchape's techniques strongly resembled the approach described by Audrey Richards during the thirties (Richards 1935: 448-49). Adam Sikaombwe, with three others, was accused of harvesting large crops with the help of harmful medicine (for details, see Pottier 1981: 298-99). His medicine horns were destroyed through ritual spraying. It is significant that the late 1970s were a time of economic hardship, not unlike the depression suffered on the Copperbelt in the 1930s.

8   Watson described the practice of *mwankole* in a passage about Adam Sikaombe's 'knowing something', the euphemism for sorcery:

He is said to know how to tame crows through magic, so that they take maize from other people's gardens and grain-bins and bring it to his own (1958: 123).

9   The practice of cyclical movement was also confirmed by visitors from Chiwindi and Iku, two villages north of the Mbala-Kawimbe road. They too had been threatened, earlier this century, by the expansion of the mentioned cattle farm. The villages had lost several inhabitants when the farm started in the mid-1920s. Some of the children and grandchildren of those who had then left returned to Iku and Chiwindi during the early 1970s.

10   See appendix 1.

11   Table 7 is complete but for two cases, [C11] and [C12]. Both men are young Siuluta who are trying hard to become progressive farmers. Their migrant careers, about which they were reluctant to give details, had been short-lived.

CHAPTER FIVE

1   Kaka's farmers are only moderately optimistic. They are well aware that

economic stagnation through dependency has hit the rural areas – a fact brought home by the disappearance of many village shops (Pottier 1983a: 15).

2 Not all registered farmers attended the celebration. The absence of farmers who were also Watch Tower members (an acceptable combination) was particularly noted. One explanation here is the suggestion by Dumont and Mottin that 'Jehovah's Witnesses ... stand on their own feet and do their own organizing, knowing that no one will ever help them' (Dumont and Mottin 1983: 45). The comment is not entirely adequate. Witnesses also know that their organization is highly efficient (see Poewe 1978: 308, 318) and, in my experience of a peripheral economy, very superior to the operations of NAMBOARD and NCU.

3 Hedlund's analysis of the position of a project-based Agricultural Assistant reveals several aspects of the administrative impotence of field-based civil servants (Hedlund 1984: 235-6).

4 Research by Bratton on VPC activity in Kasama district is congruent with my observations. He writes: 'Because VPCs are adapted from the traditional social structure they may be unsuited to the development tasks expected of them. Traditional leaders can use VPCs to bolster their own authority rather than to initiate change' (Bratton 1980b: 218).

5 UNIP held its eighth general conference in Mulungushi from 8 till 11 September 1978. The *Zambia Daily Mail* issued a special 'Independence Day Supplement' on that occasion. The following extracts from the supplement highlight the spirit of the conference:

'[The General Conference] meets normally once in five years and consists of all members of the National Council plus up to 600 delegates from each of nine provinces. One of its most important functions is the election of the President of the Party and MMCs [i.e., Members of the Central Committee].

'... This was a gathering where the high and the low freely intermingled. Peasants from rural areas and workers from urban areas shared meals and all joined in chants such as 'KK. No Change. One Zambia. One Nation. One leader'. There can be no doubt that the GC was highly representative of the mass of the people of Zambia.' (*Zambia Daily Mail*, Independence Day Supplement, page one).

6 Diverting attention from critical issues through the presentation of an abstract account of President Kaunda's major political achievements is a technique much used in local-level party politics. Chikulo's characterization of the 1978 local election campaigns parallels my own critique of the way in which the Mulungushi Conference was presented to Mambwe villagers. In Chikulo's opinion, 'Although the campaigns were supposed to provide an opportunity for propagating UNIP policies, on the whole campaign speeches were devoid of any critical discussion of politics' (Chikulo 1979: 206).

7 Weddings often take place during the slack season in agriculture. They therefore tend to coincide with the period in which cross-border exchanges gather momentum.

8 This is a difficult issue. Although farmers complain of dependents flocking to Kaka, some 'dependents' (e.g. divorced younger sisters) are undoubtedly more productive than others.

9 Maize cropping is pursued in the face of organizational problems with NCU, because peasants who live in harsh environments simply need to spread their risks and options. I have developed this point elsewhere (Pottier 1986b).

CHAPTER SIX

1 I did not observe any other 'battles with ploughs', but was struck by the regularity with which fallow land is said to belong to certain household heads. Individual ownership is a concept related to the ban on moving villages. This was very clear in villages like Chikoti (Chapter 8), where population pressure on the land is relatively high.

2 Older VPU members are likely to have their places taken by younger members of the household or family. Many people bitterly complained at the end of the 1978 Easter vacation, when village children who attended boarding schools (secondary education) were once again preparing to leave.

3 The terminology is borrowed from Arrighi (see Arrighi 1973: 198-99). Dumont (1979) demonstrates the applicability of Arrighi's terms to rural Zambia in the late 1970s.

4 Kaka's WDC chairman is also chairman of the Kaka Constituency.

5 Dumont and Mottin (1983: 43) illustrate farmers' reactions to the Zambian fertilizer crisis.

6 Insufficient attention is paid to meeting basic needs. Lagging behind is the provision of 'staple manufactured foodstuffs like cooking oil, maize meal, sugar and other such necessities as textiles and clothing, building materials, water pumps and basic transport equipment such as bicycles and buses' (ILO 1977: 15). Agricultural implements, hoes and scotch-carts for example, are also not manufactured in sufficient quantities.

7 The tables convey no more than a rough idea of the scale on which Kaka farms. The data are based on extensive interviewing, but all figures are approximations. I was able to visit fields in most cases.

8 Barnett (1975: 195) discusses credit terms and their consequences on the Gezira project, Sudan.

9 Bryson (1981: 34-35) offers a general theoretical discussion of the impact which increased labour-time expenditure for women may have on their involvement in trade.

CHAPTER SEVEN

1 A slowdown in rural outmigration has also been observed for Zambia's southern regions (Adrian Wood: personal communication; Scudder 1985).

2 NAMBOARD's organization and history are discussed by Seidman (1974: 225-26).

3 In 1978 cooking oil, maize meal, sugar, salt, soap, paraffin, etc. were extremely scarce in Mbala district.

4 The following information reveals the potential for profit-making: one bag of millet sold for K3,50 in grassland villages, but fetched between K6,50 and K7,00 when retailed in Kasama.

5 The seventies also witnessed another change, from an almost total preoccupation with fishing *indaga* to a preference for the minnow-sized herring *kapenta* (GRZ 1977b: 13; *Abercornucopia*, 19 November 1965).

6 The terms 'divorce' and 'divorcee' are used in a very loose sense, since 'divorcees' did not always (could not always) obtain divorce certificates from the local courts. A 'divorcee' is therefore defined as a woman who lives separated from her husband and receives no support from him. The husband of a woman who is abandonned (i.e. separated without divorce certificate) may claim compensation money (*ulemu*) from any man with whom she has children.

7 One common method of exchange is for middlemen to swap beans for brightly coloured tin pails (see Chapter 3). In the case of *kapenta*, small plates represent set amounts of beans.

8 Footnote to Diagram 9. Grace Nanyangwe's marriage [B10] is a special case of 'village endogamy'. Grace, from Yolam's village, had moved to Chivunzila for her second marriage. She had two children, when her husband left to take up work on the Copperbelt. The couple became estranged, but there was no formal divorce. Grace could have returned to Yolam's, but she stayed on and became the second wife of another Chivunzila resident.

CHAPTER EIGHT

1 Trapnell states, in Watson's words, 'that the Bemba have a tradition that they were hoe-cultivators in Lubaland [from whence they came in the eighteenth century] and learned ash-cultivation from the peoples they found already living in the [Mambwe] area' (1958: 24).

2 All *grassland* villages where I researched bore the unmistakable mark of "dissolution", along the lines suggested by Murray. The villages had a significant proportion of adult women who had never married, an increasing incidence of female-headed families, households with children from various unions, and complex multi-generation families (Murray 1980: 144-45). The process of "conservation", in contrast, seemed to me to be much less visible, except for political showpieces like Chele, where ideological continuity was maintained through the mobilization of unusually large communal work-parties (Chapter 6).

In Chikoti the process of "dissolution" had not yet reached the critical stage. For instance, there were no female-headed families in 1978. Nor were there any complex multi-generation families residing in the village. It is difficult to advance a comprehensive explanation for the absence of female-headed households in Chikoti (1978). My guess is that the practice of ash-planting, which involves lopping trees, makes it more difficult for women from woodland villages to achieve autonomy in food production. However, this interpretation does not preclude the possibility that (woodland) female-headed families may have resettled in the grassland zone.

3   The villagers of Chikoti loathed the long distance to their forest gardens. The important point, however, is that they did continue to grow millet in the forest. The resettled Sudanese Zande, described by Reining (1970), appear to have adopted a similar attitude: despite the heavy demands of the settlement scheme, 'they were willing to go considerable distances to find land suitable for cultivation' (Reining 1970:163).

4   Cassava cultivation is more capable of supporting sustained population growth, because starchy root crops absorb less nutrients than the protein-rich seed crops (Ellen 1982:39). There is also a reduction in the amount of time required for processing. As Reining argues for the Zande, 'the processing of cassava into flour ... is much less work than the flailing, winnowing, and grinding required of eleusine' (Reining 1970:137; for an alternative view, see Chambers and Singer 1981). On the other hand, it is equally important to take up Reining's suggestion that the proportion of cassava in the diet gives 'a rough indication of the stress under which a household or individual [operates]' (*ibid*:138). Reliance on cassava can lead to protein deficiency.

5   Reining argues for the Zande system (before resettlement) that 'the absence of rigid rules allowed for considerable adaptability, as in the alteration of the usual crop succession plan in the event of unusually good or poor yields' (Reining 1970: 142).

6   The complicated issue of cattle ownership is discussed in a paper on cattle manoeuvres among the Ila of Zambia (Cutshall 1982). Although cattle do not form the mainstay of the Mambwe economy, the notion of ownership is equally complex, and competing claims of control are regularly brought before the courts. In a hearing which I attended at the court of Mwamba (10/7/78) the alleged debt - a case of partially paid bridewealth - went back to the parental generation of two senior litigants. The case was of interest to the villagers of Chikoti, since the losing party was none other than Chief Kela. The people of Chikoti, I was told, had for a long time had their cattle looked after by Kela, as a token of their political alliance. (Chikoti villagers say they are neither Aisa nor Maswepa, but Matala – i.e. people of Kela.)

7   Ecological anthropologists tend to conceptualize migration from rural areas as the possible 'culmination of a structured set of responses to severe [hardship]' (Vayda and McCay 1975: 298; also Netting 1974). Waddell's study of responses to frost in the New Guinea Highlands is a well-known illustration (Waddell 1975). In the case of the Mambwe, however, the causal link has

worked in reverse, since hardship did not precede but followed the breakdown of circulatory migration.

8   Epstein relates that in the period before the pax britannica 'Bemba would point in the direction of Mambwe country and say "Our gardens are over there" - a reference to the raids carried out on the Mambwe in order to seize their cattle' (Epstein 1975:208).

9   One reservation to the argument (as far as Chikoti is concerned) is that Kaka may become self-sufficient in terms of its labour needs. Such a shift has been reported for at least one 'intensive development' area in Zambia (see Wright 1983:82). Wright argues for the progressive farmers of Mazabuka that they achieved self-sufficiency in labour power through an increase in the rate of polygyny. Wealthier farmers resolved the problem of labour 'by institutional changes achieved through the polygynous family and paternal power' (Wright 1983:82). I cannot comment on whether polygyny is on the increase in Kaka, as Kaka was still 'shaping up' during my stay there. The likelihood of such a development is not precluded.

GLOSSARY

cancine	crude gin
chibuku	maize beer (CiBemba)
chipatala	hospital
cikolwe	clan doyen
cipumu	millet beer
cisaka	maize
citemene	shifting agriculture
impepe	flat fields
intanta	granary
ivizule	kitchen-gardens
kalundwe	cassava
kapenta	minnow-sized herring
kapitao	foreman
katata	maize beer
malezi	fingermillet
mbalala	groundnuts
mianda	riverside gardens
muchape	witch-finder
mulozi	sorcerer
ngano	wheat
ntoyo	soya
ntumba	mound
saladi	cooking oil
simapepo	shrine priest
sinanga	herbalist
ukupula	to work for food
ukusinza	to harvest

BIBLIOGRAPHY

ADEPOJU, A. (1979) 'Migration and Socio-Economic Change in Africa', *International Social Science Journal* 31 (2): 207-25.
ADDO, N.O. (1975) 'International Migration Differentials and the Effects on Socio-Demographic Change', in J.C. Caldwell *et al.* (eds.), *Population Growth and Socio-Economic Change in West Africa*. New York: Columbia University Press.
ALDER, J. (1960) Report on Land Usage of the Aisa Mambwe in Reserve IV, Abercorn District.
ALLAN, W. (1965) *The African Husbandman*. New York: Barnes and Noble Inc.
ALLAN, W. et al (1949) *Studies in African Land Use in Northern Rhodesia*. Manchester: Manchester University Press.
AMSELLE, J.-L. (1976) 'Les Migrations Africaines', in M. Aghassian *et al*, *Les Migrations Africaines: Réseaux et Processus Migratoires*. Paris: Maspero. pp.9-39.
ARDENER, S. (1984) 'Gender Orientations in Fieldwork', in R.F. Ellen (ed.), *Ethnographic Research: A Guide to General Conduct*. ASA Research Methods in Social Anthropology 1. London: Academic Press. pp.118-29.
ARRIGHI, G. (1973) 'Labor Supplies in Historical Perspective: A Study of the Proletarianization of the African Peasantry in Rhodesia', in G. Arrighi and J.S. Saul, *Essays on the Political Economy of Africa*. New York and London: Monthly Review Press. pp.180-234.
BAIER, S. (1980) *An Economic History of Central Niger*. London: Oxford University Press.
BARNETT, T. (1975) 'The Gezira Scheme: Production of Cotton and the Reproduction of Underdevelopment', in I. Oxaal, *et al* (eds.), *Beyond the Sociology of Development*. London: Routledge and Kegan Paul. pp.183-207.
BARTH, F. (1967) 'Economic Spheres in Darfur', in R. Firth (ed.), *Themes in Economic Anthropology*. ASA 6. London: Tavistock. pp.149-74.
BATES, R.H. (1976) *Rural Responses to Industrialization*. New Haven and London: Yale University Press.
BATES, R.H. (1981) *Markets and States in Tropical Africa*. Berkeley and Los Angeles: University of California Press.
BAYLIES, C. (1980) 'The State and the Growth of Indigenous Capital: Zambia's Economic Reforms and their Aftermath', in Centre of African Studies, University of Edinburgh (ed.), *The Evolving Structure of Zambian Society*. Proceedings of a Seminar held 30 and 31 May 1980.

BAYLISS-SMITH, T. (1982) *The Ecology of Agricultural Systems*. Cambridge: Cambridge University Press.
BERG, A. (1981) 'The New Need: Nutrition-Oriented Food Policy', *Food Policy*, May, pp.116-22.
BERGER, P. (1974) *Pyramids of Sacrifice: Political Ethics and Social Change*. Harmondsworth: Penguin.
BOND, G.C. (1975) 'Labour Migration and Rural Activism: The Yombe Case', *African Urban Notes*, Series B, No.1, Winter 1974-75, pp.21-34.
BOND, G.C. (1976) *The Politics of Change in a Zambian Community*. Chicago and London: University of Chicago Press.
BOND, G.C. (1978) 'Religious Coexistence in Northern Zambia: Intellectualism and Materialism in Yombe Belief', *Annals of the New York Academy of Sciences* 318: 23-36.
BOSERUP, E. (1965) *The Conditions of Agricultural Growth: The Economics of Agrarian Change under Population Pressure*. London: Allen and Unwin.
BOSERUP, E. (1970) *Women's Roles in Economic Development*. London: Allen and Unwin.
BRABIN, L. (1984) 'Polygyny: An Indicator of Nutritional Stress in African Agricultural Societies?', *Africa* 54 (1): 31-45.
BRATTON, M. (1980a) *The Local Politics of Rural Development: Peasant and Party-State in Zambia*. Hanover, New Hampshire: University Press of New England.
BRATTON, M. (1980b) 'The Social Context of Political Penetration: Village and Ward Committees in Kasama District', in W. Tordoff (ed.), *Administration in Zambia*. pp.213-239.
BRYCESON, D.F. (1980) 'Changes in Peasant Food Production and Food Supply in relation to the Historical Development of Commodity Production in Pre-Colonial and Colonial Tanganyika', *Journal of Peasant Studies* 7 (3): 281-311.
BRYSON, J.C. (1981) 'Women and Agriculture in Sub-Saharan Africa: Implications for Development (an Exploratory Study)', in N.Nelson (ed.), *African Women in the Development Process*. London: F.Cass. pp.29-46.
BURY, B. (1983) *The Human Ecology and Political Economy of Agricultural Production on the Ufipa Plateau, Tanzania: 1945 - 1981*. Columbia University, New York: unpublished D.Phil thesis.
BWALYA, M.C. (1984) 'Participation or Powerlessness: The Place of Peasants in Zambia's Rural Development', in K. Woldring and C. Chibaye (eds.), *Beyond Political Independence: Zambia's Development Predicament in the 1980s*. Amsterdam: Mouton.
BYERLEE, D., J.L. TOMY and H. FATOO, (1976) Rural-urban Migration in Sierra Leone: Determinants and Policy Implications. *African Rural Economy Paper* No.13, East lancing.
CARLSTEIN, T. (1982) *Time, Resources, Society and Ecology*. London: Allen and Unwin.
CESARA, M. (1982) *No Hiding Place: Reflections of a Woman Anthropologist*. London: Academic Press.
CHAMBERS, R. and H. SINGER (1981) Poverty, Malnutrition and Food in Zambia. I.D.S., University of Sussex: Country Studies for World Development, *Report IV*.
CHIKULO, B. (1979) 'Elections in a One-Party Democracy', in B. Turok (ed.), *Development in Zambia*. London: Zed Press. pp.201-13.
CHIKULO, B. (1986) Availability and Access: Food Security in Zambia. *CDAS Discussion Papers* No.34. Center for Developing-Area Studies, McGill University.
CLIFFE, L. (1978) 'Labour Migration and Peasant Differentiation: Zambian Experiences', *Journal of Peasant Studies* 5 (3): 526-46.

COHEN, A. (1969) *Custom and Politics in Urban Africa: A Study of Hausa Migrants in Yoruba Towns*. Berkeley: University of California Press.

COWIE, W.J. (1979) 'Aspects of Resource Access among Villagers and Farmers in Kanyanja Parish, Chipata District', in D. Honeybone and A. Marter (eds.), Poverty and Wealth in Rural Zambia. Lusaka: Institute for African Studies, University of Zambia. *Communication* 15. pp.59-72.

CREHAN, K. (1981) 'Mukunashi: an Exploration of some Effects of the Penetration of Capital in North-Western Zambia', *Journal of Southern African Studies* 8 (1): 82-91.

CREHAN, K. (1985) 'Production and Gender in North-Western Zambia', in J. Pottier (ed.), *Food Systems in Central and Southern Africa*. London: School of Oriental and African Studies. pp.80-100.

CURRY, R.L. Jr (1979/80) 'Zambia's Economic Crisis: A Challenge to Budgetary Politics', *Journal of African Studies* (Los Angeles) 6 (4): 213-217.

CUTSHALL, C. (1982) 'Culprits, Culpability, and Crime: Stocktheft and other Cattle Maneuvers among the Ila of Zambia', *African Studies Review* 25 (1): 1-26.

DANIEL, P. (1979) *Africanisation, Nationalisation and Inequality: Mining Labour and the Copperbelt in Zambian Development*. Cambridge: Cambridge University Press.

DASMANN, R.F. et al. (1973) *Ecological Principles for Economic Development*. London: John Wiley.

DE GRAFT-JOHNSON, K.T. (1974) 'Population Growth and Rural-Urban Migration, with special reference to Ghana', *International Labour Review* 109 (5/6), May-June.

DEMESSE, L. (1978) *Changements Techno-économiques et Sociaux chez les Pygmées Babinga (Nord Congo et Sud Centrafrique)*. Paris: SELAF.

DOUGLAS, M. (1969) 'Is Matriliny Doomed in Africa?', in M.Douglas and P.Kaberry (eds.), *Man in Africa*. London: Tavistock. pp.121-36.

DUE, J.M. (1980) 'Allocation of Credit to Ujamaa Villages in Tanzania and Small Farms in Zambia', *African Studies Review* 23 (3): 33-48.

DUMONT, R. (1979) *Towards Another Development in Rural Zambia*. Lusaka: Government Printer.

DUMONT, R. and M.-F. MOTTIN (1983) *Stranglehold on Africa*. London: A. Deutsch.

ELLEN, R. (1982) *Environment, Subsistence and System*. Cambridge: Cambridge University Press.

ELLIOTT, C. (1983) 'Equity and Growth: An Unresolved Conflict in Zambian Rural Development Policy', in D. Ghai and S. Radwam (eds.), *Agrarian Policies and Rural Poverty in Africa*. Geneva: I.L.O. pp.155-89.

EPSTEIN, A.L. (1958) *Politics in an Urban African Community*. Manchester: Manchester University Press.

EPSTEIN, A.L. (1975) 'Military Organization and the Precolonial Polity of the Bemba of Zambia', *Man* 10 (2): 199-217.

FEYERABEND, P. (1975) *Against Method: Outline of an Anarchistic Theory of Knowledge*. London: New Left Books.

GADAMER, H.-G. (1976) *Philosophical Hermeneutics*. Berkeley: University of California Press. (David E. Linge, tr. and ed.)

GERRY, C. (1977) Urban Poverty, Underdevelopment and 'Recuperative' Production in Dakar, Senegal. University of Swansea: Centre for Development Studies. *Occasional Paper* No.1.

GERTZEL, C. (1972) 'Institutional Developments at District Level in Independent Zambia.' Paper presented at the Political Science Workshop, University of Zambia, 3-4 August. Mimeo.

GERTZEL, C. (1980) 'Two Case Studies in Rural Development', in W. Tordoff (ed.), *Administration in Zambia*. Manchester: Manchester University Press.
GOODY, J. (1982) *Cooking, Cuisine and Class: A Study in Comparative Sociology*. Cambridge: Cambridge University Press.
G.R.Z. (Government of the Republic of Zambia) (1971) *Village Productivity and Ward Development Committees: A Pocket Manual*. Lusaka: Government Printer.
G.R.Z. (Government of the Republic of Zambia) (1977a) 'Annual Report (1976-77).' Mbala: Ministry of Lands and Agriculture. Mimeo.
G.R.Z. (Government of the Republic of Zambia) (1977b) *Tanganyika Lake Study*. Lusaka: Government Printer. Undertaken by the Department of Town and Country Planning.
G.R.Z. (Government of the Republic of Zambia) (1978) 'Northern Province I.D.Z. Programme: Annual Report 1977 and Work Programme 1978.' Kasama: Ministry of Lands and Agriculture. Mimeo.
GRANDSTAFF, T. (1978) 'The Development of Swidden Agriculture', *Development and Change* 9: 547-579.
GREGORY, J.R. (1984) 'The Myth of the Male Ethnographer and the Woman's World', *American Anthropologist* 86 (2): 316-27.
GREGORY, J.W. and V. PICHE (1983) 'African Return Migration: Past, Present, and Future', *Contemporary Marxism* 7: 169-83.
GUYER. J.I. (1981) 'Household and Community in African Studies', *The African Studies Review* 24 (2/3): 87-138.
GUYER, J.I. (1984) 'Women in the Rural Economy: Contemporary Variations', in M.J. Hay and S. Stichter (eds.), *African Women South of the Sahara*. London: Longman. pp.19-32.
HALL, R. and H. PEYMAN (1976) *The Great Uhuru Railway: China's Showpiece in Africa*. London: Victor Gollancz Ltd.
HANSEN, K. (1975) 'Married Women and Work: Explorations from an Urban Case Study', *African Social Research* (Lusaka) 20: 777-99.
HANSEN, K. (1980) 'The Urban Informal Sector as a Development Issue: Poor Women and Work in Lusaka, Zambia', *Urban Anthropology* 9 (2): 199-225.
HARDOUIN, J. (1983) 'Possibilités actuelles dans la recherche de sources différentes d'alimentation', in *Symposium: Malnutrition du Tiers Monde / Malnutritie van de Derde Wereld*. Brussels: Académie Royale des Science d'Outre-Mer / Koninklijke Academie voor Overzeese Wetenschappen.
HARRIS, D.R. (1972) 'Swidden Systems and Settlement', in P.J. Ucko, *et al.* (eds.), *Man, Settlement, and Urbanism*. London: Duckworth.
HEDLUND, H. (1977) Towards a Village Agricultural Programme in Northern Province. Lusaka: Rural Development Studies Bureau, University of Zambia. Unpublished paper.
HEDLUND, H. (1984) 'Development in Action: The Experience of the Zambian Extension Worker', *Ethnos* 49 (3/4): 226-249.
HEDLUND, H. and M. LUNDAHL (1983) *Migration and Change in Rural Zambia*. Uppsala: Scandinavian Institute of African Studies. Research Report No.70.
HEDLUND, H. and M. LUNDAHL (1984) 'The Economic Role of Beer in Rural Zambia', *Human Organization* 43 (1): 61-65.
HEISLER, H. (1974) *Urbanisation and the Government of Migration: The Interrelation of Urban and Rural Life in Zambia*. London: C. Hurst.
HENN, J. (1984) 'Women in the Rural Economy: Past, Present, and Future', in M.J. Hay & S. Stichter (eds.), *African Women South of the Sahara*. London: Longman. pp.1-18.

HIRSCHMANN, D. and M. VAUGHAN (1983) 'Food Production and Income Generation in a Matrilineal Society: Rural Women in Zomba, Malawi', *Journal of Southern African Studies* 10 (1): 86-99.

HONEYBONE, D. and A. MARTER (1979) (eds.) Poverty and Wealth in Rural Zambia, Lusaka: Institute for African Studies, University of Zambia, *Communication* 15.

I.L.O. (1977) *Narrowing the Gaps: Planning for Basic Needs and Production Employment in Zambia*. Addis Ababa: JASPA (Jobs and Skills Programme for Africa).

I.L.O. (1981) *Zambia: Basic Needs in an Economy under Pressure*. Addis Ababa: JASPA.

JANZEN, D.H. (1973) 'Tropical Agroecosystems', *Science* 182: 1212-1219.

JOHNSON, A. (1980) 'Ethnoecology and Planting Practice in a Swidden Agricultural System', in D. Brokensha, D. Warren and O. Werner (eds.), *Indigenous Knowledge Systems and Development*. Lanham, Md.: University Press of America.

JULES-ROSETTE, B. (1982) Women's Work in the Informal Sector: A Zambian Case Study. Michigan State University: Office of Women in International Development. *Working Paper* 103.

KAINDU, C.K. (1973) 'Rural Reconstruction: Prospects and Problems', in R. Molteno (ed.), *Studies in Zambian Government and Administration*. Lusaka: University of Zambia. pp.3–14.

KANDEKE, T.K. (1977) *Fundamentals of Zambian Humanism*. Lusaka: Neczam.

KAPLAN, A. (1964) *The Conduct of Inquiry: Methodology for Behavioral Science*. San Francisco: Chandler Publishing Company.

KAPTEYN, R. and C. EMERY (1972) *District Administration in Zambia*. Lusaka: NIPA-Administration for Rural Development Projects.

KASHOKI, M.E. (1978) 'The Institute for African Studies in the University of Zambia: Problems and Prospects', *African Social Research* 25: 359-97.

KLEPPER, R. (1979) 'Zambian Agricultural Structure and Performance', in B. Turok (ed.), *Development in Zambia*. London: Zed Press. pp.137-48.

KLEPPER, R. (1980) Agricultural Research, Development Planning and the Rural Poor in Zambia. Institute of Development Studies, University of Sussex. Mimeo.

KUHN, T.S. (1970) *The Structure of Scientific Revolutions*. Chicago: University of Chicago Press.

LAPPE, F.M. and A. BECCAR-VARELA (1980) *Mozambique and Tanzania: Asking the Big Questions*. San Francisco, California: Institute for Food and Development Policy.

LELE, U. (1977) 'Considerations related to Optimum Pricing and Marketing Strategies in Rural Development', in T. Dams and K. Hunt (eds.), *Decision Making and Agriculture*. Lincoln: University of Nebraska Press.

LITTLE, P.D. (1983) 'The Livestock-Grain Connection in Northern Kenya: An Analysis of Pastoral Economies and Semi-Arid Land Development', *Rural Africana* 15/16: 91-108.

LLOYD, P.C. (1979) *Slums of Hope? Shanty Towns of the Third World*. Harmondsworth: Penguin.

LOMNITZ, L. (1974) 'The Social and Economic Organization of a Mexican Shanty Town', in W.A. Cornelius and F.M. Trueblood (eds.), *Latin American Urban Research*, Vol.4. California: Beverley Hills.

LONG, N. (1968) *Social Change and the Individual: A Study of the Social and Religious Responses to Innovation*. Manchester: Manchester University Press.

LONG, N. (1970) 'Rural Entrepreneurship and Religious Commitment in Zambia', *Internationales Jahrbuch für Religionssoziologie*. Vol.6: 142-57.

LONG, N. (1975) 'Structural Dependency, Modes of Production and Economic Brokerage in Rural Peru', in I. Oxaal et al. (eds.), *Beyond the Sociology of Development*. London: Routledge and Kegan Paul. pp.253-82.

LONG, N. (1977) *An Introduction to the Sociology of Rural Development*. London: Tavistock Publications.

LONG, N. (1984) Creating Space for Change: A Perspective on the Sociology of Rural Development. University of Wageningen: Inaugural Lecture.

LUDWIG, H.-D. (1968) 'Permanent Farming in Ukara: The Impact of Land Shortage on Husbandry Practices', in H. Ruthenberg (ed.), *Smallholder Farming and Smallholder Development in Tanzania*. Munchen: IFO-Institut für Wirtschaftsforschung, Afrika-Studien 24.

MANSFIELD, J.E. et al. (1975a) *Land Resources of the Northern and Luapula Provinces, Zambia - a Reconnaissance Assessment*. Vol.2: Current Land Use. Surbiton: Tolworth Tower, for Land Resources Division, Ministry of Overseas Development.

MANSFIELD, J.E. et al. (1975b) *Land Resources of the Northern and Luapula Provinces, Zambia - a Reconnaissance Assessment*. Vol.5: Social and Economic Factors. Surbiton: Tolworth Tower, for Land Resources Division, Ministry of Overseas Development.

MARTER, A. and D. HONEYBONE (1976) *The Economic Resources of Rural Households and the Distribution of Agricultural Development*. Lusaka: Rural Development Studies Bureau, University of Zambia.

McLOUGHLIN, P.F.M. (1970) 'Introduction', in P.F.M. McLoughlin (ed.), *African Food Production Systems*. Baltimore, Md: The Johns Hopkins Press. pp.3-39.

MENDONSA, E.L. (1982) *The Politics of Divination: A Processual View of Reactions to Illness and Deviance among the Sisala of Northern Ghana*. Berkeley: University of California.

MILIMO, J.T. and Y. FISSEHA (1986) Rural Small Scale Enterprises in Zambia: Results of a 1985 Country-wide Survey. Michigan State University: Department of Agricultural Economics. MSU International Development Papers, *Working Paper* No.28.

MIRACLE, P.M. (1961) 'The Copperbelt', in P. Bohannan and G. Dalton (eds.), *Markets in Africa*. New York: Doubleday Anchor. pp.698-738.

MIRACLE, P.M. (1962) 'Apparent Changes in the Structure of African Commerce, Lusaka, 1954-59', *The Northern Rhodesia Journal* 5 (2): 170-5.

MIRACLE, P.M. (1973) 'The Elasticity of Food Supply in Tropical Africa during the Pre-Colonial Period', *Ghana Social Science Journal* 2 (2): 1-9.

MOORE, M.P. (1975) 'Cooperative Labour in Peasant Agriculture', *Journal of Peasant Studies* 2: 270-91.

MULLER, M.S. (1976) 'Self Help: A Case of Water Projects in two Unauthorized Settlements in Lusaka', in H.J. Simons et al, *Slums or Self-Reliance? Urban Growth in Zambia*. Lusaka: University of Zambia, Institute for African Studies, Communication No.12. pp.102-18.

MUNTEMBA, M.S. (1977) 'Thwarted Development: A Case Study of Economic Change in the Kabwe Rural District of Zambia, 1902-70', in R. Palmer and N. Parsons (eds.), *The Roots of Rural Poverty in Central and Southern Africa*. London: Heinemann. pp.345-64.

MUNTEMBA, S. (1982) 'Women as Food Producers and Suppliers in the 20th Century: the Case of Zambia', *Development Dialogue* (Uppsala) 1/2: 29-50.

MURRAY, C. (1980) 'Migrant Labour and Changing Family Structure in the Rural Periphery of Southern Africa', *Journal of Southern African Studies* 6 (2): 139-56.

MWANGILWA, G. (1986) *The Kapwepwe Diaries*. Lusaka: Multimedia Publications.

NEEDHAM, R. (1975) 'Polythetic Classification: Convergence and Consequences', *Man* 10 (3): 349-69.

NELSON, N. (1978) 'Women Must Help Each Other', in P. Caplan and J.M. Bujra (eds.), *Women United, Women Divided*. London: Tavistock Publications. pp.77-98.

NELSON RICHARDS, M. (1981/2) 'Experiment on Rural Development in an African State: Zambia – The Chunga Irrigation Scheme', *Journal of African Studies* (Los Angeles) 8 (4): 146-62.

NETTING, R. McC. (1974) 'Agrarian Ecology', *Annual Review of Anthropology* 3: 21-56.

NYIRENDA, A.A. (1957) 'African Vendors in Lusaka', *Human Problems in British Central Africa* 22: 31-63.

OBERSCHALL, A. (1972) 'Lusaka Market Vendors: Then and Now', *Urban Anthropology* 1: 107-23.

OBERSCHALL, A. (1973) 'African Traders and Small Businessmen in Lusaka', *African Social Research* 16: 474-502.

PARKIN, D.J. (1972) *Palms, Wine and Witnesses*. London and San Francisco: Intertext Books.

PARKIN, D.J. (1975) 'Migration, Settlement and the Politics of Unemployment', in D. Parkin (ed.), *Town and Country in Central and Eastern Africa*. London: Oxford University Press for the International African Institute. pp.145-55.

POEWE, K.O. (1978) 'Religion, Matriliny, and Change: Jehovah's Witnesses and Seventh-Day Adventists in Luapula, Zambia', *American Ethnologist* 5 (2): 303-21.

POEWE, K.O. (1979) 'Regional and Village Economic Activities: Prosperity and Stagnation in Luapula, Zambia', *African Studies Review* 22 (2): 77-93.

PORTER, P. (1978) 'Geography as Human Ecology', *American Behavioral Scientist* 22: 15-39.

PORTER, P. W. (1979) *Food and Development in the Semi-Arid Zone of East Africa* Foreign and Comparative Studies, African Series XXXII. Syracuse: Maxwell School of Citizenship and Public Affairs, Syracuse University.

POTTIER, J. (1981) The Transformation of a Defunct Labour Reserve: The Case of the Mambwe People of Zambia. Ph.D. thesis, University of Sussex.

POTTIER, J. (1983a) 'Defunct Labour Reserve?: Mambwe Villages in the Post-Migration Economy', *Africa* 53(2):2-23.

POTTIER, J. (1983b) 'Aspects of Agricultural Intensification: A Case Study from Zambia's Northern Province', *African Studies Association (USA) 26th Annual Meeting Papers*, Vol.1983, No.111.

POTTIER, J. (1985a) 'African Food Systems: An Introduction', in J. Pottier (ed.), *Food Systems in Central and Southern Africa*. London: School of Oriental and African Studies. pp.1-60.

POTTIER, J. (1985b) 'Reciprocity and the Beer Pot: The Changing Pattern of Mambwe Food Production', in J. Pottier (ed.), *Food Systems in Central and Southern Africa*. London: School of Oriental and African Studies. pp.101-137.

POTTIER, J. (1986a) 'The Politics of Famine Prevention: Ecology, Regional Production and Food Complementarity in Western Rwanda', *African Affairs* Vol.85 (No.339): 207-237.

POTTIER, J. (1986b) 'Village Responses to Food Marketing Alternatives in Northern Zambia: The Case of the Mambwe Economy', *Bulletin of the Institute of Development Studies* (Sussex) 17 (1): 51-56.

POTTIER, J. (1986c) 'La Parole est à Deux Personnes: Knowledge, Ignorance and Power in the Context of Urban Agriculture in Rwanda', paper presented at the EIDOS conference on 'Local Knowledge and Systems of Ignorance', School of Oriental and African Studies, University of London, 8-10 December.

QUICK, S. (1978) *Humanism or Technocracy? Zambia's Farming Co-operatives, 1965-1972.* Lusaka: University of Zambia, Institute for African Studies, Zambian Papers No.12.
QUICK, S. (1979) 'Socialism in One Sector: Rural Development in Zambia', in C.C. Rosberg and T.M. Callaghy (eds.), *Socialism in Sub-Saharan Africa.* Berkeley: Institute of International Studies. pp.83-111.
RABINOW, P. (1977) *Reflections on Fieldwork in Morocco.* Berkeley: University of California Press.
READ, M. (1942) 'Migrant Labour in Africa and the Effects on Tribal Life', *International Labour Review* 45: 601-31.
REINING, C. (1970) 'Zande Subsistence and Food Production', in P.F.M. McLoughlin (ed.), *African Food Production Systems.* Baltimore and London: The Johns Hopkins Press.
RICHARDS, A.I. (1935) 'A Modern Movement of Witch-Finders', *Africa* 8 (4): 448-61.
RICHARDS, A.I. (1961/1939) *Land, Labour, and Diet in Northern Rhodesia.* London: Oxford University Press for the International African Institute.
RICHARDS, P. (1983) 'Ecological Change and the Politics of African Land Use', *African Studies Review* 26 (2): 1-72.
RICHARDS, P. (1986) *Coping With Hunger: Hazard and Experiment in an African Rice-farming System.* London: Allen and Unwin.
SCHULTZ, J. (1976) *Land Use in Zambia.* Munchen: IFO-Institut für Wirtschaftsforschung. Afrika-Studien, 95.
SCHULTZ, T.W. (1976) *Transforming Traditional Africa.* New York: Arno Press.
SCHUSTER, I. (1976) Lusaka's Young Women: Adaptation to Change. University of Sussex: Ph.D. thesis.
SCOTT, E. (1984) (ed.) *Life Before The Drought.* Boston: Allen and Unwin.
SCUDDER, T. (1985) A History of Development in the Twentieth Century: the Zambian Portion of the Middle Zambezi Valley and the Lake Kariba Basin. Clark University / Institute for Development Anthropology: Cooperative Agreement on Human Settlements and Natural Resource Systems Analysis, *Working Paper No.22.*
SEIDMAN, A. (1974) *Planning for Development in Sub-Saharan Africa.* Dar es Salaam: Tanzania Publishing House.
SHIVJI, I. (1976) *Class Struggle in Tanzania.* London: Heinemann.
SILBERFEIN, M. (1984) 'Differential Development in Machakos District, Kenya', in E. Scott (ed.), *Life Before The Drought.* Boston: Allen and Unwin. pp.101-23.
SIMONS, H.J. (1976) 'Zambia's Urban Situation', in H.J. Simons, *et al*, Slums or Self-Reliance? Urban Growth in Zambia. Lusaka: University of Zambia, Institute for African Studies, *Communication* No.12, pp.1-32.
SIMONS, H.J. (1977) 'Prologue', *African Social Research* 24: 259-73.
STAUDT, K. (1979) Women and Participation in Rural Development: A Framework for Policy Design and Policy-Oriented Research. Cornell University: Rural Development Committee. *Occasional Papers*, No.8.
STEINER, K. (1984) *Intercropping in Tropical Smallholder Agriculture, with special reference to West Africa.* Eschborn: Deutsche Gesellschaft für Technische Zusammenarbeit.
STOLLEN, K.A. (1983) 'Socio-Economic Constraints on Agricultural Production in the Northern Province of Zambia', in H. Svads (ed.), *Proceedings of the Seminar on Soil Productivity in the High Rainfall Areas of Zambia.* Oslo: International Development Programs, Agricultural University of Norway, for Zambian SPRP Studies, Occasional Paper No.6.

STROMGAARD, P. (1985) 'A Subsistence Society Under Pressure: the Bemba of Northern Zambia', *Africa* 55 (1): 39-59.
TALLANTIRE, A.C. (1975) 'A Preliminary Study of the Food Plants of the West Nile and Madi Districts of Uganda', *East African Agricultural and Forestry Journal* 40: 233-55.
TODARO, M.P. (1969) 'A Model of Labor Migration and Urban Unemployment in Less Developed Countries', *American Economic Review*, 59:138-148.
TORDOFF, W. (1980) (ed.) *Administration in Zambia*. Manchester: Manchester University Press.
TUROK, B. (1979) 'The Role of Parastatals in Zambia', *Africa Development* 4 (2/3): 44-66.
VAN DONGE, J.K. (1982) 'Politicians, Bureaucrats and Farmers: A Zambian Case Study', *Journal of Development Studies* 19 (1): 88-107.
VAN DONGE, J.K. (1985) 'Understanding Rural Zambia Today: The Relevance of the Rhodes-Livingstone Institute', *Africa* 55 (1): 60-76.
VAN VELSEN, J. (1960) 'Labour Migration as a Positive Factor in the Continuity of Tonga Tribal Society', *Economic Development and Cultural Change* 8: 265-78.
VAN VELSEN, J. (1975) 'Urban Squatters: Problem or Solution', in D. Parkin (ed.), *Town and Country in Central and Eastern Africa*. London: Oxford University Press for the International African Institute. pp.294-307.
VAYDA, A.P. and B.J. McCAY (1975) 'New Directions in Ecology and Ecological Anthropology', *Annual Review of Anthropology* 4: 293-306.
VON FREYHOLD, M. (1979) *Ujamaa Villages in Tanzania*, London: Heinemann.
WADDELL, E. (1975) 'How the Enga Cope with Frost: Responses to Climatic Perturbations in the Central Highlands of New Guinea', *Human Ecology* 3 (4): 249-273.
WATSON, W. (1954) 'The Kaonde Village', *Human Problems in British Central Africa (Rhodes-Livingstone Journal)* 15: 1-30.
WATSON, W. (1958) *Tribal Cohesion in a Money Economy: A Study of the Mambwe People of Zambia*, Manchester: Manchester University Press.
WATSON, W. (1959) 'Migrant Labour and Detribalization', *Bulletin of the Inter-African Labour Institute* 6 (1). (Reprinted in J. Middleton (ed.), *Black Africa: Its Peoples and their Cultures Today*. London and New York: Macmillan. pp.38-48.)
WHITE, C.M.N. (1959) Preliminary Survey of Luvale Rural Economy. *Rhodes-Livingstone Papers*, No.25.
WILLIS, R. (1966) *The Fipa and Related Peoples of South-West Tanzania and North-East Zambia*. London: International African Institute.
WILSON, G. (1941/2) An Essay on the Economics of Detribalization in Northern Rhodesia, parts 1 and 2. Livingstone: *Rhodes-Livingstone Institute Papers* 5 and 6.
WOLDRING, K. (1984) 'Reflections on the René Dumont Report and the State Farms Project', in K. Woldring and C. Chibaye (eds.), *Beyond Political Independence: Zambia's Development Predicament in the 1980s*. Amsterdam: Mouton.
WOOD, A. (1985) 'Food Production and the Changing Structure of Zambian Agriculture', in J.Pottier (ed.), *Food Systems in Central and Southern Africa*. London: School of Oriental and African Studies, London University. pp.138-168.
WORLD BANK (1981) *Accelerated Development in Sub-Saharan Africa: an Agenda for Action*, Washington, D.C.: World Bank.
WRIGHT, M. (1975) 'Women in Peril: A Commentary on the Life Stories of Captives in Nineteenth-Century East-Central Africa', *African Social Research* 20: 800-819.
WRIGHT, M. (1977) The Cultivator and the State in Ufipa. Paper presented to the University of Illinois Colloquium, April 1977.

WRIGHT, M. (1983) 'Technology, Marriage and Women's Work in the History of Maize-Growers in Mazabuka, Zambia: a Reconnaissance', *Journal of Southern African Studies* 10 (1): 71-85.

WRIGHT, M. (ed.) (1984) *Women in Peril: Life Stories of Four Captives*. Lusaka: Neczam.

WRIGHT, M. (1985) Sketch for a Paper on the History of the Border Zone. Background Paper for the Conference on 'Regions, Frontiers and Boundaries'. Columbia University, New York, February.

INDEX

AFC, *see* Agricultural Finance Company
agricultural extension 87, 94-5, 97, 107-8, 140, 166, 168-9
  assistant 89, 92, 97-8, 130
  demonstrator 130
Agricultural Finance Company (AFC) 21, 26, 111
  loans 89, 97, 107, 123-4, 131
  policy 25-6, 113, 140
agricultural labour
  exploited 126, 176-7
  paid 15, 84-5, 125, 133, 172
  seasonal 113
  sexual division 125, 161, 175
  specific crops 22-3, 159
  timing 135
  weeding 22, 85, 122-3, 162, 167-70
  see also cash flows; food for work; ploughing; social differentiation
agricultural policy vii, 1-3, 88, 99, 128-9, 137, 160
  agricultural shows 97, 99, 104-6
  Food First 9, 10
  Operation Food Production 1-3
  training 122
  urban food crisis 112
  see also AFC; NAMBOARD
aid
  integrated development 23
  self-help 93, 107-10
  see also IDZ
Aron 104-8

barter 9
beans, *see* cash-cropping
beer
  Chibuku National Brewery 40, 43
  commercial brewing 39-40, 51, 85, 112, 124-5, 134, 146, 149
  drunkenness 4, 104, 125
  social drinking 50, 51, 82, 83
  taste 167
  women's responsibility 162
  work-parties 9, 116, 126, 129
Bemba 6, 38, 100, 102
brideservice 8, 13, 180
bridewealth
  cash 8, 12-13, 181
  quarrels 170

cash-cropping 45, 82, *passim*
  beans 14, 23, 54-6, 99, 106, 108-9, 115, 138, 141, 145
  ecology 10, 159-73
  groundnuts 55-6
  hybrid maize 14, 20, 23, 114, 130
  inflation 145, 157
  millet 129-30
  women 39, 147-54
  see also hybrid maize; Watch Tower
cash flows 5, 8, 87, 107, 128, 131
  constraints 14, 20, 26, 76, 82, 87, 114-15, 139, 141, 177-8
  see also migration (remittances)
cassava 22, 148, 166, 168
  see also diet
cattle 72, 119, 121-2, 169-70

charcoal 15, 34
Chele 72, 112-13, 117-29, 135-7, *passim*
chemical fertilizers 14, 95, 166, 168
Chiefs
    Kela 70
    Kowa 119
    Mpande 45, 67
    Mwamba 99, 100-1, 105, 107, 109
    Nsokolo 59-60
    Penza 99
Chikoti 73, 163-73
Chivunzila 73, 138-57
Church of God 68, 84-5
class
    alliances 90, 93
    consciousness 174-5
    interests 113
colonialism 24, 28, 89, 108
cooking oil 40, 145, 178
cooperatives 1-2, 24, 26, 88, 92, 140
copper 1, 4, 23, 34, 139
Copperbelt 3, 11, 13, 31-4, 44, 48, 78, 81
    entrepreneurs 92, 106, 145, 151
    food markets 55-6
cross-border trade 18, 93, 98-9, 101, 112, 151, *passim*
    hazards 149, 157
    mechanisms 116, 141, 149-57, 174
    partners 49-51, 156
    women 139, 147, 156-7

deforestation 14-15, 163-4, 168, 170-1
Department of Agriculture 92, 102, 118, 140
Department of Community Development 93-4, 102-3
development policy 2, 14, 24-6, 28, 46, 89, 93, 101, 131, 135
    cost 14, 18, 30
    integrated 23, 92
    on settlements 14, 23, 28, 114, 160, 170, 176
    theory 16, 176
    see also agricultural policy; AFC; UNIP
development projects 2, 16, 23-4, 26, 89-93, 111, 130
    see also Chele; Kaka; IDZ
diet 99, 124-5, 128, 145, 148, 171, 179, 185
    see also food for work
divorce 8-9, 63, 127, 147, 162
    consequences 127-8, 151, 177
    women's solidarity 129, 137
drought 126, 183

entrepreneurs 55-6, 106, 141, 145, 181, *see also* Watch Tower
exchange 17-18, 29, 49, 112, 146-7, 182

Fipa 29-30, 40, 181
fish 112, 156
    kapenta 40, 46, 48-9, 57, 147
    Lake Moero 49, 146
    peddlars 29-30, 146-7, 155
food for work 116, 123, 135-7, 173
    widows 117, 125-6, 165
food markets 9, 87-8, 129, 145
    Kasama 49, 146
    Line of Rail 46, 55, 157, 182
    Lusaka 32-4, 55, 151
    Mbala 39, 55, 57
food production 5-7, 9, 116, 163, *passim*
    surplus 9, 115
    time-space perspective 159-73
    urban (Mbala) 54
    see also work-parties
food security
    in Africa 18, 184
    national x, 140, 172
    Operation Food Production 1-3
    urban 54, 78, 112
    in villages 7, 9-10, 18, 86-110, 124-5, 172
forest cultivation 159, 161-73
Fwambo 22, 59-60, 67-9, 71

gin (*cancine*) 39
groundnuts 55, 168, 170
Gwembe Valley 4

healer 119, 126
households
    female-headed 12-13, 37-40
hunger (seasonal) 28, 39, 178
    see also malnutrition
hybrid maize 20, 23, 88, 114, 139-40, 171
    inputs/timing 21, 123, 136, 172-3
    promotion 48, 97, 111, 135, 171
    see also cash-cropping

IDZ, *see* Intensive Development Zone
insecticide 4
Intensive Development Zone (IDZ) 26, 28, 89-94, 113, 119-22
    patronage 116, 130-1, 134
    policy 95
    sheep scheme 94, 131
International Labour Office (ILO) 2, 31-2, 34-5, 139

International Red Locust Control
  (IRLC) 41-2, 78

Kabwe 56
Kaka 91, 93-6, 99, 100, 107-8, 113, 129-35, 163, 171
Kaonde 7
Kapwepwe, Simon 100
Kasama 15, 49, 81, 90, 92-4, 146
Kasunga 70, 74, 97, 104-5
Kaunda, President 20, 26, 100, 104
Kawimbe 49-50, 75, 79, 118, 167
Kenya 1, 38
kitchen gardens 79, 114, 118, 138, 149, 162, 171
Kowa 58-85, 119, 135-6

labour markets
  Line-of-Rail 31, 58, 114
  Lusaka 144
  Mbala 78
  newcomers 35
  saturation 13, 23, 35, 46, 114, 160
  stabilization 10-11, 13
  see also Copperbelt; International Red Locust Control
land
  disputes 97, 119, 150
  landlessness 137
  women's rights 13, 117-18, 162, 180
  see also returning migrants
Lenje 32
Literacy (International Day) 94-7, 102-4
London Missionary Society 119
Lozi 32
Lungu 36-9, 45, 54, 59, 69, 71-2, 103, 177
Lusaka 32, 55-6, 119, 144
  see also labour markets; Line of Rail
Lwembe 71

Mali x, 18
malnutrition 2
Manchester School of Anthropology 16
markets
  food, *see* food markets
  labour, *see* labour markets
marriage
  disputes 98
  patterns 38
  politics 58-60, 63, 67, 72-3
  secondary 63, 73, 139, 147-54
  see also divorce; residence (women's)

Mbala 31-57, *passim*
migration
  abenteeism 76, 80, 82
  alternatives 114, 139, 148
  circulatory 3, 5-8, 10, 12, 23, 102, 129, 138, 144, 164
  demise 11, 14, 28, 31-57, 114, 129, 139, 144, 148
  labour histories 31, 45, 56
  remittances 24, 28, 111, 148, 165, 171, 181
  women 33-5, 43, 81
millet
  displaced 15, 21, 30, 109, 115
  hoarding 39-40, 56, 124, 146
  monocropping 22
  surplus 129
Mpulungu 46, 48-9, 55, 146-7, 171
Mulungushi Conference 99-100, 102
Mwamba 55, 87, 90-1, 93, 97, 99, 100, 102-3, 108-9, 146
  see also Chiefs

NAMBOARD, *see* National Marketing Board
National Marketing Board (NAMBOARD) 21, 49, 92, 106, 108, 145, 147
NCU, *see* Northern Cooperative Union
Ndola 56
Northern Cooperative Union (NCU) 91-3, 95, 105-6, 108-9, 130, 140-1, 148
Nyamwanga 38, 45

paraffin 124, 140
Participatory Democracy 89-90
  in Chele 117-29, *passim*
  structures 96
  Village Productivity Committees (VPCs) 26, 87, 89, 93, 96, 98, *passim*
ploughing 14-16, 22, 118, 122-4, 148, 151, 170, 173
  see also work-parties
policy, *see* agricultural policy; development policy
political economy 114, 175
population pressure 3, 10, 21, 148, 158, 160-1, 164, 168, 170, 177-8
Public Works Department (PWD) 78

residence
  and circulatory migration 6, 60, 69-70, 74, 77, 80
  dynamics 71, 74-7

and returning migrants 60, 69, 144
uxorilocal 12-13, 59, 73, 77, 179
virilocal 6
women's 67, 73-4, 77, 147-54, 178-9, 181
see also Chikoti; Chivunzila; Kowa
return migration 11-12, 31, 51, 57-8, 69-70, 76
  expectations 93, 134
  Kowa 77-80
  and land 121-2
  Mbala 37, 40-6
  and resettlement 91, 130
returning migrants
  and commerce 10, 15, 20, 48, 82
  and social differentiation 8, 85
  women 63, 150-1, 154, 177
  see also class; Kaka; Kowa
Rhodes-Livingstone Institute vii, xi
riverside (*mianda*) cultivation 138, 145, 148-9, 183
Rural Council 100
Rwanda 18

Sahel 17, 183
schools 80, 102, 130
soap 112, 124, 140, 146, 156
social differentiation 6, 16, 90, 113, 116, 128, 137, 170
  in Chikoti 164-73
  emergent farmers 21, 60, 87, 90, 107-8, 113, 119, 131, 136-7
  farmer–traders 9, 141
  in Kowa 128
soil degradation 14, 169, 177, 181, 183
Soli 32
sorcery ix, 4, 56, 74-7, 166
sorghum 168, 170
South Africa 1, 32
soya 122
squatter settlements 34-6, 146
state capitalism 25
state farms 1, 2, 46, 72, 119
sugar 112, 124, 156, 178
sunflower 131

Tabwa 38
Tanzania 3, 13, 23, 30, 46, 48, 50, 56, 83, 93, 104, 106, 146-7, 154, 182

Tazara Railway 91, 144
Third National Development Plan (TNDP) 46, 91
Times of Zambia, the 1, 2
Tonga (Malawi) 9
Tonga (Zambia) 32

Uganda 134
UNIP, *see* United National Independence Party
United Bus Company of Zambia (UBZ) 55, 94-5
United National Independence Party (UNIP) 36-7, 46, 89, 94, 97-103, 105, 131, 145
United Progressive Party (UPP) 100
United States of America 1
University of Zambia (UNZA) 100

ward organization
  committees 92-3, 97, 105, 108, 130, 140
  council 89, 97, 106
  councillor 96-7, 100-1, 150
Watch Tower 88, 105-7, 141, 144, 154, 181
  cooperation with non-members 17, 104, 108-10
  transport service 131, 156
  see also Aron
wealth 76-7, 83, 112
West Africa 10-11
wheat 122
White Fathers xii
Women's Club 134
work-parties 84, 113, 117, 127-8, 131, 162
  communal 116, 126, 151
  transformed 123-6, 163-5, 181
  underpinnings 164

Zaire 18, 64
Zambian Air Force (ZAF) 43, 54, 79
Zambian Daily Mail 92
Zambian Electricity Supply Company (ZESCO) 78
Zambian Humanism 89, 116-18, 126
Zimbabwe (formerly Rhodesia) 1, 32, 95